Relentless Struggle

AN AUTOBIOGRAPHY

EDMUND H. DALE

Canadian Cataloguing in Publication Data

Dale, Edmund H.
  Relentless struggle

  ISBN 1-55212-308-1

  1. Dale, Edmund H. 2. Geography teachers--Canada--Biography. 3.
College teachers--Canada--Biography.   4.   Geographers--Canada--
Biography. 5. Jamaican Canadians--Biography.* 6. Geography--Study
and teaching (Higher)--Canada. I. Title.
G69.D34A3 1999   910'.92 C99-911303-8

TRAFFORD

This book was published on-demand in cooperation with Trafford Publishing.
On-demand publishing is a unique process and service of making a book available for
retail sale to the public taking advantage of on-demand manufacturing and Internet
marketing.
On-demand publishing includes promotions, retail sales, manufacturing, order fulfil-
ment, accounting and collecting royalties on behalf of the author.

Suite 6E - 2333 Government St., Victoria, BC, Canada V8T 4P4
Phone   250-383-6864   Toll-free 1-888-232-4444 (Canada & US)
Fax   250-383-6804   E-mail   sales@trafford.com
Web site www.trafford.com trafford publishing is a division of trafford holdings ltd.
Trafford Catalogue #99-0059   www.trafford.com/robots/99-0059.html

10   9   8   7   6   5   4

This book is dedicated posthumously to my parents who could give me only a little, but oh, so very much.

E. H. D.

ACKNOWLEDGEMENTS

The author wishes to record his thanks to Dr. Y. Yao and Messrs M. Xing and Q. Hu for their help in the computer production of the draft manuscript, and to The Noblet Design Group of Regina, Saskatchewan, for the cover design which is in keeping with the focus of the book.

I should like to acknowledge also the sound, legal advice given me by Mr. Barrie R. Touchings of the firm of Nicholl and Akers, Barristers and Solicitors of Edmonton, Alberta, and Mr. F. William Johnson, Q.C. of the firm of Gerrand, Ratch and Johnson, Barristers and Solicitors of Regina, Saskatchewan.

To all others who helped variously in the production of the book, the author expresses his grateful thanks.

This book is an accurate record of my life. It portrays the most important challenges, opportunities, disappointments, successes, hopes and fears, and all the high and low points of my life. Except for a few fictitious names substituted for persons who are still alive and may not want their identity to be disclosed, all else is authentic, the incidents or happenings having actually occurred or experienced.

My fondest hope is that my life's story will be sufficiently interesting to capture the interest of young readers, among others, to encourage them to decide early what they want to make of their lives, then ardently, resolutely work towards that goal, realizing from the start that the road ahead will most likely be long, hazardous and uphill all or most of the way.

For reasons not always clear and often perplexing, difficulties often intrude to thwart our plans and actions, and cause many of us to falter or founder, sometimes temporarily, at other times permanently. Some attribute this to fate or destiny, others to humbug. I am of the latter group, for surely, in attempting to do what we have not done before, difficulty often arises. This is flagrantly obvious in most attempts to acquire a skill or technique in, say, learning to play an instrument, or using the computer. Clearly it would be ridiculous to blame our initial difficulty with either of these activities on fate or destiny. Properly considered, it is strength of will, that is, determination, that enables us to tackle the problem and ultimately overcome it. Giving up or withdrawing in defeat without expending much energy or resolve that the task demands could be considered a weakness of character. To train our minds to grapple with difficult tasks, to persevere, to be resolute and determined, and to inject into our thinking the idea of never giving up appear to be the solution of the problem.

There is no doubt whatever that sometimes our difficulties seem monumental, intractable, inhibiting, and, if we allow them, soul destroying. However, we should not remain moribund. It is especially at such times we must summon all the strength we can to fight the difficulty.

What I am saying here is born of experience, often excruciatingly painful, as the reader will realize as he goes from page to page of this book. My difficulties, especially early ones, were so harrowing, and tended to be so inhibiting that in retrospect I wonder how I eventually triumphed over many of them. I am compelled to conclude that though determination was an essential element in the struggle, an unseen, helping, guiding hand was ever present. It helped me to surmount the difficulties.

Certainly life is accompanied by many difficulties. It is often not easy for many of us to achieve what we want to achieve. It may seem relatively easy for others, but those who are faced with little or no difficulties are often denied those qualities that our fight against difficulties brings. So often such persons seem to miss a vital step in their march towards the fulness of life.

Yet, it is reasonable to ask why is life fraught with so many difficulties. Perhaps we may never know. What appears certain is that life is meant to be fought, from the cradle to the grave. Accepting this notion, if nothing else, gives us the desire and strength of will to tackle boldly whatever comes our way and to wrest success from it. We need to accept the fact, too, that personal sacrifices and manifold hardships are necessary weapons for the ultimate defeat of our difficulties.

CONTENTS

CHAPTER *1*

It was a gorgeous Jamaican sunset. The western sky was aglow. In luxurious splendour, the sun was descending below the horizon slowly, grandly, majestically. The few clouds witnessing the spectacle were themselves reflecting an iridescence of burnished gold. There was glory in the heavens, a solemnity touched with awe, a grandeur that defied verbal description, a silence so profound that it was audible, rising, as if it were, ever higher and higher into the far beyond. And all the while, the scene was changing; gold became crimson, crimson changed to scarlet, and scarlet ran itself into grey. Earth stood still; all nature was hushed in adoration as the sun, now a red ball of fire and shrouded in magnificent splendour, slipped slowly, gracefully below the horizon.

Sitting there on the trunk of my favourite coco-nut tree overlooking my humble home, I, hardly twelve years by the calendar, watched the westward scene, lost in the splendour of the moment. I, too, was up there in the heavens, with the clouds, witnessing the magic of the disappearing sun. But though my spirit was aloft, my physical body still rested on the coco-nut tree trunk. When both soul and body had re-united, dusk had fallen, suddenly, a phenomenon of tropical areas. Now in semi-darkness, my ears were alerted by the evening hymn of a solitary nightingale perched high up on a branch of a nearby tree. Slowly, the voices of insects in chorus, unseen, and the whistling of frogs, also unseen, began to lament the passing of day and to usher in the quiet approach of evening. Then, as it grew

1

darker, fireflies — beetles emitting phosphorescent light — flitted in a fairy-like fashion from place to place, puncturing the darkness with little bursts of light that suddenly jolted me from my reverie and reminded me that it was long past the time to begin my homework. Quickly, I jumped from the coco-nut tree, descended the hill and entered my home.

The house was built on the lower slopes of a hill, overlooking a small rural town, thus offering an excellent view of a part of the town. The house had survived many a hurricane, perhaps because of its sturdy structure. It was a three-bedroom bungalow, with a sitting-dining room, and a quasi-basement and bathroom. The kitchen and pantry occupied a small building by itself, and the toilet another structure some distance from the house. Above the house was a public foot path which separated the adjoining property with coco-nut trees. One of the young trees had been partly uprooted by a hurricane years before. Its roots were partly in the ground, while its trunk was thrown to the ground. Later it began to grow upwards, leaving a pronounced sag in the trunk. I adopted this tree and called it my horse and saddle. Often I would go to sit there to ponder what was beyond the horizon, and dream dreams about my future which I sensed was to be beyond that horizon. I had been doing this on that particular evening when the sunset caught my attention and left in me a glow which was to stay with me for the rest of my life.

Entering the house, my father, James Henry Dale, a disciplinarian of the first order, demanded to know where I had been and why I seemed to becoming slack in getting to my homework on time.

"I am sorry, Dad. It was first the dazzling colours of the sunset, then the nightingale singing in the tree, then the fireflies dancing about, and the insects chirping in chorus. I completely forgot the time."

Henry Dale (he preferred to omit the "James") made no reply, looked sternly at me, put his glasses on again and continued to read the newspaper in his arm chair. At the same time, Lydia Dale, my mother, who was at her sewing machine surrounded by yards and yards of white silk — a wedding dress she was making for a young bride-to-be — looked up at her son, saw a strange light in my eyes and said nothing. She, too, continued to do what she was doing. I went to my table quietly, turned up the paraffin lamp brighter, opened my book and began to do my homework.

My mother knew me well and was sensitive to all my moods. Still at her sewing machine, she would glance intermittently at me, perhaps because my concentration was poor on that night. I kept looking up from my book to stare at the wall opposite. Then I would read again, write again, and look away again. Mum knew that something was bothering me but kept silent.

Dad was the first to retire for the night. He folded the newspaper, took off his glasses, yawned and said, "Enough! I am going to bed," and left the room. I was the next to retire. I put aside the essay I had begun to write, got up, kissed my mother and said,

"Good night, Mum."

"Good night, son," came the reply. "Now, mind, go to sleep," she said quietly.

Mum continued to pump the pedal of her sewing machine for another hour or so. Then I heard her gathering up the long train of silk material which she had carefully embroidered and would have carefully placed the whole in a cardboard box on the sofa. She checked the doors of the house to make sure they were locked, but before she joined Dad, she peeped into my room and found me awake. I had turned down the lamp in my room but I had not put it out.

"You're not asleep?" she asked.

"No, Mum."

"Why aren't you? Is something the matter with you?" she inquired.

"I keep seeing the glow of the setting sun. It was so beautiful, so wonderful. If heaven is a place, it must be very beautiful."

Mum came closer and sat at the side of my bed, obviously touched by what I had said. She was a religious person and tried to bring up her children, I, being the last of five children, in a religious atmosphere. Before she could reply to what I had said, I continued.

"It was as though I could touch it and yet couldn't. I was so close to it and yet so far away from it." I stopped for a moment, fixed in thought. Mum waited. Then I continued.

"Looking at it, the sunset I mean, I got the feeling that I will always be reaching up to hold or get what I want and may not hold it or get it."

The dubious look on mother's face suggested that she could not believe she was listening to a 12-year old boy.

"Well, my son," she said, "you must always try, never give up. You must fight to get what you want, fight, fight, fight the odds! When I was about your age, or perhaps a little older, my mother used to say to my two brothers and me that we could make the impossible possible if we tried hard enough. What she meant was that if we really tried, we could succeed in overcoming our difficulties."

"And was she right?"

"Yes, son, right as nine pence. You see, if you try very hard and ask God to help you, he will. He is merciful and dependable, very dependable. I have always carried in my mind the words of an old German hymn that I first heard when I was a girl and had gone to either a Methodist or Congregational Church — I do not remember which — with my mother. I remember the first stanza:

> There' s a wideness in God's mercy,
> > like the wideness of the sea.
> There's a kindness in his justice
> > more than liberty.

"And the last verse went something like this:

For the love of God is broader than the
measures of man's mind.
And the heart of the Eternal is most
wonderfully kind.

I kept looking at my mother in the dim light for a long time, impressed not only by the words of the hymn but by my mother's profound sincerity, no less, her diction — always she insisted that we (her children) should enunciate clearly. Equally, she objected to our speaking the local dialect.

"Son," she said, "God is merciful, mercifully kind. He will help you. Depend on him. Call on him. Always ask him to help you. He will. I know he will, but you must also work very hard."

My questioning, reasoning, searching had long evoked in my mother strong maternal feelings, but on this occasion she was so moved that she hugged me and whispered,

"Always reach up, Edmund, for the highest and the best. Accept nothing less. The good Lord will help you. Trust him. Now, go to sleep."

With that she blew out the lamp and said good night. Quietly she left the room, did her toilet, changed into her night dress, and would have crept quietly into bed beside her husband. But he, too, was not asleep, for I heard her say in a low voice, believing I could not hear them in my room,

"Henry, "that boy of ours is very mature in his thinking. He is not like the others. I gave birth to them. I know. This one, the last, is quite, quite different."

"What is it now?" Dad asked.

"Edmund has a questioning mind. Constantly, he wonders about his future."

"Well, what is wrong with that?" Dad asked.

"You are just like a man, you are," Mum said.

5

"Of course, I am a man. Would you have me any other way?"

"You just don't understand, Henry Dale. Edmund senses that we may not be able to give him the education he wants. He has not said so, but he senses it and reveals it in his eyes. He knows that we are getting old and that your business is not doing well. He is afraid we will not be able to help him when he wants that help."

"You may be imagining it, you know."

"No, I am not. I am his mother. I know what he is thinking. How is it you, his father, don't know?"

Dad made no reply. There was silence for a time. Then, in what he thought was a whisper, said tenderly,

"Don't worry so much; try to get some sleep."

The next day my dad got the bad news of his life. The cabinet-making business, owned and operated by himself and his younger brother, William, had failed. Dad had left the management side of it to William who proved to have had little or no business acumen or management skill. He had succeeded in getting Dad to use Dad's house as collateral for a loan from the local bank, without mother's knowledge or consent. When, therefore, William was to repay the loan and could not, the bank legally claimed Dad's house. The news of this and the order for our family to evacuate the house forthwith came to mother with the force of a bomb. She did not cry; she bawled.

"How could you do this to us?" she demanded of her husband.

"Well," he said, "I left the management to William. He looked after the books and paid the bills. I knew that business had fallen off somewhat — you knew that too — but I did not think it was so bad."

"But why didn't you tell me you had mortgaged the house?"

"Well, I knew you would have objected, and William needed the loan to run the business. I thought I would upset you."

6

"And what do you think you are doing now? It is such a terrible disgrace for us to be kicked out of our own home. We will never be able to hold up our heads in the town again. Henry Dale, how could you be so easily influenced by William Dale?"

"He is my brother, Lydia, my brother!"

"Yet he did not hesitate to run his brother into this dilemma."

And so Mum and Dad continued to argue. I quietly listened to all of this and tried to console her but failed utterly. Fortunately Dad had another house, less comfortable than the one we lived in, and to this house we moved. The bank made repairs to the house they took from Dad, repainted it, fenced it off, and rented it. For months my mother refused to show herself in public, refusing even to go to church on Sundays, a duty she previously performed punctiliously. She felt ashamed, disgraced, as though she had committed a crime. Her feelings were deep. She found it difficult to forgive her husband whose loss of confidence in his brother now held him in abject grief. He became an entirely different man, without a will to fight the odds. He seemed to have lost himself and could not find himself again.

Thus the dread that I had sensed all along was now real. What was I to do? The education I had hoped to get now seemed so elusive. Slowly, after many sleepless nights, I came to the realization that I would have to help myself, to find the means of obtaining the education I wanted and felt I should have. But how could I do this? I asked myself. In my small town there were no opportunities for young people to improve themselves, much less a boy as young as I. As I wrestled with myself, the thought came that I could do a little business in buying and selling coco-nuts over the weekends. I could take my father's donkey, go to the coco-nut plantation, some eight miles away, buy one hundred or more coco-nuts at a time, and sell them in the local market on Saturdays for a little more than what I paid for them. In silence, I explored the idea further. But where was I to get the initial capital, about ten to fifteen shillings to begin? Even if I did little errands for neighbours, they would not give me money, for they did not have it. Everybody was so terribly poor.

To this day, I confess to close friends, I believe God stepped into the picture, and that what my mother had told me was right, namely, that God would help me if I tried. It was while I was contemplating becoming a little businessman that a distant relative visited the family. He asked me about my school work, how I had been getting along, and what I wanted to make of myself. I told him of my dream of going to a high school and finally to university. My relative showed a keen interest in me and my dreams, for, as he said, I knew exactly what I wanted. He discussed with me my future plans in great detail. He was somebody I could easily talk with, quite unlike my father; he even showed me how to set up my potential business. I liked him very much. To my great surprise, when he was about to depart, he slipped a pound note (equivalent to 20 shillings) into my hand and wished me good luck. I was overcome with emotion, and after thanking him, I quietly looked up to the heavens and whispered, "Thank you, God. This makes me think you approve what I want to do."

But there was another difficulty I would have to overcome, namely, false pride. My school mates would not think much of me if they saw me selling coco-nuts in the market on Saturdays. In Jamaica, such a person is called a 'higgler'. In the end, I said to myself, "Well, I do not care two hoots if they call me a higgler. I will do anything honestly to make a few shillings to pay for my schooling and get the education I want."

Having worked out the pros and cons of my potential business, I discussed the whole matter with Mum who reluctantly approved it. Dad also agreed to let me have the donkey, and so I went off on a Friday afternoon (I had to miss the afternoon school but easily made up for it afterwards) to the coco-nut plantation, bought the one hundred coco-nuts and presented myself with them in the local market the next day. My prices were lower than those of other coco-nut sellers in the market. Thus I quickly sold off my stock and made a profit of seven shillings and six pence. Not bad, I thought. With pride, I counted out the taking before Mum who looked at me with mixed feelings of pride and sorrow — pride in my determination to help myself, and sorrow because she could not help me more, as she wanted to.

The business launched, I continued it week by week. With the profits I bought my books and happily studied as hard as I could. The jeers and teasing of my school mates had no effect on me. I would merely smile at them and met their taunts with an equanimity befitting that of the bishop who presided at the restoration ceremony of our church. Soon, they realized that they could not easily upset me, and desisted. Besides, I was always top of my class. I think they admired my determination to help myself, but they would not admit it.

During all this time I had been attending the local elementary school. A new headmaster had been appointed when I was just past my twelfth birthday. The headmaster was a young man, fresh from Mico Teachers' Training College in Kingston. He was keen, resourceful and vibrantly masculine. The boys immediately took him as a role model. They liked him but feared him. He had huge, powerful eyes which sent shivers down the spine of most of us, his pupils. Added to this was his readiness to use the cane on recalcitrants. I saw this as a regrettable flaw and told my mother so. But the serious-minded pupils, including myself, responded more positively than negatively to his teaching methods. At all times his eyes, like balls of fire, indicated that he meant business, that he demanded the best from his classes, and that nothing but the best would satisfy him. There was just no nonsense about him. It seemed that his motto was school was a place where teachers taught and students learned.

We were soon to realize that the headmaster had a passion for geography. He would come alive, absolutely transported, when he taught the geography of Canada, His only teaching aid was a tattered, obsolete map of Canada which showed mountains by black lines. Slides (black-and-white or coloured) were unheard of, nor, for that matter, did our school own a slide or film projector. But our teacher, by his eyes and facial expression, as well as his voice, brought before our eyes the prairie wheat fields shimmering in the wind, the Niagara Falls tumbling down with a deafening roar, and the glaciers (solid rivers of ice, we imagined them to be) moving imperceptibly down the steep slopes of the Canadian Rockies. At such times our teacher had the whole class transfixed. We were on the Canadian scene with him. Little did I think that one day I would see the Rocky Mountains in person, or be domiciled in western Canada. Little did I know, too, that years later I would be emulating my early teacher in his method of teaching. William Wilberforce Benjamin (that was his name, affectionately called by his initials, "WWB", by all of us) left so deep an impression on my young mind that, posthumously and in silence, I often offer to him my thanks and appreciation. I wish most sincerely he was alive so that I could tell him this in person. I was very lucky to have had such a man as my teacher in my formative years.

To continue with the narrative, the response of the pupils, especially those of my class, was interesting. They competed with each other to win the headmaster's approval of their work. Years after, when I became a teacher, I wondered, if the headmaster had not deliberately but discreetly encouraged this keen competition among the pupils of his class. In my class, for example, Aubrey Allen, Shirley Jones and I were constantly competing for the top place. Always I held the lead, but only by a few marks, never by a substantial lead. Dissatisfied, I would discuss the matter with Mum, who seemed always to understand me, never with my father who often seemed distant.

"Mum," I said to her, "however hard I try, I still cannot get a good mark above them (Aubrey and Shirley)."

"Nonetheless," she said, "you are top of the class. That is very good. Doesn't it make you feel good?"

"No, not really," I admitted. "They (Aubrey and Shirley) are saying, 'It's only one mark (or two marks) above us'. I want to have a commanding lead."

"Well, next time you may even do better," she said. "Don't upset yourself. Just keep right on trying. Do the best you can and all will be well in the end. Worrying about it certainly won't help," Lydia Dale advised her son, surmising that the headmaster might well be instigating the competition among her son and his two friends.

Occasionally during the year, the school was visited by foreigners who showed an interest in Jamaican education. Always these visitors would be asked to address the whole school, much to the delight of many of the pupils who welcomed a break from the daily routine. I recall vividly one of these visits. It was by an American doctor of medicine and his wife. He gave an interesting talk on the human body and the care of it. At the end, he offered a prize to anyone from the senior class who submitted the best essay on his talk. This was my class, and every member of it wrote the essay under the strict supervision of the headmaster. He sent them off and nothing was heard of them for a long time. Lacking humility, Shirley Jones had declared that she had written what she thought was an excellent essay. She was always inclined to be boastful, one of two reasons why the boys in her class did not like her. The other was that she was not much to look at, though inordinately bright. Aubrey Allen did not say much, and I kept silent, refusing to say how I had done.

Then, quite unexpectedly one day, the American doctor and his wife revisited the school. The headmaster assembled the whole school to hear his comments on the essays. He began by congratulating those who had entered the contest. He stated that he had intended to award one prize but his wife objected to that idea, claiming that he should award a first, a second, and a third prize, as well as a few consolation prizes, because it was a whole class that had entered the contest. He made the school laugh by saying that women are always right. Thus he had changed his mind and would offer prizes as his wife suggested. The school cheered and would not stop cheering until his wife rose and took a bow. Then he added that even if his wife had not insisted on his offering a few more prizes, the essays would have compelled him to do so, for so many of them were very good.

Members of the class who entered the contest sat looking as though they were sitting on pins and needles. I looked at Aubrey and Shirley who epitomized acute anxiety. I, myself, was shaking, my heart wanting to jump through my mouth. The doctor sensed our anxiety and quickly proceeded to relieve it by first, calling out the names of those who won the consolation prizes: Marjory Hastings, Ellen Small, Harry Ingram, Joseph Williams and Carl Miller. His wife handed out the prizes, all books, as were the other prizes.

Next, he said he had much difficulty in deciding which of two essays should be awarded the second or third prize. He had to read them over several times, and decided in the end that the third prize should go to Shirley Jones and the second to Aubrey Allen. Both went up to receive their prizes as the school applauded.

At this stage of the proceedings, I could hardly breathe. I was hot and uncomfortable, visibly shaking. I could hardly control myself. Perspiration was streaming from my face which I wiped constantly with my handkerchief. I felt I would die if my name was not called, but the doctor seemed to be in no hurry. How would I live it down if I did not win a prize, I wondered. At last the doctor continued.

"Now, the first prize!" he said. Whereas I had difficulty deciding the second and third prizes, I did not have that difficulty in choosing the first prize. That essay was easily the best, the most outstanding. My wife readily agreed with me — an indication that men also know what is good."

The boys of the school cheered. Then he read the opening paragraph and a few other paragraphs of the essay to the school. I had difficulty remembering if I had written those lines, I was shaking so much. The doctor ended by saying:

"I have the greatest pleasure in presenting the first prize to Mr. Edmund H. Dale."

I rose and the school cheered. I walked up humbly to receive my prize without revealing the agony I suffered throughout the doctor's talk. It was an ordeal I would long remember. Aubrey and Shirley were pleased with their prizes, too, but clearly wished they had taken the first prize. Yet, all three of us congratulated each other. The rivalry among us was certainly intense, but it was healthy. There was nothing wrong in wanting to be number one as long as humility and modesty were not sacrificed, I thought.

It was also at this time that the headmaster decided to form a Scout Troop, for there was no youth activity, apart from sports, to claim the loyalty of the boys in the community. Readily some thirty boys enrolled. I prevailed on my parents to allow me to join, and they agreed. I bought the material for the scout uniform, which my mother made, from the proceeds of my little business, as well as the scout belt and hat. The Scout Leader (the headmaster) made a grand affair of the Investiture Ceremony by inviting the Chief Commissioner of Scouts for the island, the Commissioner of Scouts for the parish, six Scout Troops from nearby towns, the parents of the boys, and all the townsfolk to the open-air ceremony.

(The boys in my troop were secretly amused to see their Scout Master when he appeared in short pants for the first time at the Investiture.) On the whole, we all looked smart. The flags (colours) of the Troop were donated by a local resident; they looked absolutely splendid. We held them proudly and high as we marched to take our place in front of the visiting troops.

The Investiture was conducted by the Island Chief Commissioner, helped by the Commissioner for the parish and a local member of the clergy. First, the Chief Commissioner took the salute in a march past of the troops, headed by their Scout Masters and their individual Colour Parties. The whole was preceded by a Band of one of the visiting Troops. The drum beats helped the boys to keep in step as they marched crisply before the reviewing stand where the Chief Commissioner stood. As our Troop, which was to be invested, approached, the local townsfolk who attended applauded warmly, and the boys, bursting with pride, carried themselves erectly past the reviewing stand. All the Troops and their Colour Parties, with our Troop in the inside, formed a horseshoe facing the Chief Commissioner.

First, the clergyman gave a short prayer. Next, the Chief Commissioner thanked the large number of townsfolk and visiting scouts for attending, congratulated the new Scout Leader and his Troop, and made a short speech on the training of young boys to be good citizens, which, he said, was what scouting aimed to do. Following this, the member of the local clergy blessed the new scout colours (flags of the new Troop), ending with another short prayer.

The Investiture of our Troop followed. The Chief Commissioner questioned the boys who answered in unison, and in unison repeated their Scout Motto:

> I promise to do my best, to do my duty to God and the King, to help other people at all times, and to obey the Scout Law.

The Band then struck up a march. The Troops and their Color Parties marched past the reviewing stand again and were dismissed. Immediately, the newly-invested scouts were surrounded by parents and friends who extended their individual congratulations.

The ceremony was very successful. It was short, to the point, smooth and colourful. It added a measure of excitement to an otherwise dull small-town existence. The parents of the boys were proud, the town pleased, the Scout Leader (headmaster) very happy that his plans were brought to fruition successfully.

Soon, by the calendar, it was the summer season (though it is always summer in Jamaica), and the idea of a scout summer camp began to be tossed about by the Scout Troop. The owner of a property on the north coast of the island, near to Dunn's River and Ocho Rios — a tourist resort area and one of the most picturesque areas of Jamaica — had offered the site to the Scout Association of Jamaica for use as a campsite by the scouts of the island, and the Commissioner for the parish had informed all the scouts of the parish that that year's summer camp would be held there.

Once our Scout Leader agreed that our Troop should go to camp that summer and join the other scouts of the local area, we began to seek ways to raise funds to cover our camping expenses. The town's people were very generous; they provided food of all kinds. The two grocery shops in the town gave a wide selection of canned and other preserved food and drinks; one resident even lent his truck to take us and our gear to the camp site and return for us at the end of the camp. In no time, most of our arrangements were finalized, except permission from my father for me to go. He refused to agree to my going until he could be assured his son would return alive. But surely no one could give such a guarantee. Clearly I had to do something about this. Quickly, I devised a strategy which I thought would bring about the required result. I would ask my Scout Leader (the headmaster) to seek my father's permission for me to go to summer camp. But the Scout Leader should see my father in the company of the Commissioner for the parish, a successful lawyer whom my father greatly admired. If the Commissioner told my father that all would be well, I felt certain that my father would agree to my going to the summer camp. If that did not work, nothing else would, I thought. The Commissioner was to make a visit to talk to the Troop about the camp and what was expected of each scout.

Accordingly, the Scout Leader and the Commissioner paid Henry Dale a visit and complimented him for wanting to know first-hand what arrangements were being made, especially for swimming at the camp. They told him they wished other parents were as careful as he, and assured him that the boys would be under strict supervision at all times, especially when they went swimming in the sea. None would be allowed to go into the sea without a capable life-guard looking on. Their tact, diplomacy and forthright explanation won over James Henry Dale completely. He agreed that his son, already promoted to Patrol Leader, could go to summer camp. He had no idea whatsoever that that son had skilfully arranged the visit by the two gentlemen.

And so the great day came for the Troop to go off to their first summer camp by the sea. In great excitement, we packed our gear in the truck, safely deposited ourselves in it, and were off. Our excitement mounted to fever pitch when we arrived at the site.

The site was a level coco-nut grove, raised some tens of feet precipitously above the sea, and offered from every point a magnificent view of the blue sea below, interrupted now and then by the tall, slender trunks of the coco-nut trees which shaded the site from the tropical sun. The ground was carpeted with a hard grass which grew horizontally instead of vertically. Close to the entrance to the site, the Roaring River, after descending the famous, spectacular Falls further upstream, rushed playfully under a bridge on the road between St. Ann's Bay and Dunn's River Beach. The Roaring River reached the sea below by cascading over smooth rocks and crossing the dazzling white sands of the beach. The white sands extended under the sea for some considerable distance and could be seen from above. Fronting the sea was a fairly steep slope of tropical vegetation interspersed with bougainvillea of different shades, oleander and other flowering shrubs, mango trees and other fruit trees waiting to be 'raided' by the boys. The scouts thought the area was a natural paradise. Already a few tents were pitched on the site by early arrivals and gave the appearance of a small town in its nascent development.

The three patrols of my troop quickly set up their three tents at intervals from each other, demarcated their area with beautiful shells found along the beach, cleaned up the site, erected various gadgets, raised their banner proclaiming their troop, and was easily the most attractive of the tent sites. Other troops from various parts of the parish came, pitched their tents, and soon the whole place was inhabited by hundreds of young, happy, eager boys in one of the most pleasing natural settings of the island. To me this was heaven. Never before had I felt so happy, so free, so completely relaxed, and never since those sublime days have I been able to experience those splendid moments, except in reminiscence.

The camp site allowed access down to the sea by a series of steps cut into the soft sandstone cliff, but that access was strictly out of bounds, as was going into the sea, unless under camp supervision. The camp routine was strict. After wake-up call by a bugle, the day's programme began with physical exercises on the beach, then about half an hour of supervised bathing in the warm, buoyant sea, and rinsing in the cool, refreshing river water. This was followed by breakfast — those detailed for cooking on a rotating basis could not take part in the day's programme — then, parade inspection, and inspection of the tent sites and camp site. Immediately after, instruction in badge work, including first aid, signalling and swimming, occupied everybody until lunch time. An hour's rest followed lunch, during which the scouts could make or add gadgets to their tent sites — always something new and novel to win points for the next day's tent-site inspection. The tent site that scored the highest number of points for tidiness, novelty, improvisations etc. and whose patrols were smartly attired at morning inspections was awarded the coveted Scout Emblem for the day.

At the end of the rest hour, individual groups were taken on hikes up to the Falls or on nature trails, spotting types of flora and fauna, or on a visit to local places of interest. The evening meal was between 5 and 6 p.m., followed by camp fire, singing and skits. By 10 p.m., the bugle sounded for lights out; all were to be in bed, and no

17

walking about was allowed. It was a full day's activities and sleep came to the boys easily and quickly, but not to Edmund Dale who lay wide awake listening to the gentle lapping of the waves of the sea below, the distant roar of the Falls, the rushing of the water under the bridge nearby, and the gentle rustle of the leaves of the coco-nut trees above in the gentle night breeze. These sounds were to stay with me always.   It was this phase of my life, this coming together harmoniously with nature, with beauty, with sharing and living amicably with other boys that was to leave an indelible mark on my character. Unquestionably, scouting helped me. I would always be grateful for this and would rightly want to return in my later years some of what I received.

Another notable experience in my early life bordered to some extent on the supernatural and is not easily explained. But first, the headmaster of my school had approached my parents and those of my friend, Aubrey Allen, to allow him to give us extra lessons in the evenings in preparation for an impending scholarship examination. He thought we stood a good chance of winning a scholarship that would give us a place in a secondary school. Our parents gratefully agreed. The arrangement was that we would go to the headmaster's home in the evenings and under his supervision worked for two or three hours. Unmarried at the time, the headmaster lived alone in a comfortable two-bedroom house that was provided for him. Instead of going home after the extra lessons in the evenings, we would sleep in the second bedroom. What our parents and ourselves did not know at the beginning was that the headmaster was courting a young lady some six miles away and would quietly slip out of town to spend many evenings with her, returning in the early hours of the morning. Apparently this was to avoid local gossip which, in a small, conservative town, can be devastating. It seemed that he wanted to use Aubrey and me as a cover for his private activities. He would be at home when we arrived and would explain the work and set exercises for us to do, and then he would leave to be with his fiancée, whom he later married and with whom he had two sons and two daughters. The

18

light in his home, while Aubrey and I worked at our exercises before retiring to bed, would give the lie that the headmaster was at home.

What Aubrey and I did not know was that the house was haunted. But did the headmaster know? And if he did, was that another reason for him to want someone else in the house at nights with him? We wondered about this later. So while his motive for wanting to give us extra help might have been quite sincere, did he have a second ulterior motive? It was not easy for us to fathom this. At any rate, awareness that the house was haunted became evident some two weeks after we began sleeping there.

The two bedrooms of the house were connected by an inside door, and this rendered easy access from one room to the other. Each bedroom had an outside door which opened on to the sitting room. A flight of stairs led from the sitting room to a lower floor with bathroom, dining room, kitchen and pantry. The main entrance to the house was on the upper floor from the main street, while the lower floor opened on to a back yard and garden.

One night, after we had finished our work and had gone to sleep, we were awakened by a noise which came from downstairs. Startled, both of us bolted upright in our beds and looked across at each other in silent wonder. Then I whispered to Aubrey,

"Did you bolt the door downstairs after you came in? That was the entrance you used in coming in, wasn't it?"

"Yes, I am sure I did," said Aubrey.

"Let's go and see," I insisted.

We lit the paraffin lamp and went timidly down the stairs to the lower floor. There was no one there, and the door was securely bolted, as Aubrey had said. We thought it strange, for we were quite certain the noise we heard was from the lower floor. Neither of us would admit we were scared. We went back to our room and fell asleep again. We heard no more noises that night.

Two nights after, we were again awakened by the sound of knives and forks, and people talking as if they were eating downstairs. We listened intently, and there it was, very clearly, a murmur which was not quite intelligible, and knives and forks rattling as if people were eating around a table. I shot up, lit the paraffin lamp and said to Aubrey whose eyes were bulging with fright,

"Come on, we must get to the bottom of this."

Aubrey did not want to go but was afraid to be left alone, so condescendingly, he trailed behind me and the lamp. We tip-toed down the stairs and, reaching downstairs, saw the dining table unspread and everything in place, just as the headmaster's cook and domestic helper left it. We looked into the kitchen, the pantry and the bathroom, and all was normal. As we were about to ascend the stairs to go back to our room, an audible swish of air, as if blown by someone, put out the lamp, leaving us in pitch darkness. Aubrey screamed, and there was an audible chuckle, like suppressed laughter, from behind us. We bolted up the stairs with the speed of lightning, dashed into our beds and dived under the sheets, covering our heads, hardly daring to breathe, absolutely terrified. The hours passed, but we could not sleep until after the headmaster returned and went to bed.

The next day I told Aubrey that we would look stupid if we were to tell anyone about what took place the previous night. I believed we would be teased. And after all, I said, the whole thing could have been our imagination playing tricks with us. We decided therefore to say nothing about the occurrence. But Aubrey was not too keen on returning to the headmaster's house that evening. He relented only because I pressured him to do so.

Nothing out of the ordinary happened that night, nor the next night, nor for a whole week after. Aubrey and I were just coming to the conclusion that it was fear that caused us to hear things in the house when the most extraordinary thing happened. The headmaster's custom on his return early in the mornings was to enter the house from the street level. He would put his key in the lock, which would make a rattle, and open the door, which always made a squeaking noise. Then he would walk to his desk, perhaps to check to see if we had completed the work he set us to do, and next walked loudly (he was a big, athletic-type of man) across the room to his bedroom. He would then peep in on us to see if we were asleep. Invariably we were not but pretended we were.

About a week or more had passed after the hair-raising incident of the blowing out of the lamp and the chuckling sound, when one night Aubrey and I were aroused by the opening of the front door, the usual squeaking of the door, and loud footsteps across the sitting room to the headmaster's bedroom; but to our surprise, the door between the two rooms was not opened, and no one looked in on us. We heard the person who came in changing his clothes and the squeak of the bed when he lay down in it. Sleepy, we went back to sleep. An hour or so later, the same thing happened but this time the door between the rooms was opened, and the headmaster looked in. We had raised ourselves up in the beds with the opening of the door, looking terrified. Moonlight, streaming through the window, revealed the headmaster's face. Then I said,

"Headmaster, did you not come in before?"

"No," he said. "Are you having difficulty sleeping?"

Neither of us answered. If the headmaster could see our eyes more closely, he would have realized the panic we were in.

On our way home the next morning, Aubrey said,

"That's it. That house is haunted. Nobody can tell me that I did not hear what I heard last night and the times before. It is haunted. It is definitely haunted. I'm not going back there. That's it. No more!"

"Calm down," I said. "We are alive, aren't we? Nothing has happened to us except that we are scared stiff. If you do not turn up tonight, what will you tell your mum and dad?"

"The truth! The house is riddled with ghosts, ghosts, ghosts everywhere, downstairs, upstairs, in the bedroom, on the stairs, everywhere ! I would not have believed it if I had not seen it myself. It is amazing we are still alive."

"You haven't seen anything," I countered. "You heard noises; that's all."

"Well, it is the same thing. You can go back if you want to, but I am not going back there. That is definite."

Later that day in school, the headmaster called me aside and asked,

"What was all that about my coming in last night before I did?"

I told him exactly what occurred. He listened in silence, then asked if that had happened before. I replied that was the first time we heard someone coming through the front door and walking across the sitting room to his bedroom, but that Aubrey and I had heard other noises and had investigated but had found no clues. Telling the headmaster about someone blowing out the lamp, Aubrey's scream and the chuckling noise we heard behind us as we flew up the stairs threw me into fits of laughter. I laughed so much that tears flowed from my eyes; the whole thing seemed so fantastic, so utterly ridiculous to me. The headmaster laughed heartily, too. Indeed, both of us could not control ourselves. My class had been looking on, saw us roaring with laughter, and wondered what the joke, if it was a joke, was. It was the first time they had seen him laugh so freely. Later, they inquired of me what it was, but I would not say, and Aubrey, who knew, kept silent. The headmaster had asked what I made of the whole thing.

"Well, sir," I said, "If there is a spirit in the house — and I did not believe such a thing existed until now — it is a playful spirit, for it chuckled when the lamp was blown out and Aubrey screamed and

22

we scampered up the stairs." And again I began to laugh uncontrollably; he also.

"Are you afraid?" the headmaster asked.

"Perhaps a little, sir, but I sense that I am in no danger, really."

The headmaster looked at me for some time with fatherly love and affection. There was a silent communication between us, and I knew that he liked me somewhat. That realization made me feel good and very proud.

Aubrey was true to his word. He told his parents what had happened. Whereas his father was a man of few words, his wife made up for this deficiency by being loquacious. She immediately sought out the headmaster to tell him that her son did not want to return to his home because he thought it was haunted. In turn, the headmaster went to see my parents. To his surprise, he found that I had not told them anything about my experience. I was at home and was immediately summoned. I explained very briefly what had happened, that I was not scared to go back (I was, but would not admit it), and above all, I was very grateful for the help that the headmaster was giving me. Mum and Dad immediately joined in and thanked the headmaster, and agreed that I should continue going to him to get the extra help.

What came out of the headmaster's visit to my home was the startling revelation by my mother that the headmaster's house originally belonged to her father, my grand father, and that her mother lived there while her father ran a plantation some distance away. Why was I not told this before? How strange! But then, mother was always loathe to talk about the past, doubtless because of the humiliation of being descended partly from slave owners. Nor did the headmaster give the slightest hint that he knew that the house was haunted. But the news that one of my grand parents had lived in the house reassured me that no harm would befall me. Again I pressured Aubrey to go back with me, and Aubrey relented. We continued to receive extra lessons from the headmaster, which resulted in our success in the examination. The headmaster, happily married, later left the town to take another school in his wife's hometown.

The years passed, and with their passing came an intensification of my desire to obtain higher education. But without financial assistance, how was this to be achieved? As I pondered the matter, I felt the excruciating pain that poverty invariably brings. Two of my school mates, Basil Rowe and Aubyn Johnson, both of whom appeared to have had no financial problems, were sent off to good secondary schools. Yet, their school work, judged by the marks they were getting, were lower than mine. But this was no consolation for me. They could get the help they needed and I could not. Nevertheless, I continued to fight the odds, fully conscious of the fact that my own course of action must be to struggle, struggle, struggle. And struggle, I did. It was to characterize my whole life.

In the rural town in which I grew up, I was like all the other boys except that in the local elementary school I attended, I was, as mentioned earlier, always first in my class, from grade to grade. This was due in part to the high priority my parents placed on education and their insistence on my continuing school work at home, and in part to whatever native intelligence with which I was endowed. From early childhood, I was disciplined to read and think for myself. By the age of twelve, the habit of reading for knowledge was well inculcated in me.

It was also at twelve that I won a scholarship to go to a secondary or high school in Kingston, where most Jamaican youths went for secondary schooling. Except for two or three secondary schools of merit, which were distributed widely in the island, most of the others were concentrated in Kingston. The scholarship I was offered could cover tuition fees but not boarding, and my parents could not raise enough funds for this. In short, I could not accept the scholarship. My mother silently wept, confessing to Dad that they had failed their son. A dark cloud began to hang over the Dale household. I wanted so much to begin more advanced studies at a secondary school. I tried not to show how greatly disappointed I was because I knew that if my parents had the means to support me, they would send me to Kingston. They had sacrificed much to send my sister to Westwood High School, then one of the best secondary schools for girls in the island.

What other option was there for me? There was the pupil teacher's route. While at the elementary school (7 to 15 years) students could prepare themselves for and sit the First Year, Second Year and Third Year Pupil Teacher's Examinations. At the successful conclusion of the Third Year, they could be employed as pupil teachers, a kind of teacher's aid.

The secondary school route (fee-paying) led ultimately to the London or Cambridge (UK) Matriculation which qualified students from the colonies to seek admission to a British or Canadian or US university, and eventually to an academic degree in the area of the student's choice. (The University of the West Indies had not yet been established, and was not until after World War II.) Lacking financial support, I was forced to take the pupil teacher's route even though that was not what I wanted. I passed all three examinations in rapid succession and could now become a pupil teacher. Still, I was not satisfied. I thought it was all a waste of time. It was the secondary route I preferred.

My sister had obtained her Matriculation but instead of going on to university, which was what Mum and Dad wanted her to do, she entered the nursing profession and had become, by the time I was fifteen, a qualified nurse at a hospital in Kingston. She had promised to help me if I was admitted to the Mico Teachers' Training College in Kingston, then the only male training college in the island for those intending to get into the teaching profession. Accordingly, I moved to Kingston to live with my sister, attended a College (high school) for some time and began to prepare myself for the annual entrance examination to Mico. Later, I obtained a pupil teacher's position in an elementary school in Kingston, earning four pounds per month. Then, not to waste any time, I enrolled in an evening institute to begin externally the work of the first year students at Mico. To work by day and study by night was my only option, and I took it courageously.

The year passed and I took the First Year Teacher's Examination as an external student and was successful. Then I sat the Mico Entrance Examination. To my great surprise, candidates were never told if they passed or failed. They were all asked to meet at Mico on a certain evening, two or three weeks after they had written the examination, and to wait in an assembly hall while a few were called, one at a time, to be interviewed. The others waited nervously, wondering if they would be called. After the Principal of the College, the interviewer, had selected his intake of young men for the year, hardly more than twenty out of a total of nearly 200, the others were told to try again the next year. It was a cruel system, outrageously wicked, absolutely deplorable. I was not one of the selected few. My disappointment was gross. I wanted to know if I had passed or how the selection was made. I felt I had a right to know. But I quickly snapped myself out of this mood, continued my pupil teaching and began to prepare myself for the Second Year Teacher's Examination at the same evening Institute where I had studied for the First Year Examination. This was by no means an easy task. After a day's teaching and bicycling forty or more miles daily, I felt extremely tired in the evenings, just when I had to give myself fully to my studies. But there was no turning back.

Eventually, I took the Second Year Teacher's Examination (the teacher-training programme at Mico lasted three years) and was again successful. And again I sat the Mico Entrance Examination, subjecting myself to the torture of waiting for the interview which again eluded me. I was never called, not selected! I was totally bewildered, absolutely puzzled. I was able to pass not only the First but the Second Year Teacher's Examination, the same examinations that the internal students at Mico took, but still it appeared I was not good enough to pass the entrance examination to the institution. Something seemed very wrong. The Principal of Shortwood Training College for women (the equivalent of Mico) a lady of influence who had taken a keen interest in me and who knew the Principal of Mico on a professional level, inquired of him how I had done in the examination. The Mico Principal admitted to her that I had scored very high marks but that I was either the youngest or one of the youngest candidates, and there were older men who had tried repeatedly to enter the College, which had only a limited number of places. The older men had to be given preference over me. Had the Principal explained this to the waiting, anxious candidates who wanted to know the results of the examination, their anxiety would have been relieved somewhat, disappointed though they were. What was even worse for me was that two of my friends, older than myself, whom I had coached for the examination, were admitted, but I was not.

Sadly, I came to the inescapable conclusion that I was wasting my time in Jamaica. I must seek greener pastures. Life was too short for me to waste it. I felt that if I was to be a teacher, I must not only be college-trained but hold an academic degree or two as well. I must get away; Jamaica held little promise for me. Around me were highly intelligent youths who were denied the opportunity of college or university or technical training — promising youngsters who could, in the end, make an invaluable contribution to the development of their island. One by one they had migrated to Kingston in the frenzied hope of improving themselves but in the end fell prey to the evils of city life, their hopes dashed, their ambition denied, their youth spent. As was my custom from an early age, I contemplated these matters, wanting to know why life was so difficult for me and my peers, given their intelligence and strong desire to improve themselves. With rare exceptions, those from my rural town met ultimate defeat. I reflected on the poverty around me, the general air of despondency and frustration, the marked tendency of the governing authorities to provide for a large police force and many prisons, and the equally strong disposition to ignore those positive influences, including technical and vocational centres, that could counteract the negative elements. Why was this? I asked myself. Why were all the people of my home town so indigent, appeared so downtrodden, so lacking in material wealth? Why were all at the bottom of the economic ladder?

My thoughts next turned to my parents. I knew little about their background. How strange, I felt, that I did not know! As I then recollected, there was hardly any mention of my ancestors at home. Why, I wondered. For that matter, what was the background of the black people around me? Why did they possess so few of the world's goods, so disadvantaged? Until then I had given little thought to my ethnic background, except once when I wanted to study Jamaican or West Indian history in school and could not because it was not included in the curriculum. As I thought about it, I recalled that none of my school mates ever spoke of his/her ancestors — Negroes, Indians, Chinese and those who were the product of mixed marriages. Suddenly curiosity overcame me, and I turned to my mother for an explanation. I visited her during the holidays.

"Mum," I said, "please tell me who my grand-parents were — your mother and father first, then Dad's."

"Why suddenly this interest?" Lydia Dale asked. "You have never inquired before."

"But now I am inquiring. I would like to know. The time has come for me to know my roots. Please tell me about our ancestry, our history."

"You haven't been taught that at school?" she asked.

"In school, I once told the teacher that I was not interested in English history, which she didn't know very much about, anyway — William the Conqueror, Hereward the Wake, and all that stuff. I said I would prefer to learn Jamaican or Caribbean history. She reported me to the headmaster for being insolent. I was not insulting at all. I honestly wanted to know something about our people. And the headmaster punished me. That was very unfair, and I said so, and got more punishment. I still think I was not being rude."

"I remember," my mother said. "Your father did not really believe the headmaster when he told him you were being difficult, but your dad did not want you to know that he had taken your side.

29

He said to the teacher, 'Difficult because he thinks, because he has an inquiring mind, curious about most things? We brought him up to be like that."

My mother also had an inquiring mind. She read a great deal, often into the early morning hours. She knew the value of education and gave her children much encouragement to study hard. Moreover, she was always evidently stirred by my nascent ability to reason, and here I was requesting her to fill the gap left by my teachers. She dropped the lace embroidery which she was attaching to a customer's dress and proceeded to tell me the little she knew about her ancestors.

"My son," she began, "we are about the only people on God's earth who cannot trace our ancestry. That wicked institution called slavery robbed us of our African heritage which, I rather think, was very impressive. The slave owners would not allow any two slaves who could speak the same tribal language to work together for fear they would plot their escape or mutiny. They were separated and had to learn and speak the language of the slave owners. Every vestige of their culture was destroyed, or forbidden, or ignored. The name, 'Dale', or my maiden name, 'Coy', for example, is certainly not African. It is English. The English language and English customs were forced upon our ancestors. That is how we come to be speaking English and not one of the African languages. It was a terrible thing. I say to you, my son, never be ashamed that one part of your ancestry is African."

I listened intently as my mother continued. She emphasized again that she knew very little about our forebears and could go back no further than to her grand mother, Marie. She knew absolutely nothing about Marie's husband, her grand father, whether he was left in Africa or captured and forced into slavery. The British slave merchants had captured Marie and her young daughter, Annie, most likely in the hinterland of the Gold Coast, now Ghana, possibly in the northern reaches, the Mali/Chad area, because Marie constantly made mention of Timbuktu. (I read later that this was the capital of the Songoi Empire, one of the principal Negro intellectual centres of the Moslem world. It was a trading centre of some repute during the early days — the 16th century — of overland trading from the Sudan to the West African coast, much before the advent of the slave trade). Marie had a stately bearing, and Annie comely looks and a striking appearance. Both were thrown into irons like wild beasts, shipped across the Atlantic under unspeakable, inhuman conditions, according to some of the books mother had read, and sold as slaves. Contrary to the custom of the slave traders, both mother and daughter were not separated but were sold together since their bearing, looks and dignity, despite the tatters they were in, could fetch a higher price than if they were sold separately. The owner of the sugar plantation who bought Marie and Annie was so impressed by the regal bearing of the two that he spared them the customary field work to which all his slaves were subjected, and kept them in his house to do housework.

At this point, Mum paused, overcome with emotions, tears streaming from her eyes. Almost in a stupor, I sat wide-eyed looking at her.

"Mum," I said at last, "please go on. Please tell me more. I would like to know everything."

Lydia Dale wiped her eyes and continued with the story, much of which she had heard from her parents. The young girl, Annie, grew up in the slave owner's home and was allowed to play with his son who was of Annie's age. Gradually, Annie flowered into an attractive teenager, and the young boy, John, into a responsible, sensible young man. One day, to the profound surprise and annoyance of his father, John told him he had fallen in love with Annie and that he wanted to marry her. This was like a bomb exploding in the ears of his father. He would not hear of it, and quickly shipped John off either to England or Scotland or Wales (Mum could not remember which), where a cousin of marriageable age was living. The intent was that

31

John would marry this girl. John obeyed his father, went as directed, but refused to marry his cousin. He returned to Jamaica, to his father's estate in the parish of Trelawny, and married Annie, his former sweetheart.

"Bravo! Brave man!" I said with enthusiasm. "But how was he to manage without his father's help?"

"Well," said Mum, "he actually did manage. In his determination to prove to his father that he could make a success of his life without his father's help, he succeeded in becoming an overseer of a small plantation. There he took Annie, his wife, who bore him two sons and a daughter — me."

"So you are Annie's and John's daughter, and they are my grand parents on your side!" I said.

"Yes, that's what I am trying to tell you," said my mother.

"So one of my grandfathers was either English or Scottish or Welsh! I am not proud to be related to anyone who kept slaves or supported slavery because of greed. Well, what happened to John's father; that would be your grand father, my great grand father?"

"He disinherited John, and thereafter no one knew what happened to him," Mum explained.

"And your brothers? What happened to them?"

"Harold went to Australia and, we heard, made a fortune, but we were not sure if this was true. Alexander stayed in Jamaica and went into business in Kingston. Neither of them kept in close touch with me, unfortunately."

"Why didn't they give you an African name? Why 'Lydia'?" I asked.

"My mother named me after one of the early Christians by that name. The Bible (somewhere in the Acts of the Apostles) says that on one of his missionary journeys, Paul met Lydia in Macedonia. He

32

had gone to Macedonia because in a dream he saw a man, a Macedonian, pleading with him to go there and help the people. He went, and was entertained by Lydia, a dealer in purple fabric, a woman of some influence. The Bible says she worshipped God and that God opened her heart to respond to what Paul had said. She and her household (perhaps the people she employed) were baptized. So my mother had me baptized when I was a little baby and gave me the name 'Lydia'."

"Why didn't you tell me this before?" I asked.

"You never asked me," came the reply.

"Well, you are certainly like Lydia of the Bible. You are always entertaining and helping people, and you have a strong religious belief."

Mum made no reply, and I continued the interrogation.

"And how did you come to meet and marry Dad?" I asked.

Well, as you know, your father has a rich tenor voice and was a member of the local Baptist Church, also a member of the church choir. It was his voice that first attracted me to him. He could take high "C" without any difficulty whatsoever."

Here Lydia Dale's face shone like the morning star, as reminiscence swept over her. Her teenage son listened, absorbed, thinking what magical effect romantic love had on his mother.

She began. "I was then in my late teens and whenever my mother took me to any special function at the Baptist Church — my mother was Anglican but the three churches in our town supported one another — and heard your dad sing the solo part of an anthem, I would be lifted clean off the seat I was sitting on. I fell in love with the man because of his voice. Wasn't that silly?" and both son and mother laughed heartily.

"No, not really," said her son.

Mum laughed again and said, "What do you know about such things, any way?"

"But how did you actually meet him, and when and how did he propose marriage to you?" I asked.

"We will pass over that and say only that I accepted his offer of marriage when he proposed."

"Ah, Mum, you are leaving out the juiciest part. And what about his background?" I inquired further.

"His parents were also slaves. When slavery was abolished, they squatted on a piece of land where your father was born. Like me, he had no more than elementary schooling. He learned a trade, cabinet- (furniture-) making while his parents eked out a living from subsistence farming. Their bodies had suffered the ravages of slavery and in the end they became totally blind. Your father looked after them until they died. You have seen their graves in the cemetery."

Mum went on to point out that her childhood was a trifle better than that of most of the local girls in her town. After elementary school, she was taught dress-making and embroidery, both of which had helped to put food on the table and send her children to school. They had no inheritance whatsoever. She and her husband had to start from scratch and had struggled to rear a family and remain alive. She had hoped to give me what she called a "decent education" but, as I saw, matters had not turned out the way she had hoped they would. Added to that, she and Dad were becoming old.

"Don't worry," I said. "I will try to help myself; and I promise you to get back your home which the bank has taken. I will. I must. One day! I promise!"

Like most of the young people of the island, I was black, or more accurately brown, because of the intermarriage of my grand parents. As the descendant of slaves, without inheritance of land or wealth, I could now understand more fully why I was living in a climate of

34

poverty, pregnant with hopelessness and frustration. I became more acutely conscious that if I was to make a success of my life, I would have to fight to ward off the contagion of hopelessness so prevalent among my peers. They felt they had no future; they were dejected, trapped, lacking in self-esteem and a sense of purpose. What was there for them to do? Simply, nothing! Soon they become illegitimate fathers while still in their teens. Temptation to do wrong was almost irresistible. Already two of my closest friends had succumbed to it and ruined their lives. I was afraid that I, too, could fall into the trap.

Judith, a beautiful local girl who caught the eyes of most of the local boys, had eyes only for me, it seemed. I, in turn, was curiously drawn to her. I had listened to the exploits of my friends, but I had no encounter with girls up to then. Judith, however, nearly threw me off my feet. Passion or infatuation or whatever it was rose up in me with volcanic intensity. It was indeed fierce. I could hardly suppress it. But it was Judith herself who brought me to my senses. She told me one day that my friend, Lyndon, who was from a privileged family, had asked her to marry him.

"And are you going to?" I asked.

"Yes, if you don't want to marry me," Judith replied boldly.

Immediately my analytical mind snapped into action.

"You are joking," I said. "Me, a husband even before I am 18? What a joke! What sort of life would we have? A husband without any form of security, without the university education that he is determined to have, without a job, without anything? Young lady, you cannot be serious."

"Edmund Dale," she replied, "I am quite serious. I want to bear your children, to be with you through thick and thin, for the rest of my life."

"Childish talk! You must have been reading some of those 'girlie-

girlie' books. Grow up!" I said. "You do not know what you are talking about. Lyndon may be able to give you what you want, but I will not be able to do so. Besides, marriage is not a part of my dreams just now. Nor should it be a part of yours yet either."

In this vein, I continued to lecture Judith, as a father would a daughter, though I was somewhat younger than her. I encouraged her to put the thought of motherhood aside just then and seek to improve herself educationally and otherwise. I pointed out the folly of taking on such a responsibility before she was quite ready. No, she should hold her head up, aspire to other things than the marriage bed or the changing of diapers just then.

Judith Robart became angry not because of my logic and sensible reasoning but because she could not have me, or have her way with me. I was mentally or perhaps morally too strong for her. So she thought she would make me feel jealous by going out with Lyndon. But this had no noticeable effect on me. I fought as hard as I could to conceal my inner feelings. I wished her good luck and continued to pursue my goal of finding a way to get to a university.

By this time, World War II was at its peak. The Commonwealth, including Jamaica, had stood beside Britain from the day in September 1939 when Britain declared war on Germany. Although poor, Jamaica contributed greatly to the war effort, including her young sons who volunteered for active service in the Armed Forces. Even I had donated my greatly-treasured album of rare Jamaican postage stamps which I had been collecting since I was seven years of age. Years after, I wondered if it had ended up in the hands of an unscrupulous person who kept it for himself. The value of such a huge collection would have been appreciable.

Then came an urgent drive to recruit young Jamaican males to serve in the Royal Air Force (RAF) in England. Many had volunteered before and were then on active service, but recruitment was later stepped up. This caught my attention. Many of my former school friends had volunteered and had passed the rigorous medical examination which was required of all new recruits. For some time my mind played with the idea of volunteering, but always I returned to the questions which troubled me: Why should I? Why should I fight in a war about which I knew very little? War, to me, was and still is senseless, primitive, barbaric. From the little I had read, I had concluded that war brought out the worst in people. So many thousands, indeed millions had been foolishly killed in wars, especially innocent people. And no sooner we bury them, if their bodies were found, or we erect monuments in their honour, than we are back at it again, hating and killing one another. Yearly around the cenotaphs we express stirring words and shed painful tears for those who did not return. But soon, greed and selfishness, fear and hatred, bigotry and arrogance well up in our breasts and back to killing we return. The truth was that I had become ambivalent about volunteering for service in the RAF.

Some initial training was given the new recruits in Kingston before they were sent off to be trained either in Canada or Britain or both. An English resident in Kingston felt he could make a contribution by teaching the Morse code to the recruits, some of whom wanted to be wireless operators, pilots and navigators in the RAF. He had for years been a member of the Cable and Wireless Company in the island. Thus he obtained, or was helped by his compatriots to obtain, a number of wireless sets and Morse keys and turned the spacious grounds of his magnificent home in Upper Kingston into an open-air school. After work in the afternoons, the recruits would gather there and be instructed in sending and receiving Morse signals.

Intrigued by the progress of my friends who had volunteered, I would listen to them in silence as they discussed the training programme. Finally, I concluded that if I volunteered for service in the RAF, at the end of the war, if I was mercifully spared, I might stand a chance of gaining admission to a British university. Perhaps this could well be the opportunity I was seeking. Very quietly I volunteered, passed the medical examination, and was soon sitting before a Morse code buzzer with the other recruits in the open-air school, on the private grounds of the English expatriate. I thought I would say nothing about this to my parents or sister, for I knew they would certainly disapprove my action. Moreover, under Jamaican law then, a male child under 21 years of age was wholly under the control of his father; and I was not yet out of my teens. With the help of friends in the right places, I advanced my age above 21 and obtained my passport, as the recruits were asked to do well before they were due to leave. In fact, they were told that their departure from the island, when the time came, would be at very short notice. German U-boats were making havoc of North Atlantic shipping, and extreme caution was necessary.

The training continued for a few months until at the end of one of the sessions in early September 1943, the recruits were told that was their last training session and that their departure date had been decided upon. They should return to their respective jobs the next day, say nothing about their intended departure, not to relatives or friends or anyone else, until a few hours before leaving home. They should then report at 6 a.m., two days later, at a given secret destination. No other information was given, such as where we would be going and by what means we would be transported.

Our excitement reached boiling temperature. The time had come at last! Instead of going that evening to the Institute where I had begun to prepare myself for the Third Year Teacher's Examination, I went home and began to pack my suitcase. As luck would have it, my sister was on night duty and was not expected to return home until after mid-night. Next, I sat down and wrote my parents a letter, explaining what I had done, why I was doing it without their consent, and adjured them to pray for me and to believe that the good Lord would protect me and bring me back alive and well. I confessed to them that I had not settled in my mind the question of killing people in a war and that was still causing me mental anguish. I thanked them for their love, affection, guidance, and the many sacrifices they had made for me, and for bringing me up in such a happy home, even if it was deficient in many of the world's goods. Finally, I urged them to continue believing in me. I would not let them down; and they should try to forgive me for not seeking their consent to leave. Then I added a postscript: "I love you very much, Mum and Dad."

The next morning I went off to the school where I was pupil-teaching, and on the way posted the letter I had written to my parents. I tried hard to conceal my excitement and to some extent actually succeeded. During the day, I made certain that the recruiting people phone the school authorities the next day and explain my absence and the reason for the secrecy.

I returned from my school late that afternoon and completed packing my suitcase. I spent the evening tidying my room, putting away my books and little treasured possessions, took out the clothes I would be wearing, had my shower, climbed into bed, and began to read, as was my custom. I was still reading when my sister, Hazel, returned from her night duty at the hospital. She popped into my room, surprised to find me still awake.

"Reading as usual?" she asked.

"Just killing time waiting for you," I replied.

"Are you ill?" she asked.

"Heavens, no. The medical examination at the recruiting office found me in excellent health," I replied.

"Recruiting Office …."

Before she could say another word, I continued.

"You see, I volunteered for service in the Royal Air Force and have been undergoing preliminary training for the past months. I am due to leave the island in the morning, no, this morning. See, my suitcase is packed and labelled."

39

"What!" she exploded as surprise, anger, if not disappointment, flared up in her. "Going to war? Are you insane? Have Mum and Dad agreed to this?"

"No, they don't know anything about it."

"And you are going to leave without their knowing?"

"I posted a letter to them this morning. It explains everything."

"How could you be so cruel?" she demanded.

"Well, you know quite well that they would object."

I tried to explain to my sister my motive, that she knew too well how hard I had tried to get into Mico Training College and how I had failed miserably. Well, I advanced my age so that I would be accepted as a recruit. It was a wrong thing to do and I may later regret falsifying my age, but leaving the island that way was really my passport to higher education. With luck, at the end of the war, I would seek admission to a university. She should not be too annoyed with me, but have faith in me. What I was doing was the only way out for me, as I could see it.

In tears Hazel left the room. Although feeling tired, she could not fall asleep. The news was too sudden. When 6 a.m. came, she was still awake. I had hoped she would be asleep and that I would spare myself and her the "sweet sorrow" of parting, as Shakespeare puts it. The Dale family was an affectionate one, although members of it would often hide their strong family feelings. At my departure, Hazel scolded me, rebuked me, reviled me, but in the end hugged me. With determined effort, I pulled myself away, grabbed my suitcase, jumped into the waiting taxi, which I ordered the evening before, and was off.

At the appointed rendezvous, the 25 recruits had gathered, looking excited, nervous, anxious, curious. We were a motley group, drawn from upper-middle, middle and lower-middle income homes; some had attended well known schools like Jamaica College, Wolmer's School, St. George's College and other secondary (high) schools in Kingston. Black, brown, half-white, we represented somewhat the ethnic structure of the island; all ambitious, all keen, all ready for adventure. The fire of youth burned brightly in our faces. We had been well selected, but the thought that some of us might not return alive was registered in the faces of a few local officials who had come to see us off. They had brought a few ill-sorted overcoats, sweaters, scarves and woollen socks — cast-off from former days — that they thought we could use as we plunged ourselves into northern climes. The whole day was given to trying on and choosing garments, pep talks, checking of documents, and further medical check-ups. No one was allowed to leave the building or phone relatives. Even then we did not know when we would be leaving or where we would be going. The closest security was maintained until 7 p.m. when the group was assembled for the final pep talk. We were then told that we would be going first to Tampa, Florida, and there take a Pullman train to New Haven, Connecticut, thence to Moncton, New Brunswick, Canada. Although the youngest in the group, I was singled out to be the leader of the group, and to me were entrusted documents which I should deliver to the Air Force authorities in Canada. At all times, the group was told, Edmund Dale would speak for them, and at all times throughout the journey, they should give him support. We were next asked if we had any questions. No one had, except me, for by that time my head was reeling around, wondering why I was chosen to be the leader of the group.

"Yes, Mr. Dale?" the officer said.

"May I ask when we are due to leave Jamaica and whether we are flying or going by boat? Also, how long will we be staying in Tampa and in Canada?"

"You are due to leave here in one hour's time by boat. You will be taken aboard one by one in order to avoid undue notice. The doctor has provided some tablets for you to take if and when you experience sea sickness. You will be met on arrival in Tampa by British officials who will give you more information. Any other questions?" There was none, and the group was dismissed.

Immediately, most of the recruits surrounded me and voiced their approval of me as leader.

"Dale," Brian Byrne, who was to be my friend and companion throughout the war, said, "you are just the man for the job. You are fearless and you can talk. You have my support."

Clifford Jones was the next to speak. "Man, you have style. We like you. We are all in this together," and patted my shoulder in friendly camaraderie.

One by one the group voiced their sentiments. As one of them had said, our hour had come; we were going to war and some of us might not return. For the next little while, the gravity of the hour, or the realization of what we were about to do, suffocated speech. It was I who broke the spell with,

"Come, fellows, put sentiments aside. Excitement awaits. That train ride from Florida to Canada is bound to be interesting. I have not slept on a train before. Has any of you?"

The moment of dread or fear or whatever it was that for a moment had all these promising young men in self-examination soon passed, and in our youthful faces optimism returned.

At last the call came for us to move to the pier, and one, by one at punctuated intervals, we climbed the gang-way of a medium-sized boat. When all were aboard, the boat pulled up anchor and moved slowly, silently out to sea under the strictest blackout. I remained on deck in the darkness for a long time and saw the barely visible outline of my beautiful island disappear from view. Then I went into the cabin I was assigned, threw myself down on the bunk assigned to me, the one below that on which Brian Byrne lay wide awake. The cabin had four beds, two to a tier. All the other occupants were awake, but there was silence. We had been told during the day that a German U-boat had been spotted in the Caribbean only the day before. The lights in the cabin had been turned off and the blackout material over the port hole removed. As the boat made its way through the choppy sea, the rush of the water below the port hole was very audible. Still no one talked. The silence was heavy. What was each of us thinking? At last I got up, walked to the port hole, covered it with the black drape and said,

"Fellows, let us try to sleep."

At the break of dawn, all 25 recruits were on deck, looking out on the vast expanse of sea around us. The fascination of being surrounded so completely by water gripped us — our first time at sea — until a squall blew up and quickly became a violent wind. The boat began to roll from side to side, then it pitched forward and backward, then descended into the angry sea and heaved upward again — four movements that caused us to become completely unhinged. Just then the bell for breakfast rang. We tried to reach the dining room, one deck below, but the smell of food made matters worse. A few of us had to be helped by crew members to our respective cabins and were told to lie down. Gladly we complied. At lunch time, we remained completely incapacitated. I reached for an orange and tried to eat it, but no sooner it went down than it came up again. Evening came and the wind abated slightly. The rolling of the ship ceased somewhat. Still feeling dizzy, we tried to put on a good face and take solid food, but quickly retired to our cabins for fear of bringing it up again. Standing or moving caused nausea of the worse kind. Sea-sickness is truly horrible!

The next day sanity returned to the sea. It was now calm. The sun was out; it was altogether a beautiful day. Soon, good humour returned and stayed with us until eventually we saw the first faint outlines of the Florida coast. But it seemed ages before we could reach it. The hours passed as we watched US. coastal patrol boats busily dashing about. About a hundred or more miles out from the coast, our boat, which had been reducing its speed, suddenly stopped. Immediately, a US patrol boat drew alongside with a US pilot and immigration officials. They came aboard, and the pilot took charge of the boat and guided it into Tampa harbour. Thus the first leg of our journey was at an end.

43

CHAPTER 3

As we were told before leaving Jamaica, immediately the boat docked in Tampa, British officials boarded it and sought us out. The officials saw to immigration and customs formalities, and took us to a hotel in the city where we would stay for two days, "getting our feet," so to speak, before boarding the Pullman for Connecticut. The group was pleased to have this time to explore Tampa and see something of the vaunted American way of life.

To the shock of all of us, everywhere we looked we saw signs with 'White only' and 'Colored only'. Coming from Jamaica where economics rather than race decides where people live, where social mixing of the races is common place, and where the colour of one's skin is not a barrier to entry to shops and other public places, we were greatly astonished by what confronted our eyes. If we had felt little national sentiments before, now we began to feel proud that whatever may be said of our homeland, at least segregation of the races there was not as strikingly obvious or blatantly ridiculous.

Soon, all the recruits were to meet this absurdity head on. As the American spelling of 'coloured' omits the 'u', I wondered at first if the word meant something other than what it purported to mean. At any rate, I ignored the signs and walked about as freely as I would in my native Jamaica. I had a few American dollars in my wallet and, passing a shop advertising peanuts, I thought I would pop in and buy a few boxes to take with me on our forthcoming train ride. I walked

44

into the shop and realized by the large number of expensively-dressed customers busily shopping that it was indeed an exclusive place. The chatter and general buzz of the customers, though inordinately surprising to someone unaccustomed to the general tempo of American life, failed to capture my attention. Not so the decor of the place which immediately fascinated me! Everywhere I looked, I saw peanuts in the husk, in geometric patterns, in various colours, cleaving to the ceiling and the walls, and hanging from trellises. Always touched by things beautiful, I stood, on entering the shop, and ran my eyes from ceiling to walls, in delightful admiration. Gradually, the noise and chatter of the shoppers ceased. There was a marked silence which drew my attention away from the decor. I looked around and saw all eyes focused on me. The stares were ugly, decidedly wicked, unquestionably hostile, intensely charged with anger. It was the look of hatred, which spoke louder than words, once seen or felt, never forgotten. Suddenly, I realized I had entered a 'white only' shop. Strangely, I was not one little bit afraid. Youth is often fearless. Well, I thought, if they thought I was going to make a dash for the door, they were going to be disappointed. I held my ground, smiled and walked boldly, but calmly, up to the girl at the cash desk, whose make-up effectively made her appear, I imagined, like Jezebel of the Old Testament. With withering scorn, she looked at the young man facing her. Still smiling, I advanced closer as she almost shrank into the wall, her eyes seemingly spitting fire and essaying the words, "dare you to come closer!" I smiled even more sweetly and in modulated cadence, said for all to hear, and all in the shop could hear, for the loud chatter had ceased,

"What a beautiful place! The artistry! The designs! It is exquisite! Everything is so beautifully harmonized. Indeed, it is unique!" And I meant every word of it.

The sincerity of my words, together with the sheer delight that shone from my eyes, obviously brought about a change in the girl's face which now mirrored considerable curiosity.

"But you are not an American," she said, descending from her lofty heights of assumed superiority.

Before I could reply, the manager of the shop, apparently hearing the silence in the place, rushed out of his office at the back to see what was going on. When he saw me, a black man in his 'lily white shop', he rushed to confront or assault me. But, still smiling and looking calm and confident, I blocked his speech with:

"Presumably, you are the manager of this beautiful shop. I was just saying to her, pointing to the cashier, how splendid the decor is. If you are not an artist, you certainly know what good taste is. Where did you get the idea to do this place so effectively?"

The tightened face of the man slackened.

"But you are not an American," he said dubiously. "Are you?"

I laughed outrightly and, pointing to the girl again, said, "She has just asked me the same question. Does it matter if I am or am not an American?"

Ignoring my question, he asked,

"You are a tourist?"

"Well," I said, "I am just passing through your city. My first visit!"

"So you are a tourist!" his manner completely changed. He held me by the hand and led me to his office and said, "Please sit down," offering me his chair. He sat on another chair and proceeded to tell me all about his shop, how he started with only a few dollars, and how he sacrificed and worked hard (the credo of the American dream) to make it into the business that it became. At the end, he loaded me with boxes of peanuts, without accepting a cent, some in candy form, wished me an enjoyable 'holiday,' and expressed the hope that I would visit Tampa again.

I was still laughing and chuckling to myself over the incredulity of what I had just experienced when I mounted a bus of the local transit system which would take me back to the hotel where we were staying — a 'colored only' hotel. I climbed in at the front door, walked mid-way to where the conductor sat collecting fares, paid the fare and walked to a seat at the front so that I could see where I was going. I sat beside a passenger, a white woman, who made a suppressed scream and fled to another seat. I thought the boxes I was carrying had accidentally poked her, so I began to tie them up more securely. I was thus engaged when the conductor, of brownish complexion, not black and not white, came and stood before me, looking menacingly, and rudely thundered,

"You can't sit here. You must go to the back."

I shot a glance quickly to the back and saw only black people, all with wild eyes staring at me. In my pre-occupation with the boxes of peanuts I had in my hands, I had not taken note of the segregation on the public bus when I climbed into it (and even if I had, it would have made no difference). Loudly, clearly, slowly, emphasizing every word, I shot back to the conductor,

"I have not the slightest desire to sit at the back. May I know why you want me to sit there?" There was general laughter in the bus.

"**You** (emphasizing the word) must sit at the back," he said.

"Why?" I demanded vehemently. "I do not want to, and I have no intention of doing so."

The conductor stood looking helpless and I sat looking defiant. The atmosphere in the bus had suddenly become tense. The Negroes at the back looked terrified, apparently thinking that a lynching was inevitable. Just then, I felt a poke in my back. With a dramatic, if not regal, turn of my head, I looked at the woman who had poked me and said,

"Madam, you are actually assaulting me. Can I be of some help?"

47

She, laughing (I could not tell if she was being supportive or sarcastic) said, "I take it you are not an American."

"I am not." said I, with delight, "nor do I want to be one, nor to be treated as one. I am a visitor and expect to be accorded the civility and common courtesy that any civilized country shows to visitors. I was under the impression that these niceties were practised in your country. Perhaps I am mistaken. Any more questions?" I asked.

"No, thank you," she continued laughing but this time more heartily, clearly extremely amused.

While all this was going on, the bus had stopped. The driver turned round in his seat and looked at me, his eyes almost shouting "murder." And I looked steadfastly into those grey, murderous eyes, my eyes belching fire, and stared him down. Finally, he turned round again and continued driving the vehicle.

I was not sure of the stop where I should get off the bus for my hotel, and would not ask. At last I recognized a large advertisement board which I had seen from the hotel that morning. I rang the bell; the bus stopped, and I dismounted. Then I looked back and saw the eyes of all the passengers on the bus staring at me. I shook my head with a disdainful smile and heard myself asking myself, "Is this the United States to which so many Jamaicans want to migrate? Surely the darkness that exists here is much thicker than that in Jamaica. Certainly in race relations Jamaica could teach these people a useful lesson or two."

On my second day in Tampa, I decided to look up a pen-friend, Ben Sutherland, with whom I had been corresponding for over two years. I consulted a city map and located the street on which he lived. It was some distance away. I decided to walk so that I could see and observe more of the city. My walk turned out to be most interesting. Eventually, I reached the address, a large house with a decorated iron gate. I pressed the bell and a black maid admitted me. Ben was out but his mother was at home. She came forward to receive me most warmly. She told me that she had heard about me through her son, and that he would be home shortly. She appeared unaffected, genuine, very kind, and without pretence. But how could this be in a city so steeped in racial prejudice? I thought my powers of judgment might be failing me. Yet, I told myself that if the family was prejudiced, I would know. Cold drinks were served, and Mrs. Sutherland entertained me graciously until her son returned. On his arrival, he was told in the hallway that his Jamaican pen-friend was paying him a surprised visit. Ben dashed into the room and, seeing me, gleefully extended his hand and shook mine forcefully.

"You look very much like your photograph but more handsome. Why didn't you tell me you were coming?" he asked.

"I did not know myself until four days ago and then not until just before we departed," I said.

"We?" asked Ben.

"Volunteers for the Royal Air Force. I suppose I can tell you that 25 of us, all Jamaicans, are on our way to Canada, thence to Britain, to join the RAF. We are spending only two days in Tampa."

Ben whistled and said, "Boy, oh boy, you have taken the war to heart, all right. But why do you want to leave your beautiful, peaceful Jamaica to go to be shot up by the Gerries?"

Mrs. Sutherland answered for me, reminding her son that Jamaica was a British colony and had been British since the 17th century. That much she said she knew, and that when Britain declared war in 1939, not only Canada and Australia but the whole British Empire, including colonies like Jamaica, threw their weight behind Britain. From his looks, it was clear that Ben did not regard Jamaica's action rational. He quickly changed the topic and proceeded to tell me about the university to which he had been admitted a few months before. Fortunately, he had come home for the weekend, otherwise he would have missed seeing me.

49

Noon arrived and I was about to leave but was invited to stay to lunch with the family — Ben, his mother, his elder sister and younger brother. His father was a Colonel in the Army and was away. The lunch was good and the conversation agreeable and convivial. I liked Ben's repartee and did more laughing than eating. He had a care-free attitude which, with his peculiar mannerisms and boyish humour, made every one laughed. He was really an attractive young man, clearly idolized by the Negro maid.

After lunch, Ben decided to show me about the city. I was hesitant to go, knowing full well what was likely to take place. However, I went at Ben's insistence. He took me first to a public park, then to a museum, and the City Hall. It was a very hot day and both of us became thirsty. Ben insisted on having a cold drink or ice cream soda, and reluctantly I agreed to go to a nearby soda fountain parlour with him. Ben led the way and I followed. As I was about to enter the building after Ben, a white commissioner in an elaborate red uniform and gold trimming and tassel blocked my way and said in tones decidedly unfriendly, "Are you sure you know where you are going?"

I looked up and saw the sign 'white only'. I felt insulted, and anger flared up in me, but I shook my head with a scornful smile and began to retrace my steps when Ben came running to me and asked,

"Why didn't you come in?"

He could see that I was angry. I pointed to the sign above the door and to the commissioner, and said,

"He wouldn't let me."

Ben's face flushed red. So accustomed to his society's privileges, and seemingly indifferent to its treatment of black people, he suddenly felt ashamed. He held me by the hand and said.

"Come, we will see a movie and have a cold drink there."

At the cinema, Ben was allowed to go in but I was not. The

50

'white-only' sign was there also. Now utterly frustrated, Ben apologized to me for the restrictions.

"You have come to my city and because of racial stupidity I cannot show you around freely. I am sorry, very sorry, Edmund."

"Never mind," I said. "Look, there seems to be a quiet avenue along there," I pointed. "Let's walk along there for a little while."

The avenue ran past a cemetery, for 'Whites Only', and I began to laugh uncontrollably.

"Ben," I said, "even over there in the cemetery, stupidity has gone stark mad. Do they think that they are not going into the same ground? Do they think that on the other side they will be received by a 'white' God who will usher them into a 'white' heaven? This is more than laughable. It is madness. Really, Ben, this is gross stupidity, and in 1943, almost the middle of the 20th century!"

Both of us stood, looking at the 'White-only' cemetery, and we laughed, laughed, laughed. At the end, Ben held me and said,

"We have a lot to do, haven't we? I mean our generation."

I agreed wholeheartedly.

Finally, we said good bye to each other, and I returned to the hotel with extremely mixed feelings. I was pleased that I had met Ben and his family and that they revealed no obvious signs of racial prejudice. True, their black maid seemed to fit, painfully to me, the stereotype black maid of former days. Could it have been that because I was a visitor, the family was hiding their real feelings? I wondered about this. But surely I was, I thought, quite able to detect insincerity. Ben seemed sincere enough, though apparently lacking the fighting spirit, that is, seemingly unable to stand up fearlessly for what he believed in, and seemingly insensitive to the insulting treatment of the black people around him. He seemed also to be comfortable with the privileges he enjoyed as a white member of his society and obviously insensitive to the 'colored only' signs

51

around him. His eyes appeared to focus mainly on the 'white only' signs.

I was acutely disturbed, indeed, indignant about the way Negroes were treated in Tampa, more so because they appeared to accept the treatment without much obvious resistance, possibly because of the fear of what would happen to them if they actively resented it. Everywhere in the city were manifestations of the contempt with which they were held. I wondered how I, a Negro, could possibly survive in an atmosphere which, in 1943, was so charged with bigotry and racial hatred, and which had a penchant for lynching what they call the 'uppity' Negro.

I went to bed, feeling very troubled in spirit but I could not sleep. I got up, paced the floor, and began a dialogue with the Almighty.

"Dear God," I said in the darkness of the room, "why do you allow this wicked thing? How can you allow this? If you are a God of fair-play, justice, love and mercy, if in you there is no east or west, no north or south, as the hymn says, why do you allow this injustice, this, this, this terrible thing?"

And the good Lord said to me in my heart,

"Edmund, I made all of you good and gave all of you a free will to choose and distinguish between good and evil. Are you asking me to rush in now and overcome all choice? I cannot do that. If you do good, you help to carry out my will on earth. If you do evil, you subvert my will and will eventually reap your reward."

"But," I argued with the Lord, "in the meanwhile, look what is happening to those on whom racial hatred is unleashed."

" This," said the Lord, "is the misuse of man's free will or the fruit of his folly or his sin. Remember, they did it to my son, too. He had done nothing wrong, but they murdered him in the most painful, barbaric way imaginable."

But I persisted: "Should you not help them? The Negroes, I mean."

"I am helping," said the Lord. "In my own time, I will bring about change. The fact that you are so concerned is an indication that you want to help, too. You and others will help me to bring about the change that is needed. Yesterday, in the peanut shop and on the bus, you made the racially prejudiced **think**. That was a change for many of them, you know, a beginning at any rate. It is not guns and bombs that will bring about a change in the thinking of these people. It is an attack of conscience, a change of heart. I am working at it. Be patient. Do what you can to help me."

It was this seeming dialogue with my Creator that gradually subdued the chaos which had risen in my mind, and reminded me that evil had never triumphed over good, not even on Calvary, for Easter vanquished what insignificant little man in his blindness and folly had done. Gradually, I was led to see that white men also fought and died to put an end to the slave trade, and that it will be people of all colours — black, brown, yellow and white — who in concert will overthrow Hitler and his evil clique in the war in which I was about to take part. Albeit, the racial segregation which I saw in Tampa, and which I was to continue to see and experience elsewhere, was and would continue to be most unsettling to me. Finally, tiredness overcame me and sleep plunged me into unconsciousness.

The following morning the 25 recruits were escorted to the train station. A whole coach was reserved for us on the Pullman, clearly because as Negroes we would not be allowed to travel with the white passengers in the same compartments. The compartments were clean and comfortable. By day each was converted into something like a sitting room. By night the porters prepared them as bedrooms. Meals were served in a restaurant car several coaches forward. Always our group was served last, after the white passengers, an observation that did not escape me. In reflecting on this, I was again plunged into deep thought. I could not understand how the black people could put up with this sort of humiliation, or why they did not fight back (or were they fighting back and I was not aware of it?). I was itching to vent my pent-up feelings on this forced subservience and status quo.

At each stop of the train, I saw black porters carrying people's bags, doing the menial tasks, cleaning men's shoes — never the other way round. My blood boiled. But it was the speech of the black porters, many obvious strangers to a good education, that filled me with the greatest discomfort. They spoke a kind of lingo that made for ridicule. I could not understand it; my ears were not attuned to it; and whenever I was addressed by one of the porters, I found it difficult to make a reply because I did not understand what was said. Resentment, repugnance, abhorrence welled up in me like the rising magma of a volcano, ready to erupt. I saw the status of the black people painfully humiliating. I became intensely indignant. The other recruits, however, seemed able to shut these matters out of their minds. Or did they?

As the train hurried furiously along, black men, black women and black children could be seen picking cotton in the fields. In my heart, mind and soul, the mental anguish, wrought by the spectacle from the train window, was excruciating, utterly unbearable.

Brian Byrne who was sitting opposite to me, had been watching me and he, too, had felt the same anger as he followed my eyes to the glistening, perspiring faces of the black cotton pickers. Still looking through the window, Brian said, as if both of us had been conversing,

"What troubled me most in Tampa as I walked the streets was the constant humiliation to which these people are subjected; they are really made to feel and think they are inferior, and their general demeanour gives the impression that they are sorely diseased with an inferiority complex."

I looked at Brian with surprise and said,

"So you feel that way, too? I thought I was the only one who felt that."

Ken Thomas, who had entered the compartment while Brian was speaking, announced,

"Fellows, the porter is saying something, but I cannot make him out. Edmund, I think you should find out what he is saying."

"I am sure," I replied, "that if you cannot understand him, I will not either; anyway, I will go and see."

After I left the compartment, Brian informed me afterwards, the conversation continued. Ken Thomas said,

"What's this, Brian, about inferiority complex?"

"Well," said Brian, "I have been conjecturing that if the racial segregation we saw in Tampa, and are still seeing as we go along, is characteristic of the whole country, then it would be most difficult for the black American not to be injected with a generous amount of the poison of inferiority complex."

Now, Ken was a product of Jamaica College and was given to rational thinking, judged by his discussions with the other recruits. Brian had attended Wolmer's School but had not yet matriculated. Both had read of the racial animosity that existed especially in the southern states of the United States. What they were then seeing and experiencing was what they had expected. However, Ken was more thick-skinned than Brian or I, and perhaps a little less disturbed by what he was seeing.

To Brian, Ken replied,

"Well, have you not seen this in Jamaica, too, but perhaps in a more subtle way? At present in Jamaica, the highest positions are held by whites; jobs of lesser significance by people of lighter complexion, and mundane, low-paying jobs by blacks. Surely, Brian, you must have observed that in Kingston; in fact, this pattern holds true throughout the island."

Rodney Black then joined in the discussion. He had entered the compartment unnoticed.

"You are right, Ken, but in Jamaica we are beginning to see signs of a strong, emerging national feeling. I believe this will gather momentum by the end of the war and put to flight this nonsense in job orientation or deference to skin pigmentation. Watch and see."

Ken, wanting to comment on what Rodney had said, was interrupted for a moment by my return to the compartment. At last he said,

"Yet, the social hierarchy will continue. Why? Black Jamaicans are descendants of slaves, and in them the poison that Brian was talking about was also injected. Inferiority complex is still the companion of many Jamaicans, especially the so-called lighter-skinned Jamaicans. They seem to think they are superior to black Jamaicans."

"At least," I said, returning to the discussion, "Jamaicans have realized or are realizing this, and are gearing up to fight it. If black Americans do not fight this handicap, this contemptible thing, if they continue to remain docile and subservient, they will never change it. They must make a stand, fight it, even suffer martyrdom. It sickens me to death to see how much insult they take. I would fight it every inch of the way, even if I am lynched or thrown into prison a thousand times. I just would not take it."

To this Ken said,

"Really, I suppose we should thank God we were born and educated in Jamaica by black Jamaicans who inculcated in us, all of us, pride in ourselves, dignity and ambition."

To this all agreed. The discussion continued. It was somewhat of a self-examination, a catharsis and acute stirring of pride in being Jamaicans. This feeling had been lying dormant in us, and now we were beginning to see and understand more fully that although our country was poor and lacked the gloss of the United States, it was nevertheless a good country if the winds of change could blow away the dross and all that may hinder its development. The saying that nationals are born outside their countries seemed to have some credibility among us, young men of Jamaica on a Pullman train bound for New Haven, Connecticut. Others of the recruits had piled into the compartment, and each was very vocal about his experience in Tampa. All had come to the same conclusion: Jamaica may be wanting in many respects, but each was proud to be a Jamaican. It was I who brought the discussion to an end with:

"It is time for lunch. This was what the porter was announcing, Rodney."

To lunch we went but we did not eat what was served: frogs' legs were on the menu, and that was enough to turn us off. We returned to our compartment to munch on stuff we had bought in Tampa.

At long last we reached New Haven. Our coach was shunted to another line, then hitched to another train after what seemed an eternity, and we were next on our way to Moncton, New Brunswick, Canada.

CHAPTER 4

The first impression that the recruits had of Canada was the relative coolness of the weather and the colourful maple trees heralding the approach of autumn. A flight sergeant of the Royal Canadian Air Force received us at the train station in Moncton, escorted us to a bus and drove us to the Air Force base. The conditions there were most agreeable and the food excellent: milk, eggs, fresh fruits, cheese, fresh fish, meat — quite unlike the stuff we were offered on the Pullman. Besides, one could eat as much as one wanted. Equally, the billets were clean and comfortable, with hot and cold water, clean sheets, warm blankets, washing machines and dryers, indeed, we were impressed and felt reasonably happy, except for one thing. The coolness of the September weather compelled us to don the overcoats and other cast-off items we were given just before we left Jamaica. These were ill-fitting and woefully out of style. Consequently, wherever we went, we drew curious stares. Well-dressed civilians and smartly-attired airmen always looked at us as though we were species from another planet.

Left on our own for some two or three days, without even a tentative programme, and without spending money, we met in conference and agreed to request some kind of explanation. My skill in talking and persuasion, as the recruits would have it, but questionable to me, was then to be put to the test. I sought audience directly with the Wing Commander in charge of the base, a procedure which was seemingly unheard of in the forces. An airman

58

must first make his complaint to his sergeant or flight sergeant.

"Well," I said, "I am not an airman yet. I am still a civilian and I demand to see the officer in charge of the base."

Another day passed without a response, and I went into action. First, I located the office of the Commanding Officer, then I went back to my billet, discarded the ugly, ill-fitting overcoat I was given, and requested Bruce Lindo to accompany me. We went to the Commanding Officer's door, knocked and entered at his invitation to enter. Respectfully but without being subservient, shivering, and in clear, precise English, I explained that we, twenty-five Jamaican recruits, had heeded Britain's call for volunteers to serve in the Royal Air Force and were sent to Canada, there to be sent to Britain. Coming from the tropics, we were without warm clothing and were feeling extremely cold. Neither did we have Canadian currency, that is, pocket money. But worse, since our arrival five days ago, no one had come to inform us what arrangements had been made for us. I had given to the flight sergeant who came to the train station to receive us the papers with which I was entrusted to take to Canada, and had heard nothing from him since. As the appointed leader of the group, I, indeed the whole group, would like to know what arrangements had been made or are being made for us.

The Wing Commander was obviously impressed by this succinct statement and query, apologized for the breach in communication, and assured me that the recruits would be informed of their programme the following day.

We all slept a little better that night. The next day we were met by a flight sergeant who told us that we would remain in Moncton for another week and then sent to Britain. I asked about our request for warm clothing, and the flight sergeant stated that would present a problem unless we volunteered to join the Royal Canadian Air Force (RCAF). If we did, we would be issued with uniforms immediately. But the recruits would not hear of that, a decision that was to be to our disadvantage at the end of the war, for we would have been returned to Canada and helped to continue our education without much difficulty. Nevertheless, I pressed for warm clothing. In the end we were attested in Moncton and issued with RCAF uniforms, including a warm overcoat, jacket and pants, shirts, underwear and shoes, as well as a month's Canadian airman's pay which, we found out later, was far higher than that of the RAF. Equally, the RCAF clothing was far superior to that of the RAF.

On the whole, we were very favourably impressed with what we saw of the Canadian way of life and the surrounding countryside. What a contrast it was to what we saw in Tampa, Florida, and all along the train route to New Haven! If there was colour prejudice in Moncton, we saw none of it, or it was certainly more subtle than the vulgar, blatant prejudice we witnessed in the United States. Everybody on and outside the Air Force base seemed so kind and friendly, so hospitable and accommodating. There was not one member of the group who was not impressed.

When the day came for us to leave Moncton, we were put on a troop train with thousands of airmen and soldiers. As in Jamaica, the departure was at night, for security reasons. In the morning, we found our train and other troop trains converging on a harbour, possibly Halifax harbour, and hundreds of people along the rail lines leading to the pier handing out boxes of fruits, nuts, candies and K rations (dry-packed, air-tight, well-balanced meals) to the airmen and soldiers. The men were hugged and kissed as they descended the trains and made their way to the pier. It was a touching scene. The troop ship was there in the harbour, the SS Acquitania, which had been converted for the purpose. At last the men, thousands of us, climbed the gang-way. The ship was so crowded that many of the men were assigned to sleeping in hammocks which had been slung all over the ship. What a tremendous loss of life, I thought, if the boat received a direct hit from a German torpedo in the North Atlantic and went down! But what a dreadful thought! I must think positively, I told myself.

The crossing was extremely rough. Apparently to avoid detection by enemy submarine, the Acquitania zigzagged its way across the Atlantic. One day we were sweltering, the next day we were freezing. On a few occasions, the ship stood still in the sea, engines turned off, and under the strictest blackout. But in all this, the men aboard were most cheerful. Even Shan Turner, one of the Jamaican recruits, was heard to say, "Man, we are really in it (the war) at last! Any minute now and it could be good-bye for all times." The others laughed heartily.

There is a certain daring, adventure, if not heroic streak in the young. It seeks to express itself on occasions in mirth, sometimes even in the most tragic circumstances. Here was a ship with thousands of young men on board and in the midst of danger, yet listen to them as they lie in their bunks or swing to and fro in make-shift hammocks, making jokes and dispensing banter as though they were on their way to a well-earned holiday. Perhaps the good humour was itself a psychological reaction, a defence mechanism, against the imagined savagery of war. Whatever it was, the conviviality continued until the boat safely docked at Birkenhead, Cheshire, England.

On arriving, most of the men, including my group, were sent to West Kirby, a distribution centre for the RAF. It was pitch dark when we arrived in West Kirby, for nearby Liverpool had been taking a prolonged pounding from the air by German bombers. The men were led to various camouflaged tents and there given blankets, hot drinks and a meat pie so tough that it almost needed a sledge hammer to break it apart. It was fortunate that my group still had many of the boxes of K rations that were given to us before we left Canada. These were to supplement the relatively poor meals that Britain at war and with food rationing could provide.

Early the following morning, the Jamaican recruits and a group of the Canadian airmen were assembled for briefing by a Wing Commander who gave frightening statistics of the war. The RAF was desperately short of gunners and navigators, more so than pilots. Gunners, especially those at the rear of the aircraft, were easy targets for the German Messerschmidts, and their loss was phenomenal. The Wing Commander made no bones about it: the RAF wanted gunners quickly. Volunteers would be quickly trained and would quickly "get a crack at the enemy." He illustrated his talk with black and white slides. Rarely did he show a Spitfire of the RAF squadron going down. Then he urged the men to rethink their enlistment. Most had volunteered to be trained as pilots, navigators and wireless operators. The Jamaican volunteers who had preceded our group, as well as many Canadian airmen, had distinguished themselves (if their being shot down could be regarded as distinction); and many of their bodies were never recovered. The Wing Commander brought his talk to an end, distributed remuster forms and asked the recruits to fill them out and return them by that afternoon.

To their tents the Jamaican recruits returned, solemnly and in deep thought. They sat on their beds lost in thought. It was Lionel Lopez who broke the silence with,

"By gollies," he said, "I am going to have a crack at those Gerries. I am remustering as a gunner."

"Me, too," said Granville Sharp.

"No," said Ken Thomas. "I volunteered to be trained as a navigator, and navigator it will be."

"Same here," Rodney Black chimed in. "It is pilot or nothing at all for me."

Then there was silence. Everyone was now looking at me. Slowly I looked up from the floor where my gaze had been fixed for some time.

"Well, chaps," I said, "your lives are your own to do what you want with them. For my part, I am going to ask to be transferred from the air crew to the ground crew, without change in the capacity in which I volunteered to serve, namely, that as a wireless operator. It may be, as the officer has stated, that the RAF is acutely short of gunners, but the question I am asking myself is whether the RAF wants to spend much money and effort on training colonials to be pilots who will not be of use to them after the war. Perhaps this could be considered parochial thinking, but I am forced to wonder why they want to rush us quickly into active service, with very little training. Arguably, the shortage of gunners may be acute, as the Wing Commander stated."

One by one we filled out the forms and in less than forty eight hours we were sent to various training bases across the country to begin initial training. To my surprise, Brian Byrne had remustered to the ground crew also. Both of us were sent to Padgate, Lancashire, to do our initial training, then to Blackpool for another month of training.

The training at Padgate was most unpleasant. Winter had descended by then and my fingers were always frozen. Holding the butt of a gun was murderous for me. More than once I dropped the gun. On the parade ground this was considered a sacrilege, and the corporal or sergeant in charge of the drilling would almost explode with anger. However, the weeks of initial training passed and Brian and I survived; and again we were posted together to the RAF training school at Compton Basset, Wiltshire, to begin training as wireless operators. That training lasted over three months.

One of my experiences at Compton Basset is worth recording. The daily routine of the training school was morning parade before the recruits went off to their respective classes. In charge of the parade was a flight sergeant, short and small in stature, who sported a frightfully-looking mustache. His speech was virtually incomprehensible when he barked out an order or command. To my keen eyes, he seemed to be suffering acutely from a complex based either on his small build or on the realization that the recruits were having difficulty understanding his commands on the parade ground.

I silently humoured his marching orders, always taking my cue from the airman in front of me, until one morning my slowness caught the eye of the flight sergeant who, focusing his gaze on me, bellowed something which sounded like:

"Blackie, two steps forward, march!"

I remained where I stood, whereupon the flight sergeant crisply marched (he could do this very well) up in front of me and shouted again,

"Blackie, I repeat, two steps forward, march!"

There was then no mistaking whom he was addressing, and with equal lung power, I shouted back,

"Flight Sergeant, if you are referring to me, my name is not 'Blackie'. I am Airman 605712 Edmund Dale. I expect you to address me thus."

There was a ripple of laughter among the recruits who had been left to stand at ease. The face of the flight sergeant went red with anger, which added to the redness of his mustache and red hair. He looked as though he was on fire. He marched me to the Squadron Leader's office nearby and charged me with insubordination.

"Well," the Squadron Leader said, looking sternly at me, "what have you to say for yourself?"

"I should like to know, sir, what was the insubordination to which the Flt. Sgt. referred," I replied.

The Squadron Leader looked to the Flt. Sgt. who said I was cheeky. The Sqd. Ldr. turned his gaze back to me, and I told him that the Flt. Sgt. addressed me as 'Blackie', and since that was not my name, I corrected the Flt. Sgt. and requested him to address me by my correct name, and the recruits on the parade ground could verify the accuracy of my statement. With that the Sqd. Ldr. dismissed me and told me to return to the parade ground, but he detained the Flt. Sgt. Smiling a wicked smile, I returned to my place in the ranks. The

Flt. Sgt. next returned, his eyes wild with anger, and dismissed the recruits. Whatever the Sqd. Ldr. had said to him, no one knew.

After the recruits were dismissed to go to their classes and were safely beyond the glare of the Flt. Sgt., they crowded around me to hear what had happened.

"Were you mad," said one, "to answer back like that?"

"Look out," another said, "from now on he will be after you"

Still feeling angry, I would only say, "We will see."

The recruits were to be proven right, but I was quite capable of looking after myself. Before the morning session came to an end, I volunteered to help the Instructor with those airmen who were having difficulty learning the Morse signals. Willingly, gratefully, the Instructor wrote a permission note for me to return to the classroom in the evenings after the evening meal to instruct airmen who needed help. I folded the note and put it in the breast pocket of the battle dress tunic I was wearing.

After lunch, the recruits crowded around the notice board to see who were on 'fatigues' that evening. My name headed the list.

"What did I tell you?" Airman Stone said to me.

"Stone," I said, "I did not leave my beautiful Jamaica to come here to peel spuds (potatoes). I won't be 'spud-bashing' tonight or any other night. No way!"

And I did not turn up at the kitchen, as I was detailed to do.

On the parade ground the following morning, the Flt. Sgt., his face reflecting boiling pools in hell, again stood before me and barked out a few unintelligible words, to which I replied coolly but again as loudly and clearly as I could for all to hear:

> ... man, proud man,
> Drest in a little brief authority,
> Most ignorant of what he is most assur'd,
> His glassy essence, like an angry ape,

65

Plays such fantastic tricks before high heaven
As make the angels weep.

"Shakespeare, Flight Sergeant. I cannot speak as he speaks but I speak English. Will you speak in English so that I may understand?"

Again there was laughter in the ranks, and again I was marched before the Squadron Leader who, on seeing me, said,

"Again? What is it this time, Flight Sergeant?"

"Two charges, sir, insubordination and not turning up for fatigues in the cook house last evening."

Certain that he had me 'nailed' this time, the Flt. Sgt. looked quite pleased with himself.

"Squadron Leader," I, addressing him, said, "May I stand at ease and respond to the charge?"

"Of course. Stand at ease, Airman Dale. That is the name, isn't it, and explain why you seem to be causing so much trouble."

"No trouble at all, Squadron Leader. The Flt. Sgt. addressed me in incoherent English and I told him that although I could not speak the language of England's greatest poet, some of whose poetry I quoted, nevertheless, I could speak English. Would he therefore speak in English so that I might understand his commands. Surely such a simple request should not be conceived as insubordination."

The Squadron Leader laughed openly, then affected a stern look.

"And the second charge? What can you or will you say to that?"

"Well, that is easy, sir, I have been assigned to help those recruits who need extra help in the evenings. Here is my assignment slip. (I took it from my breast pocket and handed it to the Sqd. Ldr.) If the Flt. Sgt. had asked me why I had not turned up for the fatigues to which he assigned me, I would have gladly explained, but he did not."

The Sqd. Ldr. turned to the Flt. Sgt. and asked, "Is that true?"

"Well, sir, er, er, …" He found it difficult to deny it.

Whereupon the Sqd. Ldr. turned to me with an unmistakable suppressed smile and said, "712 Dale, dismiss and report to me here at 1.30 p.m. today before you go to your afternoon class."

Again, with a triumphant smile I marched back to my place in the parade. Once more the Flt. Sgt. returned, hurt, the wind obviously knocked out of his sail. He quickly dismissed the men and disappeared. Everyone wanted to know what took place in the Sqd. Ldr.'s office and could not believe that I was not carted off to the Guard Room.

When I returned to the Sqd. Ldr.'s office at 1.30 p.m., as I had been requested to do, the Sqd. Ldr. said,

"I looked up your file, Dale. You seem to be quite a guy."

"Am I right in thinking that you are a Canadian, sir?"

"Yes, how did you know?"

"You used the word 'guy' whereas the English say 'bloke'."

"But Americans use the same word, too."

"But not with your accent, sir."

"You win. What I want to know is exactly what it was from Shakespeare you quoted to make your Flt. Sgt. so upset?"

I repeated Isabella's words to Lucio from Act ii, Scene 2, of "Measure for Measure," and the Sqd. Ldr. roared with laughter.

"Dale," he said, "you are the devil himself. You did not throw one but two stones of ridicule on your Flt. Sgt. Was that not cruel?"

"Not really, sir. If he is to handle young men who are not really dumb, he should know how to do so. More importantly, the RAF, and you, his Sqd. Ldr., should insist that he dispenses with racial slurs. Why should he call me 'blackie' and not the white airmen 'whitie'? I object to 'blackie' because he used it with derision, and I will fight this kind of treatment the best way I can."

The Sqd. Ldr. listened pensively to me. Contrary to Air Force policy, he had invited me to sit. He looked long and hard at me seated there before him.

"Where did you go to school?" he asked.

"In Jamaica," came the answer, "but I interrupted my studies to come here to serve in the RAF, not to be insulted or to be the butt of ridicule and derision because my skin is black. Admittedly, the war showed me a way how I might be able to obtain the higher education I seek."

"And what is that?" the Squadron Leader asked. "That is, if you care to tell me."

I had detected in the Squadron Leader's voice and eyes an empathy, an understanding which officers of his rank rarely show to men under them. I hesitated to reply to the question. But, a shrewd judge of people from my early years, I thought the officer was sincere. Whereupon I said:

"I would like to go to university at the end of the war, if I could. In order to do this, I intend to keep up my studies in the evenings when the men are out of the billets carousing in the town."

Again the Squadron Leader looked kindly at me and said,

"You will succeed, Dale. You have what it takes. I wish you every success. I say this most sincerely."

I thanked him politely and the Squadron Leader rose from his chair, crossed over to me, and shook me firmly by the hand with the words, "Good luck, Dale."

The day came at last when the course came to an end. All but three of the recruits had passed it, I heading the list. We were then posted to various air bases around the country. I was sent to Tarrant Rushton in Dorset, along with Brian Bryne, who had done well in the final examination also.

Soon after arriving at the base, Brian and I were informed of Lionel Lopez's death. He had completed his gunner's training in eight weeks and was on his first bombing raid over Germany when his aircraft got a direct hit and went down somewhere over the borders of Germany and the Netherlands. His body was found and buried in a grave in Arnhem. The news left both of us stunned for weeks.

"We were right," Brian said, "to remuster to the ground crew. What is the point of getting killed like that? Isn't that a young life wasted? God in heaven, to die like that!"

In trying to console my friend, I reminded him that all the recruits knew what they were doing when they enlisted. True, they may not have been fully conscious of how horrible war is. Lionel's main desire was, as he put it, "to have a crack at the Gerries." His life was not wasted. It was one of many that were being sacrificed to prevent Hitler, a mad man, from getting his way. I concluded that Lionel was perhaps braver than myself and Brian.

"Or was he more foolish?" countered Brian. "Nothing you say, Edmund, could make me feel he was not foolish to offer himself as cannon fodder, because that is what it was."

"But you, we are all doing that. We actually volunteered," I said. "No, Brian, you cannot look at it like that. It could have been you or me ... ."

"But it was not you or me," Brian interrupted, "for we had the good sense to change to the ground crew. Had he done what we did, he would be alive today."

But war is war. Once a person takes up arms, his life is in jeopardy.

The news of Lionel's death was a devastating blow to both of us who found it difficult not to brood. We were just about rebounding to normal when news came again that Rodney Black was missing over

Germany. After everybody was asleep in the billet that night, I knelt quietly by my bed and prayed earnestly that Rodney would be found alive and well. At the end, I felt as if a great load had lifted from my back. I woke Brian, whose bed was beside mine, and whispered that Rodney was alive.

"How do you know?" Brian asked.

"I just know," was the reply.

Weeks after, news came again that Rodney had been found. A farmer, who had been co-operating with the Underground Movement, had found him with a broken leg in his field hiding among bales of hay. He piled up the hay around him a little higher so that he could not be readily seen, and reported Rodney's location to the Underground people who recovered him during the night and had him flown back to England. His one request was for the authorities to inform me and his other friends that he was safe and would be in action again soon.

Brian and I were attached to the Wireless Section of the air base. Known to remain calm under stress, we were detailed to man the homing device equipment in a unit some distance from the aerodrome, but in the flight-path of the planes, during thick fogs when visibility was virtually nil. Radar was already in use but many of the pilots lacked or did not have much experience in landing an aircraft by radar signals in fog, especially if the aircraft was badly shot up during a night-bombing raid. Often their radar equipment was damaged. They were forced to resort to the old homing-device procedure which required the closest co-operation between the officer on the base in charge of the homing, the wireless operator of the aircraft, and the wireless operator on the ground. The procedure was simple. The ground operator would take exact location bearings of the aircraft on a goniometer, and pass them by phone to the homing officer on the base. In turn, the officer would correct the bearings for wind speed and pass them by radio (speech) to the pilot of the aircraft. The pilot would then fly on those bearings, reducing the height of the aircraft at the same time. Throughout the operation, the wireless operator in the aircraft would be giving Morse signals so that the wireless operator on the ground could plot his bearings and pass them by phone to the homing officer on the base. Many were the times when Brian or I was rushed to the wireless station whenever the procedure was to be used, regardless of the hour of the day or night. The experience gave us the rewarding feeling that although we were not dropping bombs on Germany, we were nevertheless "doing our bit" to help to bring the war to an end.

It was during this time on the aerodrome that I decided to push my studies. I had the equivalent of the London Matriculation except in name, and since I was planning to gain admission to the University of London at the end of the war, and admission required Matriculation, I thought I should sit the London Matriculation Examination to avoid any delay later. The evening meal was served at 6 p.m. on the base, immediately after which the airmen would dash to the buses and be off to the pubs, dance halls and what amusement places in the neighbouring towns they could get to — Tarrant Rushton, Wimborne, Poole or Bournemouth, — and be back by midnight. My billet would then be left peacefully empty. This would give me the opportunity I wanted to study without interruption, and this was exactly what I did, night after night, week after week, month after month until the time came for me to write the examination. The University of London made arrangements with the Commanding Officer of the base for me to write the examination on the base under conditions set by the University. Brian Byrne, who had refused to make the effort or to sacrifice pleasure to study at nights, eyed me with a degree of admiration, so it seemed, as had the other airmen of my billet.

The week of examinations came and went, and I felt I had 'bagged' the Certificate but would not say this to any one. I waited patiently until the result came. All the men in my billet were waiting too, and when it came, they crowded around me as I opened the

71

envelope with the University of London crest on it. Yes, not only had I passed the examination but had obtained high marks in all the subjects. "Whoopie," the men of my billet shouted, and tossed me to the ceiling. Quickly, quite miraculously, they provided all that was necessary for a party, despite strict rationing. Although I do not drink rum, my relatives in Jamaica had sent me a bottle of the stuff which I had kept for such an occasion. The real Jamaican rum!!! The rumpus the men made drew other airmen from neighbouring billets and a "good time was had by all."

By 1945, the German armies were retreating, and German city after city was being pounded from the air. The end of the war was imminent, and in May 1945 Germany surrendered after initiating so much destruction of life and property, and causing so much suffering. The hopes of those who suffered were now rekindled.

After demobilization, men and women whose education had been interrupted by the war sought admission to the universities, colleges and institutes, much the same as I had planned to do. I hoped that I, too, would gain university admission. Accordingly, I applied to enter the University of London, and my friend, Brian, applied to Bristol University for admission to its School of Dentistry. Brian was admitted, but he died of a heart attack a year after he began his studies. I took the news badly. For days I kept saying to myself, "Brian, Brian, how very sad! Why is life so cruel at times?" For the rest of my life I would be thinking of him and calling his name with affection: this young specimen of manhood, over six feet tall, most agreeable, remarkably kind, honest and sincere! A silent bond had been established between us, as if we were brothers.

It was a joyous day for me when the University of London informed me that I had satisfied its entrance requirements and would be admitted to the College of my choice, University College. I thought my hopes had been realized at last. My happiness knew no bounds. Unfortunately, it was short-lived.

I was demobilized a year after the end of the war and was looking

72

forward to beginning my studies at London. But in response to my application for a scholarship, I was instructed by the Colonial Office in London that the Jamaican authorities wanted me to take the Emergency One-year Teachers' Training Course (as the name suggests, a stop-gap programme, introduced in Britain to satisfy acute, post-war needs) to finish my teacher training. They stated that I had already completed two years of the teachers' training programme in Jamaica before I volunteered for active service. I refused this outrightly and stated my preference for a degree programme at the University of London. Despite the energy I expended going up and down in seeing officials, I was unable to change the official stance. The intransigence of Colonial bureaucracy was insufferable. A teacher's certificate, not a university degree, was all that the authorities would allow. If I refused, I would be shipped back to Jamaica at the earliest possibility. Still I refused to enrol in the one-year Emergency Teachers' Course, because I thought that would be a waste of time. This much I was able to point out convincingly. It was only then that the authorities allowed me to enrol in the normal two-year teachers' training course in Britain. I was provided a scholarship and was bonded to teach in Jamaica for two years after my studies were completed. Arrangements were made for me to go to King Alfred's Teachers' College in Winchester, Hampshire, a highly respected residential College. Reluctantly, I requested University College to postpone my acceptance of the place it offered me; and reluctantly, I went to King Alfred's College, wondering why it was that circumstances seemed always to militate against what I wanted to do. Was it sheer bad luck or was it destiny, if there is such a thing, that was deciding what I should or should not do? From a boy I had the prescience that something — but what, I did not know — would always thwart my efforts to reach my goal, and that if I were to reach it, I would need to develop and exercise the twin traits of determination and perseverance, coupled with patience. Here at the end of the war, the real struggle had begun. But I was prepared for it.

CHAPTER 5

I went to King Alfred's College, Winchester, Hampshire, as I was directed. Throughout my time there, I was unable to discover the connection, if any, between the College and King Alfred who was said to be the greatest of the early Saxon kings. Perhaps the College was named after him, just as many things in Winchester carry his name. At any rate, King Alfred's statue dominates the High Street in the centre of the city which, according to recorded history, Alfred made his seat of residence, as had William the Conqueror. But Winchester, it is said, was not only the capital of a United England but also the capital of a Scandinavian Empire. Also, its roots extended to Roman and pre-Roman times. Thus there is a certain quaintness about the city, in my estimation, little reminders here and there of a vanished past — timbered houses, little passage ways and narrow streets, old ruins, especially around the massive Cathedral, iron bridges, stone bridges and other relics of antiquity. At first I was not sure I would like the city.

I was told I was the first overseas student to be admitted to the College. Quickly, I adapted myself to the College routine, and settled in with the other freshmen. It was a male institution. Its female counterpart was in nearby Southampton. The lectures and discussions proved to be stimulating, largely because the new intake were men who had been on active service and whose experiences were wide and varied. They were forthright in their views, and their questions were challenging. Always they kept the lecturers on their

74

toes whenever they had views that were contrary to those presented by the lecturers. I, for example, would be on my feet, given the opportunity, to punch holes into an educational philosophy or recommended teaching method if I disagreed with it. I was soon noted to be fearless and outspoken, critical and analytical, characteristics respected by the instructors who declared it was good to have my 'kind' in their respective classes.

To illustrate, before going out on practice-teaching, the students were recommended to prepare and write up 'notes of lessons' to be presented to and checked by the instructors. My view was that it was absolutely necessary, especially for young teachers, to prepare thoroughly the lessons they were going to teach before facing their classes, but for them to spend hours laboriously writing up notes of lessons to show how they would begin to do this or that was hardly more than waste of time — time that could be better spent on a more thorough preparation of the lesson. I was challenged in one of the lectures to explain myself, and I rose to the challenge gallantly, I said:

"Once the teacher has a thorough knowledge of what he is to present to his students," I argued, "the method of presenting it is secondary. Deciding on a fixed method of presenting it beforehand prevents the creative juices from flowing, so to speak, and blocks out spontaneity altogether. But spontaneous action is often most effective, more so than pre-conceived ideas."

This was to trigger excited discussion, controlled rigidly by the Instructor. He would allow only a few owners of the hands that shot up to speak, after which he turned the discussion back to me.

"Mr. Dale," he said, "may I ask you to explain yourself more fully?"

"Gladly, I will," said I. "Suppose your class came into the classroom in high spirits and there was a definite need to calm them down a bit. And suppose you had planned, according to the 'notes of lesson' you had prepared, to start by mentioning something humorous or exciting to raise their spirits, clearly, it is more than likely that you would lose control of the class altogether. On the other hand, suppose you had not previously committed yourself in your 'notes of lesson' to begin in a certain way — I believe the psychologists call this a 'set or fixed action' — surely you could more readily, quickly, spontaneously reverse gears and resort to another method that, you hope, would have a calming, more desirable effect. And if you did that, clearly the hours you spent on writing up notes of lessons would be all in vain."

No one attempted to refute that argument. There was silence. You could almost hear the brains of the students in the class working. Then the Instructor said,

"But, Mr. Dale, the beginner usually lacks confidence and may need to resort to his notes from time to time. If he had no notes, would it not be more difficult for him to proceed with certainty?"

I was quick to reply. "Preparing the lesson is one thing, but writing up notes of the lesson is another. I am objecting to the latter. It is my belief, because I have found it to be so, that once the neophyte prepares himself well and knows the subject matter he is going to teach, confidence becomes his companion and helps him to meet any eventuality. Of course, what I am advocating has to be put to the test. I am sure I could demonstrate convincingly what I am saying."

"You will get the chance, Mr. Dale," said the Instructor.

Whereupon the class laughed, giving the impression that I 'had let myself in for it'. I was nevertheless surprised that many of the students had supported my point of view.

King Alfred's College had a most enlightened method of training teachers. Before the students could go out to the local schools to do practice-teaching, they were introduced to the classroom situation in the College itself. On Monday afternoons, classes of primary school children would be brought to the College for teaching exercises by

76

the College students. One of the first of these exercises was to describe to the pupils for ten to fifteen minutes a scene, without recourse to pictorial illustrations or the blackboard or any teaching aid except the student's voice and gestures. The aim was to secure the full attention of the class. The students were free to choose any topic.

The exercise was very much up my street, and fortunately for me, I was one of the students detailed for it. When my turn came, I quickly introduced myself to the class and told them I was going to take them with me to a land of sun and sea, in imagination, of course. I began. They should imagine an island, surrounded by a blue, blue sea. The waves of the sea are gently lapping the white sands of the beach. The sun is shining down from a blue, blue sky. They can feel the sun's warmth on their hands and faces. They can hear the gentle breeze and the gentle lap of the waves breaking on the shore. The water is quite warm; it is easy to swim in it; it is like floating in it. Behind them is a beautiful waterfall descending from a cliff above the sea. Not far away are fruit trees — oranges, grapefruit, mangoes, star apples, guineps. They can easily stretch their hands up and pick an orange (here I made a little jump upward as if to pick one of the oranges). Just then a boy gasped, "Ooh!" and the class laughed, breaking the spell. The question then was whether I could recapture the riveted attention. Yes, I did. I described the Doctor Bird, one of Jamaica's national symbols — a very small bird with a long tail exceeding two feet, hanging down behind him. On its tiny body are shiny, intensely green feathers, on its head black feathers, on its wings red feathers, and its beak red and pointed. It is a humming bird. It likes water and darts about with a hum when the garden hose is running. It is a very beautiful little bird.

"But ah," I said, my face and eyes glowing with delight, "look at the flowers," and I proceeded to name them, emphasizing their colours so that if the class could not imagine what they were like, at least they would react to the colours — scarlet, yellow and white hibiscus; the flaming poinsettia; the red passion flower and the scarlet passion flower; the blue morning glory; the pink crepe myrtle; the red and the pink ixora; the flaming red lobster claw; the flame of the forest; the white trumpet lily; the red, the blue, the white, and the mauve bougainvillea; the royal poinciana (flamboyant); the yellow and the pink poui tree; the pink and the white frangipani — oh, there are so many and so beautiful. Can you see them?" I asked. In this fashion, I held the young faces transfixed before me as I used my hands to emphasize a point, or close my eyes to transport them to the tropical wonderland. I used the full fifteen minutes. At the end of my description one boy voiced the opinion of the whole class with "Oh, sir, it was beautiful. I would like to go there," and the class spontaneously clapped heartily.

The custom, after the dismissal of the class(es) was for the College students to assemble and criticize the attempts of those who had done the exercises. As observers, they were allotted discreet seats in the large hall where the class was held, out of sight by the pupils but within sight of them.

The exercise was said to be an ordeal for some of the students, terrifying for others, and welcomed by a few, including myself. It made them either a good teacher or it broke them completely, for no error on the part of the performing students escaped the keen eyes and critical minds of their peers who were looking on. In that sense, the exercise was very good training. Yet, so many of the students dreaded that particular exercise.

When it was my turn to be criticized, Ralph Turner, one of the group, said that I succeeded in getting and holding the attention of the class only because I am an exotic person (meaning perhaps that I am of another ethnic group) and that I described an exotic scene. The Instructor, an educational psychologist, shot Turner down with, "The exercise gave everyone freedom to choose any topic, anything you wanted to do, therefore Turner's criticism about the choice of Dale's topic was not tenable and must be ignored." But this did not satisfy me one bit. I indicated I wanted to reply to the first part of Turner's criticism, and was allowed to. I said,

"If Mr. Turner had observed closely, he would have seen that the pupils were responding not so much to me, the 'exotic', Mr. Turner's word, narrator, as to the vivid scene I was trying to bring before them, that when the boy shouted 'ooh' it was not Edmund Dale he was seeing but the actual picking of the orange. Yet, it was interesting to know that Mr. Turner thought that my black skin was an advantage. But I want to assure him that it 'ain't' necessarily so."

It was the last sentence and the comical way in which I said it that caused the whole group to burst into uproarious laughter, in which I readily joined. Yet I was not satisfied, and requested the Instructor to give me another chance to do another of the same exercise, and as soon as possible. The Instructor told me that was not necessary because I had done well and scored a very high mark, but at my insistence he acquiesced.

For the next exercise, I chose to describe an early Roman burial scene on top of St. Catherine's Mound overlooking Winchester city. This is a noted local historical spot, known to be a Roman burial ground. The afternoon came and I stood solemnly before the class of some thirty pupils, aged eleven/twelve or thereabouts. As luck would have it, St. Catherine's Mound was visible from the classroom. I began in a sombre mood, my voice somewhat muted but well projected for all to hear:

"This afternoon, I would like you to witness the burial of a Roman soldier on top of St. Catherine's Mound. (I pointed to it, and the class, still seated, looked through the windows to the Mound. Then they looked back at me).

"Listen, there is a solemn drum beat," I said, "like the slow tolling of a bell — boom, boom, boom. There (pointing, my eyes far away) a group of people are going up the hill, slowly, very slowly. It is a cortege, a funeral procession. There are six pall bearers, but they are not carrying a coffin. Look, it is a stretcher with the dead body on it. It is wrapped in white cloth. Go up closer and look. The face is uncovered. It looks mummified," my voice almost in a whisper.

Then I looked from the Mound to the silent, intense faces before me and continued:

"The pall bearers are all of the same height. Their hair is cut with a fringe covering the forehead. They are wearing short skirts instead of pants. Around their waist is a black sash, and the ends fall to the left side . And they are wearing leather sandals... ."

In a hushed, subdued, mournful voice, I made the students hear the continuing slow drum beats, the footsteps of the stretcher carriers, the wailing of the relatives in the procession. Softly, as though I was an eye witness, I described the grave, the lowering of the body into the grave, the gasp and shrieks of a woman (perhaps the mother or wife or sister of the dead man), the loud blast of a trumpet in salute to the dead man, the filling in of the grave, and the heart-rending moans of the relatives. Indeed, I was not standing before the students but at the grave side. My voice was husky from grief. Tears were rolling from my eyes and from those of many of the pupils in the class. Then I stopped, turned my face to the class. There was complete silence, as though no one was breathing; an air of mourning, a sadness true and deep settled on the class. No one said a word. Then I turned my gaze again toward St. Catherine's Mound. The class followed my eyes and looked to the Mound too, still in silence. It was drama of the first order, broken after a few seconds by a girl's voice.

"Sir, was that how it really was?"

"Yes," I said, "that was more or less how it was."

When the College students met to discuss the afternoon's exercises, the Instructor called on Ralph Turner, who had criticized my previous attempt, for his comments, but Turner had no comments. Then he called on the whole group, and there was silence.

"No one is willing to make a comment?" the Instructor asked.

Still, there was silence. At last Richard Templeton volunteered a comment. He said that bearing in mind the requirements of the exercise, he thought Edmund Dale had succeeded most admirably, and that Dale did so by his voice, which he knew how to use effectively. He also knew how to evoke emotions suitable for the occasion, how to use his face, eyes and gestures. Indeed, Templeton declared, he was quite sure that Edmund Dale had chosen the wrong career, and that he should be an actor on the legitimate stage. There was then general laughter and thumping of desks. Again I joined merrily in the laughter and hoped I had exorcised the previous negative criticism of Ralph Turner.

During my two years at King Alfred's, what little spare time I had was fully taken up with extra-curricula activities. I was always in demand as a speaker, as a result, I secretly broke College rules and studied far into the morning hours in order to keep up with my classmates. I addressed an Anglican Lay Readers' Conference held in a magnificent mansion, not far from the College, where Queen Elizabeth and Prince Philip spent their honeymoon; I spoke at Women's Institute meetings in Winchester and environs, at men's clubs and at church gatherings throughout Hampshire. As secretary of the Student Christian Movement (SCM), I was instrumental in staging a medieval religious play in the College Chapel, the proceeds of which were used to pay the expenses of 14 students to attend an SCM conference in Derbyshire. And I assisted with the 1st Wimborne Minster Scout Troop in taking the boys to a summer camp near Corfe Castle, Dorset, when their Scout Leader fell ill at the last minute and could not take the boys himself.

My experiences in Wimborne went beyond the local scout troop. Invited to spend two weeks of my summer holidays with friends there, I accepted the invitation gratefully. While there, I was prevailed upon to give an illustrated talk on the West Indies at the nearby Merley Park German Prisoners of War Camp. I was assured that most of the POWs could speak English.

With projector and slides of the landscapes of the islands, showing the way of life of the islanders, I arrived at the Camp on the appointed evening to find to my surprise some one hundred or more POWs assembled, eagerly waiting to hear me, or, I would like to think, see the slides. My intent was to help them take their minds off themselves for an hour or more, and to bring before them the sunshine, warmth and exotic ambiance of the West Indies. Enthusiastically they listened. Readily they laughed at my jokes. At the end, they all wanted to ask questions, or more likely practise their English. Consequently, the questioning period was extended. Gladly, I encouraged them to talk, and eagerly, I tried to answer their many questions concerning the social life, the educational system and facilities, the economy and the development potentials of the region.

At the end of the session, while attempting to ease the dryness in my throat with a cup of tea, one of the POWs, a tall, blonde, young man, with very blue eyes, engaged me in further discussion. But this was soon interrupted by a signal for the men to return to their billets. However, my hosts fought Army red tape and obtained permission to invite this POW to tea at their home. They saved a whole week's ration of butter and sugar so that they could make a few tea cakes and cookies for the occasion. It was a great sacrifice on their part — rationing of food was still in force in Britain, and for a long time after the war — which left a marked impression on both the POW and myself.

The POW was Kurt Bienzeisler. He told his hosts that he was forced to discontinue his university education and serve in the Luftwaffe (German Air Force). Except for his very blonde complexion, the denims (with a dark diamond-shaped patch sewn on the back of the tunic) that all POWs were compelled to wear, and a guttural pronunciation of certain words, his German background could have escaped notice. The conversation over tea went smoothly, and my friends (hosts) were delighted. They had lost their only son in the war and had been struggling to ward off feelings of bitterness

82

and hatred by engaging themselves in voluntary work in the POW Camp. Entertaining a German POW in their home was truly a test of their Christian faith.

After tea, I attempted to show Kurt around the town. But the stares from many of the townsfolk eloquently registered their disdain, if not hatred, of the POW. I tried to take him to public places — a cinema, a cafe, a restaurant, but was politely told that I was attempting to break the law which forbade POWs to enter public places. Reminiscence of my experiences in Tampa, Florida, flooded my mind. Here in Wimborne it was in the reverse. Kurt was feeling humiliated and I regretful that I was unwittingly subjecting him to the humiliation. I had completely forgotten that the law against POWs was still in force. Then in extreme anger, Kurt exploded:

"Edmund, why are you bothering to show me kindness? Can't you see, I am a German?"

I was completely thrown off my guard, and should not have been. I did not reply immediately, and Kurt continued:

"The war, the bloody, bloody war! Germany! Germans! We will never be able to live down this war. It is terrible, terrible, terrible!"

I continued to remain silent, and both of us walked on. We were on the main road leading out of the town to Bournemouth. Then I said,

"Please continue slowly on. I will catch up with you in a minute."

I popped into a small shop, bought two bottles of soft drinks, and rushed to join Kurt. Handing him one of the bottles, I said:

"Kurt, I have something to tell you. Let's sit on that bench over there for a while."

We sat on the bench and I proceeded to tell Kurt about my Tampa experience, what I saw of racial intolerance there, how the society denied Negroes in Tampa and throughout the United States of ordinary human rights, and the pain, degradation and humiliation it subjected them to. I went further to declare my belief that ultimately injustice, whatever the kind or brand, would be defeated, for the law of the universe was that good would always triumph over evil.

I did not want to lecture Kurt. That would be counter productive. But I felt I should try to make him understand that there was justification for the whole world to be angry with Germany which had plunged the nations into war, robbed them of so many of their sons and daughters, killed millions of Jews because they were Jews, and caused so much destruction and suffering. And I wanted Kurt to know that whereas rebuilding and reparations would in time bring change in Europe, and Germany and her people would one day be brought back into the European community, white supremacy would not be easily supplanted, not until the diversities among humankind are admitted as our common humanity, not until nations disregard the black or brown or yellow pigmentation of the skin and overthrow racial and colour prejudice.

"You asked why I am I attempting to show you common civility. The answer is simple. Those who have suffered know what suffering is, and can easily feel empathy for others who have suffered also. I understand fully your annoyance, frustration, humiliation because I have felt and endured them, too. But I doubt very much if you could ever feel the repugnance, the painful trauma that I feel when, because of my black skin and a very persistent, despicable colour prejudice, I am sometimes denied openly or subtly, here and there, privileges that members of the white race reserve exclusively for themselves solely on the ground of their white skin. No, Kurt, your hurt is temporary. It will definitely pass. Mine will continue because the changes that may remove them are very slow in coming. Sometimes I wonder if they will ever come."

As I spoke, my face was contorted in pain, and Kurt Bienzeisler fixed on me a long, penetrating stare, his blue eyes seeming even bluer. Then he said,

"I admit that before the war I practised racial discrimination, more in ignorance of what I was doing than anything else. I know now what it is to have it returned to me, and your candour is helping me to see things differently. I am glad I met you. You have opened my eyes to so much. Thank you."

Years later, Kurt entertained me in his home in the Black Forest, and in the presence of his parents, sister, brother and a few friends thanked me again for allowing him to feel some of the pain I feel as a Negro when I see or experience racial prejudice. He confessed that more than anything else, I had helped him to give his life a new focus. He was then heading an agency that sought to bring understanding between Germans and other Europeans.

My plunge into race relations was to take me further. Before my two years were up at King Alfred's, I attended a summer International Students' Conference held at the International High School at Elsinore, Denmark. It was a beautiful complex with spacious courtyards and grounds, not far from Copenhagen. Over 200 students attended. They came from the four Scandinavian countries, Western Germany, Belgium, the Netherlands, France, Britain, Northern Ireland, the United States and Palestine, among other countries. All were bent on forging friendly relations in an attempt to vanquish misunderstanding, hatred and bigotry, so rampant among the peoples of the world. The sessions during the day were most stimulating, but there was very little to do after the evening meal. On the third evening, just before the students were to leave the dining room, I got up and shouted, "What about a sing-song?" to which came a chorus of voices, "Yes, yes," and quite spontaneously, without any prompting or fuss, I jumped forward before the group and said, "Do you know Clementine? I will sing the verses and you the refrain." Everybody cheered, and into the song I plunged, my 'not-so-bad' tenor voice filling the room:

"In a cavern, in a canyon, excavating for a mine

Dwelt a miner, forty niner and his daughter, Clementine."

And everybody came in with the refrain, "Oh my darling, oh my darling ... ."

No sooner had I brought this to an end, everybody clapping joyfully, than I dived into "My Bonnie Lies Over the Ocean', and the other 200 or more voices came in with, "Bring back, bring back, oh bring back my Bonnie to me." Next, I taught the group "Roger Rum," a camp-fire ditty I learned during my Boy Scout days in Jamaica. It is a parody on the biblical story of the Rich Man and Lazarus, in Latin-sounding words. This went over very well. It was to become the signature tune of the Conference and gave me the title 'Mr. Roger Rum'. The sing-song was a beautiful end to a beautiful, long summer's evening, close to the land of the Midnight Sun. All went to bed in a good mood.

At the evening meal the next day, Peter Manniche, the Principal of the School, came to sit at my table for a few minutes and inquired what I had up my sleeves for the evening's entertainment. I had not given any thought to this, nor did I want to be the organizer of social activities in the evenings. But Peter Manniche merely said, "Well, Mr. Dale, everybody is expecting something similar to last night." Before I could say another word, Manniche left the table and my brain became a race course for various ideas. At last I thought of something that might be appropriate, namely, everybody would sit on the grass outside in the quadrangle court yard and teach one another some of the native songs and dances of the respective countries from which we came, beginning with the Scandinavian countries. At the end of the meal, Peter Manniche announced that he was certain Mr. Dale would undertake to lead the evening's entertainment. Approval rang out from the students, and I got up and told them what I had in mind. They approved readily. I asked them to bring what musical instruments they may have in coming to the courtyard.

Now, there are numerous Danish, Norwegian and Swedish folk

songs and dances, and there were many students from these countries at the Conference who were ready to demonstrate these dances, and they did so most expertly. The Norwegian "Spear Spellman" was the one that the students learned quickly and could dance to quickly. It became the favourite. Once everyone learned both words and tune, I suggested that everybody should get on their feet and learn to dance it, with the help of an accomplished Norwegian pianist (a piano had been brought on to the court yard in a hurry). Conservatism and reservations were thrown to the wind, and everyone entered into the spirit of "Spear Spellman" — song and dance. Other Scandinavian tunes and dances fascinated the group, as in youthful bliss, they danced and capered on the green, beautiful grass of the courtyard. Again, the evening went well and from then on I was given another title, "Master of Ceremonies," perhaps because of what Peter Manniche called my "unbridled enthusiasm and seemingly limitless energy."

One of the most memorable day of the Conference was a visit to a nearby rural town at the invitation of the townsfolk. A special tourist train took all the students to this town. On arriving at the station, festooned with garlands to welcome us, an excited group of the townsfolk of all ages, including the Mayor and other officials in ceremonial dress, welcomed us and led us to the local church nearby — the only building in the town large enough to accommodate us. Here an official welcome was given by the Mayor and officials, after which our names were read out. As each name was called, individual families of Danes would indicate their wish to host the student(s).

Before my name was read out, a family seated behind me, touched me and asked in surprisingly good English (most Danes speak very good English),

"You are Mr. Dale, aren't you?"

I answered in the affirmative and said, "How do you know my name?"

"We saw your photo in our local newspaper. You were listening to a young Dane who was telling you how the Nazis crushed his fingers in an attempt to get him to reveal vital information. Everybody here was touched when we read that tears ran down your face as the young man told you of his terrible ordeal. We would be very pleased if you would be our guest."

"Thank you very much," I said, "I would be delighted to accept your kind invitation."

When at last my name was read out, six families indicated they wanted to have me, but the family who had spoken to me was the first to signal their invitation, and to them I was assigned. When all the students were allocated to their hosts, we drove off in different directions, some in delightful horse-drawn buggies and carts.

The day was largely spent on the farms. The aim of the visit was to show the students Danish farming and Danish co-operatives in action, and we saw much of this — the rearing of pigs (bacon) for the British, German and French markets, the making of butter and cheese by the co-operatives, the rearing of chickens for eggs and meat, the growing of crops, the intelligent management of the farm, and other facets of farming and farm life. The most conspicuous thing, however, was the remarkable cleanliness of the barns. There was no unpleasant smell in them. Indeed, they appeared not as places where cows were kept but as places where people could live.

Immediately after arriving at the farm, coffee was served, with the most delicious Danish cake. The four other students who were also guests of the same family and I 'did justice to the cake', much to the delight of our hosts who were too ready to bring out another huge cake and sliced it for their guests. After we had toured the farm we returned to a magnificent lunch and again ate heartily. But it was the evening meal that I thought was "the knock-out punch." It was most memorable! Then, absolutely stuffed, we were taken back to the church for farewell speeches. Without prior notice, I was asked to express to the various hosts the thanks of the students. I had to. I could not get out of it, and I rose and gave what I hoped was a stirring 'few words' about the marvellous gesture of the towns people who epitomized the true, friendly, hospitable spirit of the Danish people. I spoke of how much all of us had learned about Danish farming in a single day. I expressed the profound gratitude of all of us and assured the hosts that we would be taking back to our respective countries the happy memories not only of our visit to the town but of our month's stay in Denmark. I ended by calling on the students to join me in singing "For they are jolly good fellows." This was followed by prolonged cheering.

We were next taken to the railway station where we boarded the waiting train after saying an emotional farewell. It was a singular, enjoyable, memorable experience.

Equally memorable was the last week of the Conference. I insisted that it should be something that each student could look back on with fond memories. I suggested that the farewell function should be a dance, sprinkled with floor shows (singing, sketches etc.) A band should be engaged, the hall gaily decorated, refreshments provided and as many as possible of the former Hitler youths, who were being rehabilitated (de-programmed) in a nearby institution, invited. I formed a committee comprising Hans Henriksen of Denmark, Marianne of France, Inger of Norway, Lisette of Belgium and myself. With this committee, I approached the Principal of the school. Mr. Manniche listened keenly to me. It was obvious that he had a warm regard for me.

"First," said Mr. Manniche, "how will you pay the dance band?"

"Pay?" I said, "we will be asking them to play without expecting to be paid."

Mr. Manniche laughed, as if to say, 'this man is impossible', and I waited for him to finish.

"Do you really think," he asked, "the band, especially the one you have in mind — 12 players —would give up a whole night to play unpaid for us?"

"Yes," said I, "if I could tell them and convince them of the excellent work you are doing here to bring healing to the nations who are just coming out of a bloody war, and to encourage international understanding and mutual respect. Yes, Mr. Manniche, I really think if I could make them understand, they would join us."

For a long time Peter Manniche looked at me, then said,

"You are an extraordinary young man, Mr. Dale. Assuming you succeed with the dance band, and I doubt that very much, I am almost certain you will not prevail on the military people to allow those German young men to attend."

"Well," I said, "we will just have to try very hard."

With that, my committee and I jumped into the school's old van and dashed off to Copenhagen, Hans Henriksen's city, where he had many friends. Thus it did not take much time for him to find out where the dance band was practising. To the hall we dashed, sat at the back and listened to the rehearsing of the band. During a convenient pause, we went up on the stage, and Hans introduced us in Danish. The Band Leader, a genial gentleman, welcomed us to Denmark in very good English. In fact, all his men could speak English. Then I took over, and without wasting time told the Band Leader and his men how many students had made the financial sacrifice, a very difficult one indeed, to come to the Conference. We did it, I told them, because we feel it is the young people of the world who will have to bring sanity to a world that has gone completely insane. We came to get the experience of living together, though it was only for a few weeks, and share in the marvellous spirit of friendship and understanding for which the International School at Elsinore is famous. At Elsinore, the students, dwelling together in unity, had been touched by the international camaraderie, and would be carrying this feeling of comradeship back to their respective countries. They wanted their last meeting together to be as memorable as the experience they had gained during the four weeks. Then I mentioned the planning of the dance and entertainment, and

90

the need for a good dance band. Without the band, I declared, the whole thing would be a flop. Thus we came to request his band to play for us, voluntarily, because we could not pay them. The rest of the group had remained silent as I made my plea, at the end of which the Band Leader smiled, and the band members smiled, and the smile became a laugh, in which we also joined. Then one of the band members said,

"But why not? This is the sort of public relations we should have."

Mr. Sorensen looked at his band members, and they all nodded, signalling approval.

"You see," he said, they are all agreed. But there is one thing, we could make it on Friday night but not on Saturday night."

I did not have to answer. The others of the group said in chorus,

"Oh yes, we could easily change the date."

And so it was agreed that one of the leading dance bands of Copenhagen agreed to give their services free at the students' farewell party at Elsinore. Even Hamlet's ghost in the Castle at Elsinore nearby must have felt pleased.

One difficulty overcame, I calmed my committee and pointed to the other difficulty of obtaining permission for the German young men to join us at the party. Consequently, to the military precincts we went next. I told Hans I wanted to speak to the Commandant and not any one else of lesser rank. But Hans remonstrated,

"You cannot just see him like that; he is a big shot. We will have to make an appointment."

"There is no time for that, dear Hans," I said. "Remember, we have just moved up the date of the party from Saturday evening to Friday evening. There are only three days to go. We must try to see him today while we are here in Copenhagen, otherwise we will have to come back tomorrow."

We read the information board in the main building, ascertained who the Commandant was and his room number, and we marched to it, Hans and I leading the way. We knocked and were admitted. The secretary's desk had a notice which said, "English is spoken here." So I pushed forward and said to her,

"I wonder if the Commandant would be kind enough to see a few students (I pointed to the others). We are from the International Students Conference at Elsinore. We promise we will not keep him for more than a very few minutes."

The secretary looked surprised, somewhat bewildered.

"Well," she said, "er, er, ... Just wait a minute."

She knocked at the Commandant's door and went in, and the others of the group looked at each other in doubt. I scolded them with:

"Oh, ye of little faith! Think positively!"

Just then the Commandant's door opened, and a mighty bulwark of a man came out, his face wearing the wicked look of army authority, like that of a sergeant major on parade. I dashed to him, extending my hand, saying,

"Sir, it is most kind of you to see us without an appointment. We regret very much to come and disturb you, knowing full well that you must have a mighty lot to do."

Not waiting for a reply, I introduced myself and the others, and very succinctly told the Commandant about the Conference at Elsinore, the countries from which the students came, the precious moments and experiences we were having, and how words were trite, wholly inadequate to express our appreciation for the wonderful treatment and hospitality we were being given by the Danish people.

The look on the Commandant's face had been changing while I spoke, and at the end the Commandant was actually smiling.

"Yes, I read about your Conference in the papers," he said, "and, now to think of it, saw your photo in the papers. I am pleased to hear that everything is going on so well. Peter Manniche is a good man and is doing good work over there in Elsinore. But what can I do for you?"

I explained that we wanted to invite the German youths who were living not far from the International High School to attend our farewell party at the school. I noticed that the expression on the Commandant's face had changed slightly while I spoke, but I continued. I said I was sure that the experience of these German young men, mixing with the international students, would accord nicely with the magnanimous contribution that Denmark was making to re-educate these young men whom Hitler had taught to hate. It was such a wonderful opportunity for them to see how normal people of their age accept each other and have fun together that I was almost certain the Commandant would approve. I stopped suddenly and fixed the Commandant with a kind stare.

"Well, Mr. Dale," the Commandant said, "you are making what is a difficult request. I commend you and your group for thinking of these young men, but permission for them to attend or join in public functions at this stage requires more than my approval. So many people will need to be consulted."

"I am sure, Commandant," I said, "that they will agree when you consult them, given the international nature of the exercise and its aim of promoting understanding and friendship which, I believe, is Denmark's salutary aim in the re-education of these men, mired as they have been, in the slough of racial hatred."

"Nicely put, Mr. Dale. I agree entirely with your sentiment and will approve the request if there are no serious objections from those above me. Leave the matter with me and I will speak by phone to my seniors and then to Mr. Manniche."

The others of the group joined me in thanking the Commandant and left. When we reached the van and jumped in gleefully, mission accomplished, the excitement which we had succeeded in suppressing, exploded. Looking at me, Hans, who was always calm and was not easily excited, almost shouted:

"Edmund Dale," said Hans, "I have never met anyone like you. It is extraordinary. I didn't think you could pull it off. I came merely to be your translator if that was necessary. Although I was actually there, I still don't know how you did it. The confidence you have in what you do astounds me. Peter Manniche will never believe what we are about to tell him. Seriously, Edmund, are you ever afraid, do you ever think of failure?"

My reply was simply, "I learned from a boy not to anticipate failure before attempting a difficult task. In other words, Hans, 'never say die'. Always try to make the impossible possible. That is my motto."

On our return to the school, we quickly broke the news first to Peter Manniche. In stunned disbelief, all he could say was, "Mr. Dale, you will have to stay with us at the school because you can work wonders."

Feverishly, the students began to prepare for the farewell party. Committees were formed to look after the decoration of the hall, the programme itself, refreshments and other mundane matters. The next day, the Commandant telephoned Peter Manniche to congratulate him for the splendid work he was doing, and to inform him that approval had been given for the German youths, 30 to 40 of them, to attend the farewell party. Manniche was dumb-founded.

Friday evening came at last. The 12-piece band arrived to a tumultuous welcome by the students who lifted the Band Leader clean off the ground and thus carried him to the hall which had become a glittering spectacle. (Some of the students had crossed over to Sweden by ferry to obtain the decorations.) And when the band struck up with a youthful, popular dance tune (Scandinavian, of course), in the twinkle of an eye, the students were on the floor, including every one of the German youths, enjoying themselves. I had asked the female students not to wait for the Germans to ask them to dance. Rather the girls should do the asking and try to make them feel at home, and they had agreed. I was the Master of Ceremonies, and during one of the pauses, invited Peter Manniche to say "a few words." He accepted the invitation and praised and thanked all the students for helping to make the Conference the success that it was. But especially he thanked the dance band and their leader for their outstanding generosity and understanding.

The dancing, skits and fun continued until mid-night. Just before the last waltz, the band clashed its symbols and signalled for silence. The Band Leader made a speech, telling the students how pleased he and his band felt in coming to play for them and to catch a little of the spirit of the fraternity for which the school is noted. I was then 'arrested' and led to the stage while the band played a march. Next, a group of the students advanced from the back of the hall, gaily attired, the two in front carrying purple cushions on which were gift packages. Solemnly, they presented one to the Band Leader and the other to me. And all broke out singing, "For they are jolly good fellows". Peter Manniche then moved forward, offered his thanks to me in a moving speech, followed by sustained applause. Two, three decades later, I can hear the uproarious adulation I received from those students, something I would always remember.

To Winchester I returned and completed my teacher training successfully. But before the end of the course, I applied to University College, London, for re-admission. I was called for an interview and ultimately admitted to the B.Sc. Honours programme in Geography. On this occasion my joy was tempered by the dread that something might go wrong again to prevent me from entering the University. I hoped that what I had saved from my Airman's pay and from the grant I was given to attend King Alfred's College would see me through my first year in the University.

From Winchester I moved to London, found accommodation ('digs') and began to attend lectures, but before the end of the first week of lectures, I was summoned by the Head of my Department. He wanted to know who would be paying my tuition fees. I explained that I would be paying my way through university, that I had saved enough money to take me through the first year. I did not know how I would manage the next and succeeding years, but I was taking one year at a time.

"Well," said the Professor, "I do not understand. The Colonial Office has written to say that you should not be here, that they want to see you. Please go right away to see them. Do you know where the Office is?"

I said I knew where it was, and in extreme agitation, went to the Colonial Office. In a haughty manner, the secretary brushed me aside, condescending to say that I could not see the officer without an appointment. In retrospect, I do not know how I managed to contain my mounting anger. I waved the secretary aside, marched up to the door of the Director, knocked, did not wait for an answer, opened the door and entered. I summoned inner strength and suppressed the volcanic anger that welled up in me, and introduced myself.

"Ah, you are the fellow at U. C.," the Director said. "Well, you should not be there. You must return to Jamaica."

"And why?" may I ask, choking, shaking, livid.

"Your government says you must return. They say you agreed to return after you completed your teacher training."

"Correction," I said, " 'after my studies are completed'. Those were the actual words of the agreement. My studies are continuing. You know that, for you rudely pulled me away from them to come to see you."

"It is your government, not me or anyone else here, who say you must return. They insist that we make arrangements for your immediate return. You cannot proceed with a university degree programme."

At that point, I found speech quite impossible. My self control was being tested brutally. Like a raging fanatic, I pounded the Director's desk with my fist for a few seconds, to the utter consternation of the Director. When at last speech returned, I told him that from a boy my main aim was to obtain a university education; I had worked hard — very hard, for a very long time — to gain admission to the University of London, and now that I had at last gained admission, the Colonial Office, or the Jamaican Government, as he said, or both in collusion, wanted to prevent me from proceeding to the degree programme at my own expense. I demanded to know why. The Director restated what he had said, namely, that he had been instructed to make arrangements for my return to Jamaica. He suggested that when I return to Jamaica, I could take the matter up with the Jamaican Education Office in Kingston. Still I protested, but to no avail. I had come so near to pursuing my goal, and again I was prevented for reasons beyond my control. It was strange. It was frustrating. It was downright cruel.

Within days, I found myself on the SS Acadia bound for Jamaica. Long I stood on the deck of the ship as it moved out to sea. Once more my fond hopes of obtaining a university education were dashed. Disappointment, resentment, anger washed over me, and hot tears flowed down my cheeks. Standing there alone, surrounded by the mighty sea, I remembered that I had confided to my mother that far-off feeling that I would not obtain easily what I wanted. And now I remembered her words: "Never give up, my son, fight, fight, fight the odds!"

In this mood of utter dejection, I arrived in Jamaica. The plan I formulated on the boat between bouts of depression was that I would try to clear up the misunderstanding, and return quickly to continue my studies. Instead, what awaited me was what I experienced before — the rigidity of colonial red tape and the intransigence of colonial bureaucracy.

CHAPTER 6

The SS Acadia arrived in Kingston, Jamaica, as scheduled, and my sister, Hazel (now married), and other relatives and friends were on the pier to meet me. They had been informed at short notice of my returning date and time of arrival. Welcome and greetings given, Hazel was the first to sense that something was wrong with me, and she actually asked me why I seemed so troubled in spirit.

"Hazel, I see that your imagination is still very active. Certainly no change there!" I said.

"From the moment you stepped off the boat, I sensed that something was troubling you. You could never fool me," she said.

"But before I left for the war, you did not know I had been planning to do so," I replied.

Hazel was stumped for a reply and in the end said, "You are trying to side-step the issue."

I certainly side-stepped the issue and began to point to changes in the cityscape as I drove with her and her husband to their home where an elaborate home-coming party had been planned for me. Other relatives and friends had gathered there, and soon all were sitting down to a real Jamaican meal of chicken, curried goat, rice and peas, fried fish, fried plantain, sweet potato, fruit cocktails, rum punch, home-made cakes and cookies, and home-made ice cream.

Hazel had tried hard to give me a warm welcome, but my low spirits were much in evidence. I found it difficult to be my usual self. All who were present sensed it and attributed my low spirits to tiredness, caused perhaps by a rough voyage. They were understanding enough not to prolong the welcome past midnight.

It was true that I was tired. Yet, on retiring, I could not sleep. The realization that I had returned without achieving the goal for which I had left the island weighed heavily on my mind. I got up, paced the room, sat down, got up again. My remorse was profound, the feeling harrowing.

"Why, why, why?" I whispered, and soon found myself talking to God as if he was standing there before me. Perhaps he was. "You see how I have tried," I said to him. "Can't you help me? I have been trying so very hard. But you know this, so why haven't you helped me? Please help me. I have no one to turn to but you. Please give me strength to keep fighting and please increase my faith. Please stand by me."

Then I climbed into bed again and fell asleep. It was a troubled sleep, but in the morning I felt a little better. At breakfast, I told my sister the whole story, exactly why I was so angry. Then I telephoned for a taxi and went to the Education Office which was still on East Street. I announced to the receptionist that I would like to speak to the Education Officer, failing him, his deputy, about an urgent matter.

"May I know what it is?" she asked.

I was in no mood for bureaucratic nonsense and replied sharply, "No, you may not know. It is a private matter which does not concern you."

Ridiculously affecting the part of a prima donna, obdurate and unyielding to a degree, she dismissed me with silent contempt. Anger, which I had been trying hard to suppress, now flared up in me again to fever pitch. I pushed past the receptionist, knocked at the inner door and entered, she rushing in, explained to the man sitting at the desk — the deputy Education Officer — that I had refused to tell her why I wanted to see him. The officer looked at me and asked,

"May I know why?"

"Certainly," said I, "if I may sit down."

Without waiting for an answer, I sat and forthwith related that after years of struggle to gain admission to an institution of higher learning, I succeeded at last and began my B.Sc. Honours programme in the University of London. No sooner had I begun than the Colonial Office in London informed my College that I should not be there and hurriedly shipped me back to Jamaica. The excuse the Colonial Office gave to my College was that the Jamaican Government had ordered my return because the island was short of teachers and I had agreed to return to teach.

The deputy Education Officer told me that the Education Officer was out of the island for three months and that he, the deputy, did not know anything about the circumstances to which I referred.

"Surely," I interrupted, "the files should help you."

The deputy Officer looked hard at me, and I met his eyes with equal defiance. Somewhat reluctantly he summoned his secretary and requested her to bring my file. In it was a statement that I was bonded to the Government for two years and would be required to teach at Clarendon College, a government-funded residential high school in rural Jamaica, where my services were required.

My protest served only to harden the disposition of the officer who was, it appeared, accustomed to receiving acquiescence to his behest, if not downright subservience. I pointed out, as I had to the Colonial Office in London, that the scholarship I received to do my teacher training at King Alfred's College bonded me to teach in Jamaica after my studies were completed, but I was removed from my studies before they were completed, and in so doing, the Colonial

Office or the Jamaican Education authorities had abrogated the agreement.

"I know nothing about the nature of any agreement between you and the government," the officer snapped. "All that this document I have in my hand says is that in return for the scholarship you received, you are required to teach in Jamaica for two years, and you are now required to fill a vacancy which exists at Clarendon College, beginning in early January, that is, three weeks hence." He closed the file, handed it back to his secretary, turned to me and said, "That's it, Mr. Dale. Good morning."

I knew I was defeated. I had not the time nor the means to fight officialdom. I left the office in burning anger. In concert, anger and frustration washed over me like furious waves of the sea pelting a sea cliff. My hopes of obtaining a quick, favourable settlement so that I could return quickly to my studies, despite the catching up that the interruption necessitated, went out the window. Even when I visited my parents in the country during the week of Christmas, the feeling of despair still clung to me. What was to have been a happy re-union with my parents became hardly more than purgatory, as I confessed to them, for I had not achieved what I had set out to achieve before returning. It was not until I had spent a quiet time on my favourite 'horse', the bent coco-nut tree on the hillside above my home, looked out to the distant horizon, and was lost in silent communion with my Maker that I found the inner strength to continue my struggle and determination to bring my early dreams to fruition. Though the coco-nut tree had withstood the assaults of many hurricanes, it was still standing and readily welcomed and comforted me — so I believed, anyway.

The school to which I was sent had a sad history. It was founded by a black minister of a local Congregational Church. He had seen aspiring, young people — pushed by poverty, the lack of educational and job opportunities, and the dullness and boredom of the countryside, and pulled by the promise of better educational and employment opportunities in, and the bright lights of, the city of Kingston — leaving the rural areas for Kingston. Unhappily, many of them ended up as failures in the city. The reverend gentleman, with good academic credentials, thought he could help to stem the drift by providing an educational opportunity for these local youths. He resigned his ministry, and with the support of a few dedicated members and friends of the church, rented an old Great House of the slavery period at Chapelton, Clarendon, and began a private secondary school which he named Clarendon College. It was an act of great courage, anchored on faith. But shortly after he opened the school, he was killed in a railway accident. The local people rallied to keep the project alive as a suitable memorial to their selfless son, but their cumulative financial resources were inadequate for the task. They sought the assistance of the London Missionary Society in London, England. The Society passed the request to the Commonwealth Missionary Society which provided a measure of assistance for a time. In the end, the Government of Jamaica was asked to take over the school.

The College (high school) was (still is) located on high ground in the middle of the island. A part of the hillside on which it was (is) sited had been levelled to provide playing fields, beside which stood the main building — the converted Great House - then used as the boys' residence, years after razed by fire. Other buildings hugged the hillside, the whole surrounded by the most spectacular, most majestic, most awe-inspiring scenery imaginable, a natural paradise par excellence. Below, a U-shaped valley, with a meandering stream, accommodated stands of sugar cane and a mixture of orange and grape fruit trees, mango trees, coco-nut trees, and other tropical fruit trees, like the bread fruit and the ackee. The surrounding landscape offered vistas of mountains, not far distant, their lower slopes showing a patch-work of subsistence farming, and their higher slopes a medley of flowering trees and shrubs, dominant among them were the royal poinciana, the African tulip tree, the flower-silk tree, and the pink and yellow poui trees. It was indeed a vibrant, exotic landscape.

But the decrepit entrance gate to the school grounds belied the magnificent view from within, which awaited the visitor, though the scattered poinciana trees lining the untended driveway into the school grounds proper gave the impression that the grounds were once properly cared for.

When I first drove into the grounds and saw the breath-taking view of the surrounding landscape, the heavy mental load I had been carrying lightened dramatically. I had always been touched by, and sensitive to, Nature, and the surrounding landscape greatly impressed me. But I am also easily angered by manifestations of poverty and the insensitivity or unwillingness of people to capitalize on what Nature offers. I saw at a quick glance all that could and needed to be done to improve the immediate surroundings. I sighed, and my heart sank again under the weight of it all.

At a welcoming session by the School Board, members of which comprised local residents and those of surrounding rural towns, the school secretary (the English minister of the local Congregational Church), and the Principal of the College (a black Jamaican), I was asked for my impressions of the school. Without hesitation, I stated that I had read about the history of the school, admired the vision of its founder and the considerable effort of the Board and the local people to keep alive the passionate dream of the founder. That dream, as I discovered, was to provide an educational institution to cater, even partially, to the educational needs of the local young people. I said I knew quite well that it was a very tough, pioneering venture.

"We are pleased to hear that you are so well informed about the school, Mr. Dale," said Mrs. Harvey, a half-white Jamaican. "However, coming as you are from an English institution where you were trained, and having visited, we are told, a number of residential schools in England and the Scandinavian countries, we are, at least I am, anxious to hear what you think of the facilities here."

"If you want an honest answer," I said, "I do not think much of them."

There was an obvious unease among a few of the Board members, including the secretary and the Principal. Always practical, down-to-earth, if not fearless, I continued:

"For example, this building that we are in is, I am told, quite new. But why is it left unpainted? I am told further that it has seen little use, yet it is already looking old, drab, shabby, rude, crude, second-hand, indeed, dreadfully depressing."

The school secretary rushed to the defence. He had supervised the building of the structure.

"Mr. Dale," he said, "do you know what the cost of paint is in Jamaica these days?"

"I really do not know, Rev. Wade. What has to be acknowledged is that the teaching block, for example, apart from being opened on one side and thereby allowing rain and dust to be blown in, is painted white. The whiteness intensifies the sun's glare in a tropical climate and hurts the eyes. Surely the money that bought the white paint could very well have bought a pastel colour paint which would lessen the intensity of the glare — the same money used to better advantage!"

Hardly allowing for a response, I proceeded to support my observations by reminding the Board of the demands of education which they were attempting, or should be attempting, to satisfy. Drawing heavily on a paper I had researched during my teacher training, I pointed out that properly conceived, the real aim of education is not mainly to cram facts into the heads of the young solely for them to reproduce these facts on examination papers, but to train the whole person to become more intelligent, more thoughtful, more reflecting, more understanding, to enjoy with greater discrimination, to reason with greater judgment, and to live life more fully than before. It was necessary, then, that careful attention should be given to the environment in which young minds are nurtured and developed. Ideally, it should help to stimulate, inspire, influence. Such an education, given in such an environment usually fosters gentility and refinement, confidence and self assurance, dignity and poise — qualities which, I observed, were characteristics of both boys and girls of those English Public Schools which I visited, or where I spent week-ends and was asked to give lectures. Whatever else may be said of these schools, they offered a certain refinement which was very noticeable and very admirable.

I continued. I argued that the omission of suitable environmental influences leads inevitably and irrevocably to crudeness, vulgarity, brashness, even insensibility. No where in the immediate College precincts could I see, for instance, a bed of cultivated flowers or shrub, or a well-kept lawn, not the slightest aesthetic touches anywhere. The place was rough, wholly out of harmony with the surrounding, attractive landscape. Was the focus only on getting students to pass examinations? What was it that the Board was aiming to do? I asked. What was their objective? Categorically I ruled out limited funds or lack of funds as the main handicap to creating a more pleasing school environment. I insisted that limited funds in concert with imagination could, I was certain, give aesthetically pleasing results. I paused, looked at the Board members in whose faces recognition of the truth of what I was saying and annoyance were curiously blended. The Principal looked extremely angry. The idea of 'a specimen of the new breed' coming to tell him and the others who had been struggling to keep the school going about the demands of education! It was more than he could take. He shifted from side to side in his chair. There was an awkward pause. I wanted my words to sink in and kept silent for a moment.

The silence was broken by Mrs. Harvey, always the chief spokesperson, who had asked me for my opinion. She said that she admired my candid remarks and my courage to present them to the Board so forcefully and with such deep conviction. She, too, had felt all along that they were not providing the right educational environment, along the lines that I had pointed out, and that the time had come for the Board to reassess what it was trying to do. She thought the forthright criticism they had just heard should be a help. This gave me the opportunity I wanted to suggest what improvements I would like to attempt, with the Board's approval, and with a minimum cost to the Board.

I told the Board that my intent in criticizing what I had seen was not to denigrate what had been achieved, clearly with considerable effort, and that I wanted to be constructive. I requested the Board to provide me with the services of a day-labourer and I would get the students to help me first to improve the college grounds and thereby demonstrate in a positive way and to a small degree, I hope, what I had been talking about. Having said that, I left the meeting quickly.

Later that day, I was informed by Mrs. Harvey that the Board had approved my request and the labourer would be mine the very next day. That night I made a list of all that I would attempt and in the morning swung into action before I went up to my classroom. I showed the labourer what I wanted him to do first, namely, repair the stone wall bordering the driveway into the College grounds, reducing the height to about two feet, then cut the irregularly-spaced border shrubs to the same height as that of the wall. The irregular spaces would be filled in later with similar shrubs, and the border would be planted with annuals and biennials — flowers and flowering shrubs which, with the scattered, flowering poinciana and poinsettia trees, would form a most pleasing driveway.

The man proved to be too slow a worker, and I was in a hurry. Thus I offered to provide him an incentive by contracting pieces of work at a time and at a fixed pay instead of the hourly rate that he was offered. As soon as he finished one piece, he would be contracted another piece. This proved to be most satisfactory. The man put much effort into the work and completed each piece in record time.

While the labourer was thus engaged, I turned my attention to another part of the College grounds, the central part which, I

106

thought, could be transformed into a pleasing lawn. In former days, it was obviously kept as a lawn. It was full of brush and tough weeds. I tried to enlist the help of Form 5B, the form I was responsible for — each teacher was responsible for a Form — but obtaining that assistance was difficult at first because the students all had the notion that working on the grounds was demeaning and should be left entirely to the 'yard boy'. This was a reaction to the slave period which doomed their forebears to menial tasks. It was only after I had donned a pair of shorts, taken a machete (a versatile implement in tropical countries), and set about working side by side with Philip, the yard helper, that one by one members of my Form came to realize that I meant business. At first they watched me in silence and I them, without their knowing that I was doing so.

"Philip, how many machetes have you in the tool house?" I asked. "We are going to need every one of them."

"You mean, sa, for the students to use?" asked Philip.

"That's right. They will be helping us before the week is out." I said.

"Naw, sa, not dem. You are new; you don't know dem. Dem tink dem is too ejucated for dat, and mustn't dirty dem hands."

"Well, Philip," I replied, "you may have to change your mind."

And Philip did change his mind a few days later. After the second afternoon of hard work on the grounds with Philip, I was asked to meet a delegation of four students from my Form. I received them in my room most cordially. The speaker of the group stated in no uncertain terms that I had brought embarrassment to their Form, for I, their Form Master, was working on the grounds like a common labourer. They requested me to desist, for they were being teased by members of the other Forms who made them the laughing stock of the whole College. I smiled, then laughed heartily. I offered them glasses of lemonade and cookies which the College Matron had left for me, and I proceeded to tell them what I had in mind for the

College grounds, namely, beautiful lawns interspersed with beds of flowers, clumps of shrubs at strategic locations, here a clump of yellow backed by red, there two or three royal palms in silent communion with beds of canna lilies before them, and all the way into the College a beautiful border lined with flowers and shrubs — all of which in the end would make for a very pleasing environment; they would feel very proud to show their parents around the grounds when the parents visit them.

"And, gentlemen, am I to understand that you would not like me to do that? Clearly your idea of education is not the same as mine. To me, it does not mean you must live in drabness, crudeness, ugliness. Rather, the educated person desires to surround himself with those things that elevate the mind, soothe the spirit and give endless enjoyment. I suppose I am wrong in thinking that you would like to live in an environment that is refined and beautiful. Gentlemen, you are wasting my time. Please go and hang your heads in shame."

I opened the door for them, and they left sheepishly. Their Form Master had scored a bull's eye!

After classes the next afternoon, I dashed from my classroom, changed quickly and, with Philip, continued to chop down the veritable wilderness where other members of the teaching staff attempted to play tennis. I proceeded vigorously and even surprised Philip who constantly gave me incredulous side glances. After their games, a few of the students passed us, looked but did not tarry. They returned the following afternoon, giving up their foot ball practice and looked at Philip and me hard at work. I pretended I did not see them. Then they moved forward and said:

"What do you want us to do, sir?"

"Oh, Clarence, Darby, it's you. You gave me a start. You really want to help? Well, let me see. Philip, do you think you could find another machete or two for Clarence and Darby to cut over there?"

Philip hid his smile and brought the machetes which were ready, waiting. Then two or three more students came when they saw the first two cutting, and carried away what they had cut. The following afternoon all members of Form 5B were present, and were soon followed by Form 5A, and finally most of the students. Under my direction, they prepared flower beds, helped to turn most of the College grounds into a beautiful lawn, strewn with flower beds, and they white-washed the bases of trees along the drive-in.

Then a few went with me in a truck to the Botanical Gardens in Kingston and collected palm trees, a variety of flowering shrubs, flower seedlings and other plants — most already well grown. Insisting that they were for educational purposes and that the Botanical Gardens should be encouraging the growing and supplying of plants to all the secondary schools in the island, I succeeded in convincing the Director of the Gardens to donate the truckload of plants, shrubs and flower seedlings to the improvement of our College grounds. The boys who went with me were as impressed with my rationale as the Director himself who found it difficult not to acquiesce to what I called a valid request. Mission accomplished, and very pleased with ourselves, we returned to the College that Saturday evening. After church the next day, the students and I set about planting the palm trees and flowering shrubs along the drive, and the flower seedlings, canna lilies and other plants in the beds already prepared, grouping them according to a strict colour scheme.

It is well known that in tropical countries, certainly in the West Indies, constant warmth and frequent showers aid rapid plant growth. Thus within a few short weeks, the school grounds were completely transformed. It was a magnificent sight. I did not have to ask the students to weed or water the plants; they did it voluntarily. Everybody was now taking a keen interest in keeping the grounds attractive. They were obviously feeling proud in helping to bring about the transformation. Early in the mornings before breakfast and late in the evenings before "prep", they would be seen watering the young plants.

At the next meeting of the Board, held in the College as usual, I was summoned. The members were almost ecstatic. They could not believe the sight they saw when they drove on to the College grounds. With the exception of the Principal of the school, they showered me with compliments which, of course, I brushed aside. I pointed out that there was much more to be done, for instance, the male students did not have a Common Room where they could read magazines and journals or write letters home. They were doing these things on their dormitory beds. I told the Board I had seen a spare room in the old Great House, cluttered with junk and full of dust and cobwebs, which, I felt, could be knocked into shape for the purpose. I requested permission to do so. All that the Board would need to provide were a sand-blaster (for the floors), drapes for the windows, and fibre-matting for the floors. The boys and I would do the sand-blasting, scrape the windows and wall, and paint them. On the floor matting, I would get the boys to design and dye geometric patterns in permanent colours. I thought also that a few pieces of furniture which had been given to the College in a previous "College Shower" and stored away could be placed in the room.

"Splendid idea," said one, then the other, then all, and I obtained what I wanted. After all, it was self-help, and cheap. They would have been foolish to turn down my request.

Accordingly, the room was transformed in record time. Groups of boys attacked the floor and the walls, the windows, while others used the College Matron's sewing machine to make the drapes themselves — from material which I obtained from a local shop (at a very reduced price!). Other boys worked on the matting, drawing the patterns and dyeing them with strong dyes — all this in their spare time. The project was really a practical exercise in co-operation and fraternity. When the work was completed and the furniture, books, magazines and journals put in place, the room took on the appearance of a real study. The dark stain of the wooden floor had been blasted away, and the floor, now highly polished and revealing the natural grain of the wood, shone beautifully.

Next, I suggested that Mrs. Harvey should be invited to open the room because she had shown much interest in the project and had helped a great deal. Willingly, she agreed to open the room, and willingly, at my tactful suggestion (knowing she had a first-rate cook), she agreed to provide refreshments for the evening — cakes and cookies, ice cream and soft drinks. I suggested also that the boys should invite the girl students and the whole teaching staff to the opening of the room, and attempt to make of the occasion a social evening. My real aim was to give the boys an opportunity to be hosts, to learn to meet and entertain friends with ease, grace, charm and self assurance. Of course, this involved much preparatory work. Mrs. Harvey was most understanding. She knew and understood what I was trying to do and supported me all the way. Admittedly, at first, she balked at the idea of "boys and girls dancing in a Christian institution." But I soon knocked the cobwebs from her eyes and plunged her into the mid-20th century.

The evening came at last. There was a grand turn out, everybody was 'dressed up", and the boys performed their duties as hosts most admirably, even the senior boy whom I had coached to invite Mrs. Harvey for a waltz. During the party, I walked about discreetly helping to forge 'small talk' or easing stiffness or little awkward situations caused by shyness. On the whole, it was a successful social event. More than that, the students were beginning to realize what could be done if one really tried and exercised a little imagination. It was the first event of its kind in the College. Regrettably, the Principal did not attend.

The outcome was predictable, exactly what I had hoped and was ready to encourage: the girls were sufficiently inspired to want to provide themselves with a common room to equal or rival that of the boys, copying the self-help method that the boys had used.

From the beginning of my tenure at Clarendon College, I

attacked the false notion of many of the students, namely, that the educated person is exempt from manual work, and thus far I was winning the battle. But I wanted to do more and decided to teach them leather work in their and my spare time (what little I had) — making small leather articles, like wallets, purses, among others, which they could then sell at functions at the school when parents and the general public were invited to attend. In this way, the boys could earn their pocket money without having always to rely on the meagre resources of their parents. It was while I was at King Alfred's College that I took an evening course in leather work offered by the City of Winchester. An added incentive for me to teach the skill to the boys was the availability of the materials required.

To my surprise, the students mastered the skill quickly and produced excellent pieces of work which, offered for sale, were bought up quickly, while orders were made for more of the same pieces. So successful was their effort that some of the boys earned their pocket money themselves instead of relying on their parents for it. I knew that the parents of many of them were struggling to raise enough money to pay the school fees, no less provide pocket money. I saw no reason why the boys could not help themselves. However, I had not been fully aware of the real hardship of some of them until one rainy day I found a senior student in bed. I inquired why he was in bed and soon had a thermometer in his mouth. The thermometer registered normal reading, and the young man looked at me with considerable dread. I consulted the Matron who told me that he had only one change of clothing. When he was wearing one, the other would be in the laundry. That day he was caught in the rain and had been soaked, so he had to stay in bed until his clothes were dried.

Immediately I went to the phone and ordered from a friend's store in Kingston a couple suits, two extra pairs of pants, shirts, underwear, a pair of shoes, a pair of slippers, two pairs of pyjamas, and a dressing gown for the student. The Matron provided me with the sizes. These were sent by the evening bus which passed the

College daily. While the Matron and I were checking these articles on their arrival, Mrs. Gladys Knight, one of the female staff members and a very kind and understanding lady who had two children in the school also, was sufficiently moved to offer to contribute one-half the cost of the clothes. While the students were at 'prep' that evening, the Matron and I quietly placed the suits and pants in the student's cupboard, the pyjamas under his pillow, the shoes beside his bed, and the other articles in his drawers. Before lights out that evening there was a gentle knock at my door. It was the "sick" student. Tears streaming from his eyes, he held my hand and shook it, and shook it, and shook it, without saying a word.

"Well, what is all this about?" I asked. "A sick man should not have such a firm hand shake."

The tears still streaming, he smiled and left, still without saying a word. I dashed to the Matron's quarters to chastize her verbally, but she stopped me before I could say a word.

"He came and asked me if I had 'done it'. I said I did not know what he was talking about. Then he said, 'It is Mr. Dale, isn't it?' I told him that I still did not know what he was talking about, and he left."

That night in bed I felt good, very good! It is the feeling that comes with sharing what one has with others. Always the donor feels he receives more by giving than by receiving, far more than the recipient. But how was I to let the student know that the gift was not from me alone? I thought I would leave the explanation to the Matron, and I did.

Next, I formed a Scout Troop in the College, and after successfully launching it, encouraged Mrs. Knight to form a Girl Guide Company, which she did. Again, from the sales of their hand-made leather articles, a few of the boys were able to finance their scout uniforms. The climax of their activities was a summer camp which I organized for them and conducted near Dunn's River, the very spot where I went for my first scout camp as a young boy. Similarly, Mrs. Knight organized and conducted a summer camp for the girl guides.

Also I tried to introduce to the boys a semblance of the kind of co-operatives I had seen and studied briefly in Denmark. It was to be based on chickens (for eggs), goats and pigs. This proved to be most difficult, demanding more time than was allowed for extra-curricula activities. It was regrettable we could not continue the project, which was aimed not merely to produce eggs or pigs or goats, but to demonstrate how co-operation can produce good results; it was really training for adult life.

No less, I encouraged dramatics and succeeded in getting a few of the students to stage and act a play in the College. It was a major challenge since the students had to be coached in speaking clearly, enunciating, voice projection, poise and deportment. But they were co-operative, highly intelligent, highly talented and highly imaginative. They learned quickly.

The play was opened to the public and proved a success. The student enjoyed acting and felt proud of themselves. It seemed as if their abilities, lying dormant for some time, had suddenly been activated. They were becoming willing to face any challenge and this excited me all the more. I could see the results of my efforts, and with this came intense satisfaction.

Then I requested the Principal's permission to invite one of Jamaica's leading artists (oil painter), Albert Huie, to spend a week-end at the school to demonstrate his painting skill. I had seen an exhibition of Huie's work at one of London's famous art galleries a few years before and had met him in person. The exhibition had taken London by storm and had launched Albert Huie as one of Jamaica's famous artists; yet, at that time he was little known at home. My plan was to ask the artist to paint a landscape scene in the presence of the students and lecture to them as he went along. Huie should try, if he could, to excite their curiosity and to get them to try their hand at painting too. The visit was approved by the Principal, but only after Mrs. Knight and I agreed to cover the cost of Mr. Huie's week-end boarding in the College, for the Principal refused to do so from College funds.

This was another experiment that was most successful. Huie painted a part of the local landscape, pointing out to the students as he went along, and as they looked on, subtleties of shades and colours in the landscape before them. He also used one of the girls and one of the boys as models and painted them also. The three paintings were completed after he returned to Kingston; and at my urging, he donated them to the school, again, Mrs. Knight and I paying for the cost of the materials. The school Board was so impressed with the experiment that it appointed Mr. Huie to teach art in the school on a part-time basis — my intent in the first place.

Generally, this was a remarkable group of students who, I predicted, were destined to leave their mark on Jamaica. (I was right, for, to leap the years, many became doctors of medicine, lawyers, economists, planners, professors, entrepreneurs, among other professions.) I was so fully occupied with them that I had no time to brood over my own personal problems. Besides, the students were appreciative. Years later, one of them, Professor Bert-Fraser Reid of Duke University, North Carolina, United States, who was nominated for the Nobel Prize in Chemistry, wrote me to say,

> When I talk to my own students these days, I caution them again and again about the importance of learning how to write clearly. I still remember the drill and scolding that you inflicted upon us in our English classes. It took me a long time to realize that even more important than the benefit to the reader, is the benefit to the writer himself ... When I think of the enormous debt I owe to people like you ... for inspiring confidence in me when I needed it most, and who have not tried to take any credit for what I have been able to achieve, I feel truly humbled.

Before the end of the calendar year, the school was inspected by government inspectors, a custom in all the government-funded secondary schools in Jamaica. The inspection lasted a week. The inspectors checked not only to see if the curriculum was followed, but if the academic performance of the students and teachers, the facilities of the school, and the social life of the students, including their extra-curricula activities, were satisfactory. Then they submitted their detailed report to the Department of Education in Kingston. In turn, a copy of the official report was sent to the school.

To my considerable surprise, the report commented in detail on my contribution both to the academic and social life of the school. It was totally embarrassing for me to be singled out in the report. Even more surprising, I received a letter from the Department of Education, congratulating me on my "outstanding achievement at the school" and releasing me from my agreement with the Government to teach for at least another year. The Department stated that what I had accomplished in the school in one year was equivalent to more than two years of hard work. Whether the intent of the Department was to give credit where credit was due, or diplomatically to keep me in harness now that I had established myself was not known. What the Department might not have considered was my irrepressible desire to improve myself academically, indeed, to finish what I had begun at the University of London.

It was on a Wednesday morning that I received the letter from the Department of Education, and before the day had ended, I had put a call through to London, inquiring about the availability of my "digs" (accommodation) should I return during or immediately after the Christmas season. The response was positive. Two days after, I visited Kingston to see if I could book a berth on any steamship plying between Jamaica and London. I drew a blank at all the shipping companies I visited, except the last one. The SS Acadia — the very ship on which I had returned to Jamaica the previous year

— had a first-class cabin, and was due to sail from Port Antonio on the northeastern side of the island on Christmas Eve. Though expensive, I booked the cabin, paid a deposit, and rushed back to the school to write my letter of resignation which I handed to the Principal and requested him to treat the matter confidentially. The regular meeting of the School Board was only a week away.

However, news of my letter of resignation was leaked to the whole College, and for the last weeks of the school year I was inundated with visits and calls, all wanting to know if the rumour was true. When at last the news was confirmed, I was pressured by members of the School Board to stay. I had requested that my resignation should be accepted without question, but this proved too much for the Board which invited me to attend their meeting. They demanded an explanation for my notice of resignation. I was grilled for nearly an hour, and still I refused to say anything, only that they should accept my resignation without question. Categorically, the Board stated that if anything was wrong in the College, they would rectify it, for they wanted me to stay. All was not well, but on that I preferred to remain silent. Besides, how could they understand my deep-seated yearning to seek more advanced academic training which I had been denied? I refused outrightly to explain myself. It was difficult to draw myself away from the students who pleaded with me to change my mind, but I steeled myself against their petitions. The last day of the term was an emotional one, wholly unforgettable. The good-byes were harrowing for me, but I lived through it and took my departure from the College.

First, I rushed to spend a few days with my parents who also wanted me to stay in Jamaica. Next, I went back to Kingston to spend a few days also with my sister. And on December 24, I arrived in Port Antonio, taken there by one of the teachers of Clarendon College, and boarded the SS Acadia for London, England. Once more I saw the shore line of my beloved island disappearing from view. I stood on the deck for a long time with profound sadness, while a gentle wind brushed my face, and twilight approached quickly. My heart was heavy and I was tired, very tired and terribly alone. Could I dare contemplate what lay ahead? It was certain to be difficult. But I said to myself, "Edmund Dale, the future beckons, full of difficulties. You must face them with courage and determination." Still I felt harnessed to an invisible yoke. I had a quick shower, and with tears in my eyes, I brushed my teeth, put on my pyjamas, threw myself into the bed, and was soon fast asleep.

CHAPTER 7

Unlike the university system of North America, which is largely based on a four-month semester system, that of Britain had always been based on a term of ten months, beginning in September or early October and ending in June or July. I was fully aware of this before I left Jamaica, but hoped somehow I would gain entry to University College or one of the other Colleges of London University on my arrival in January, but I could not. I was now faced with the annoying dilemma of what to do next. The money I had saved to pay my way in London was being used up despite my valiant attempts to be frugal. Thus I thought I would seek a teaching position until the beginning of the university year in September or October. I consulted the Educational Supplement, an educational professional journal, noted the advertisements of six teaching positions in my major field, Geography, and set about applying for them. My references were salutary and my optimism high. I thought I would apply in person, though by so doing, the bus and tube (underground train) fares would eat up much of my capital, for the distances to be covered were considerable. The London area also includes the Middlesex County, but the Middlesex County Council was separate and independent from the London County Council.

In three days, I succeeded in calling in person at the Education Offices of the London County Council, which had advertized the positions. At each, I was told that the position advertized had been filled and that I should try the next educational jurisdiction. Then I called at the head office of the Middlesex County Council. The Education Officer received me well. He had been associated with the Boy Scout Movement all his life and, seeing the Boy Scout pin on the lapel of my jacket, he inquired about Scouting in Jamaica. Both of us had a friendly chat about scouting and, as a scout, I expected him to be honest, if not frank. He was both. He told me that up to that time, as far as he was aware, not a single black person had been appointed to fill a permanent teaching position in any school under the jurisdiction of the London or Middlesex County Council, and that racial prejudice would militate against my finding a position. He offered to demonstrate what he meant. He took the phone and rang the Education Office in East Finchley, close to North Finchley where I was residing. East Finchley had advertized for a Geography teacher and told the Officer that the position was still vacant. In turn the Officer told East Finchley that he would send an applicant to see them. He gave me the address and requested me to phone him back to report what East Finchley had said.

I went, as directed, but was told that the position had been taken. I went immediately to a public telephone booth and rang the previous Officer. He asked me to hold the line while he used another line to talk to the East Finchley officer. Though faintly, I could hear their conversation:

"Did you not tell me a little earlier that the position you advertized for a Geography teacher is still vacant?" he asked.

"Yes, it is," came the reply.

"Well, I sent an applicant to you just now but he was told the job was taken."

"I was surprised you did that. We have never employed a Negro before and will not be doing so now."

"Why not? You may well be denying your young people a good opportunity to learn about other people, you know."

"I am sorry, but I want to keep my job," was the reply.

Then I heard the Officer at the other end close the phone.

He returned to my line and, clearly upset, said to me,

"Mr. Dale, I had warned you that you would have difficulty finding a teaching position. You have just seen the first indication of this."

I was not really surprised by the false statement given me by the East Finchley officer, but had hoped that my British teacher's qualification would be respected. I was perhaps too naïve to think that the colour of my skin would not be an obstacle. However, the Middlesex County Education Officer gave me a list of Education Offices I should try, and wished me luck.

I felt somewhat crushed. As a Negro, my contribution, however minuscule, was sought during the war, given and accepted, but my ability to teach in a British school seemed now to be frowned upon. Yet, I refused to allow the negative response I had so far to deter me. I added a few more likely places to the list the Middlesex County Education Officer had given me over the phone and set about calling on them in person.

After six weeks of riding the London buses and underground trains, and visiting Education Office after Education Office without success, I came to the last entry on my list. I was to have an appointment at the Enfield Education Office at 4.30 p.m. On arriving there, I was asked by the Education Officer who interviewed me,

"Have you tried Palmer's Green nearby?"

"Yes," I replied.

"What did they say?" the Officer asked.

"Have you tried Enfield?" I replied.

The Officer laughed and asked where exactly I had tried. I

showed him the list of the 26 Education Offices I had been to, including Wood Green, Palmers Green, Southgate, Wembley, Hornsey, Edmonton, Hendon, Tottenham, Willesden, Harrow, North Finchley, East Finchley, Cricklewood... .

"You went to all these places?" he asked.

"Yes, I have been to all of them. I am determined to show what I can do if only I am given a chance. All I want is a chance. I think it is so unfair for them to write me off because of the colour of my skin. Indeed, it is stupid, grossly stupid, blatantly ridiculous. They don't know what I am able to do, and they refuse to give me a chance to show them."

I was thoroughly overcome and tears which I had held back for weeks gushed freely from my eyes. This was exactly what I did not want to do. I was not seeking pity or begging for anything. My pride would not allow me to do that. I felt I had much to offer and wanted to offer. I thought my inability to hold back the tears could imply that I was seeking pity, which was repugnant to my pride. The Officer watched me wrestling with my emotions, then said,

"I have had only one son. He was killed in the war. You remind me so much of him — determined, refusing to give up even when he could see no light at the end of the tunnel."

Then he got up, walked to the window, there paused in thought, then came over to me, put his hand on my shoulder and told me to go home — I had to, anyway, for it was then after 5 p.m. — and promised he would see what he could do. I should wait at home for his call. Still, I was angry with myself for losing self-control which I had fought so desperately to maintain. My pride was sorely wounded.

I did not sleep too well that night and was restless the next day. At 9 a.m. the second day, the phone rang. It was the Enfield Education Officer. He inquired if I was free to go to the Technical School in Enfield to fill in for a few days for a teacher who was ill. I

122

accepted the invitation and turned up the following morning at the school. The Principal was most accommodating and showed me around the school, introduced me to the senior class to which I would teach Geography and English Language.

The next day saw me giving my first Geography lesson to the senior class, young men between 17 and 19 years of age. At once I secured the attention of the class. True, the students' eyes were on me. They were listening, but still not listening. They were looking through me and beyond me. I stopped, then said,

"You are giving me rapt attention and yet you are not hearing me. You seem to have many questions on your minds. I do not know you by name yet, therefore you must excuse me if I point to you. You over there (pointing) have you a question to ask?"

No, he had no question. I pointed to others, and they had no questions either. Then I turned to one young man sitting in the front row.

"I know you have a question. Your eyes tell me so. (They all smiled.) Will you be the only one in the class with enough courage and backbone to say exactly what is on your mind?"

"Well, er, er...(and everybody laughed, including me) may I ask where you were educated? In Jamaica?"

"Partly," I replied. "My early education, yes, and part of my teacher training which was interrupted when I volunteered for active service in the RAF. After the war, I applied to the University of London for admission to the B. Sc. Honours programme in Geography and was admitted, but, unhappily, I could not get any financial assistance from my government for this. They wanted me to complete my teacher training instead of going on to university work. The Government would offer assistance only if I acceded to their request. I was obliged to do what they wanted me to do. I was made to sign an agreement to return to Jamaica to teach for at least two years after my studies were completed. I went to King Alfred's

College, Winchester, Hampshire, specializing in Geography, and took and completed successfully the two-year teacher training course. At the end, I applied again for admission to the University of London and was admitted to University College, but the Colonial Office in London (Jamaica was still a colony) soon rushed me back to Jamaica to fulfil my commitment to teach there. Pleased with my teaching after only one year, the Government released me from my agreement with them. I lost no time in returning to London to see if I could gain admission yet again to the University of London. But I must teach in order to pay my way. So here I am."

"Was it difficult for you to get an early education in Jamaica?" the young man continued.

I told him, the class, how difficult it was for me to get my schooling, how hard I tried, how I had to buy and sell coco-nuts to raise money to buy my books and pay my school fees (elementary education was free but not secondary education), and how determined I was to succeed, so determined that I was prepared to sweep the streets if it came to that. By then, the questions began to come freely and fast. I answered them honestly and with equanimity, indeed as freely as they came — the language spoken in Jamaica, the people and their ethnic background, the system of education, the sports played, the economy of the island, the politics — they wanted to know as much as I could tell them. Yet, it seemed it was the person, Edmund Dale, about whom they wanted to hear most. Flashing my usual smile, I told them I was very much like them only that my skin, hair and facial features were different, that I had not come from Mars (loud laughter), that I had the same desires and yearnings, the same hopes and aspirations, the same needs, the same feelings as themselves; that the similarities between me and them were far greater than the differences which were insignificant. If they looked at me closely, they would see that everything was in the right place — eyes, mouth, ears, hands, feet, indeed, everything. They roared with laughter. In this heart-to-heart exchange, I used the

124

whole period to get through to the students. At the end of the period, the curiosity and strangeness which their faces previously mirrored had disappeared. They seemed to think that their Mr. Dale was all right, and accepted me for what I was, a warm human being whom they later found to be friendly, understanding and helpful. The speed at which this was achieved surprised the Principal who, intermittently, had been keeping an eye on me and the class from his office close by.

My relationship with the teaching staff was equally good, though they took a longer time to see me as their equal. In this, I exercised patience and understanding. It was to be expected that much time would be necessary for whatever stereotypes, especially long held, they may have had of the Negro to be eradicated. I was quite able to handle this. I recalled asking one of the teachers why was it he always referred to my colour and with such apparent delight, even to the point of ridicule. Was it because of a complex on his part? Surely, I assured him, one does not always go about thinking that one is white or black or brown or yellow. I certainly did not do that. If he thought that, something was wrong with him, or he was mentally living in the Victorian age. He should therefore shed that notion and swing quickly into the mid-20th century. Throughout my time at the school, I found myself attempting to dispel some of the misconceptions some staff members and students held of the black man, more by deeds than by words.

The temporary position which I had filled, substituting for a teacher who was ill, did not terminate with the teacher's return. Instead of asking me to relinquish the position, the Principal became more and more interested in what I was able to do, and invariably did successfully. One of the school functions that he was obviously not satisfied with was the school's morning assembly on Mondays, Wednesdays and Fridays. He solicited my help. I promised I would help but I would need at least a week to make the necessary preparations.

125

During that week, I called a committee from my class to help me plan the week's morning assemblies. I knew that a few members of the class sang in local church choirs; a few played musical instruments, and one young man in particular was on his way to becoming a concert pianist. All were eager to demonstrate what they could do. It was important not to dampen their enthusiasm, but it was equally essential that they should realize that they would be contributing their talents in a religious and not a secular function; and that worship, reverence and defacement of self would be the goal of the morning assembly. Carl Jenkins, the promising pianist, had a flair for conducting. To him I assigned the task of putting together quickly a small choir and something of a chamber orchestra. They would need to practise for the three morning assemblies, the first being the most crucial. I inquired of Jenkins if he thought they could attempt the Chorale from Back's Cantata, "Jesu Joy of Man's Desiring"? Jenkins saw no reason why they could not, and immediately went into rehearsals after school. In the meanwhile, I chose suitable bible readings and a short prayer. When Jenkins thought his quickly-assembled choir and orchestra were ready, I requested a rehearsal with them. The school time-table allowed no more than thirty minutes for the assembly, including notices, and Jenkins and I tried to limit ourselves to that time. At the rehearsal, the boys demonstrated that they fully understood the meaning and purpose of the assembly and entered into it solemnly, reverently and meaningfully. I was convinced that their contribution would leave a lasting impression, and informed the Principal that I would be ready for the assembly the following week.

On the Monday morning, the boys were assembled in the main hall as usual, and the Staff members were seated in their places on the platform. As the Principal and I, led by the senior student, entered the hall, the students and Staff stood. The procession led to the stage while Jenkins played something on the piano, befitting the occasion. The Principal walked to his chair on the platform and stood with his Staff, and I to the lectern and signalled with my hands for all to be

126

seated. Silence fell upon the hall. Carl Jenkins and his group were at the ready, waiting, as pre-arranged, for a signal from me to begin. Then I turned my head slightly to Jenkins and slightly nodded. Jenkins began the Introit, playing the piano and directing the orchestra and choir. Quietly, reverently they began "Jesu, Joy", the voice of one of the choir boys rising above the others in sublime beauty. I held my stance, looking far beyond my audience, inspired, moved. The Chorale came to an end as quietly as it began, and I, still looking transfixed, in soft but clear tones, said:

"Seek the Lord and His strength. Remember the marvellous works that he has done. O Lord, how manifold are your works! In wisdom have you made them all; the earth is full of your riches."

This was followed by a hymn, "Immortal, invisible, God only wise." Next, I read a few passages from the Book of Genesis about the Creation, and offered a short prayer which, in part, ran:

> God, Almighty, we dare not to go forward alone. We are insufficient for ourselves and there is no one else who really understands and to whom we may turn. So in timidity we draw near to you and seek your courage, your love, your guidance, your help. Here and now we dedicate all our gifts of mind and body to you. Open our minds that we may hunger for knowledge and wisdom. Grant to those who learn understanding, a discerning mind, common sense, and to those who teach, wisdom, understanding, patience, and a keen sense of humour. Remember our maintenance staff, the office staff, our nurse — all who work here. Remove from this place all that offends, all that breeds discord and annoyance, and help us all to find new ways of serving you and one another. May your spirit be with us this day, during the week and always. Amen.

Then, quietly, softly, the orchestra and choir played and sang the Lord's Prayer, and I pronounced the benediction and took my seat with the rest of the Staff. There was still silence, still an air of reverence in the hall. It was usually at this point in the assembly that the Principal read out his notices. He got up, walked to the lectern and said,

127

"No, to give notices here would be to spoil a most beautiful and meaningful morning worship that Mr. Dale, Carl Jenkins and his orchestra and choir conducted for us. They have also shown me and all of us the talents and resources we have in this school, if only we could use them well or exploit them properly." Whereupon the assembly broke forth into prolonged applause. Just then the bell went for the change of classes, and the Principal dismissed the assembly.

When I reached the Staff Room to collect my books, my colleagues eyed me curiously. It was Mr. Stevens, a self-proclaimed agnostic, who spoke:

"Well, Mr. Dale, a few more encounters like this morning would land me right over on the side of the converted," and all laughed.

The next encounter was my class, from which the members of the orchestra and choir had been drawn. They stood, as usual, as I opened the door and entered to a burst of applause.

"What is all this for, I wonder?" said I.

They laughed. I congratulated and thanked Carl Jenkins, the members of the orchestra and the choir, who were all smiles. But I reminded them that they had two more morning assemblies to prepare for, and that I would meet them after school. Without any more discussion, I plunged into the lesson for the period.

Immediately after lunch, the Principal sought me out and took me into his office. He confessed that he had tried repeatedly to capture the atmosphere that I so easily secured in the hall that morning, and had failed repeatedly. He thanked me and told me, "You are a truly remarkable young man" — the times I was to hear that statement and, in all honesty, could not see what, if anything, was remarkable about me.

To me the secret of success, whether in teaching or anything else, lies in careful preparation. I tried always to be well prepared, and I really loved to teach, especially a large class. I seemed to be at my best with a large class, though equally good with a small one.

The second week after I began at the school, I noticed that a different person each day, for just over a week, would slip into the room through the rear door, unnoticed by the students, and listened as I taught — sometimes it was a woman, at other times a man. And always he/she would disappear before the end of the class. Who was this person? I did not know. However, the ghostly appearance failed to unnerve me. What really caused me a measure of concern was the arrangement for me to substitute for a teacher who had been ill and had returned, yet I was still in the position. Although I was secretly pleased about this, curiosity and suspense made me inquire of the Principal about my temporary appointment. The Principal explained at length.

The School Board had mixed feelings about my appointment. They had voted as to whether I should be hired and had come up with a tie vote. But the Education Officer broke the tie by casting his vote in favour of hiring me. That was why a few members who opposed the appointment took it upon themselves to visit my class and hear me teach. One even attended one of the morning assemblies I conducted, without my knowledge and at the Principal's invitation. The Principal said that without exception each was favourably impressed and that gave him the opportunity to press for another permanent teaching position which he could offer me, because he did not want to lose me. The matter was being considered and before the end of the term, three months after I had accepted the position, he expected to be given a reply to his request. The reply came eventually, but it was in the negative. My appointment terminated at the end of the term. I was now to face a difficult summer. I had saved my salary, less expenses, and thought I would try to live on that for the time being.

Early in August, I had another phone call from the Enfield Education Officer. He was pleased that I had done so well at the

Technical School and had silenced the critics.

"I have a permanent position for you if you have not found another yet. Are you interested?"

This was surely answer to prayer, I thought. But if I took a permanent position, would I be able to continue my studies? I had to think quickly. I could support myself only by teaching during the day, therefore I would have to study at nights. I told the Officer I would be pleased to accept the position. I was still living in North Finchley and could get to Enfield easily by changing buses. I went the same day to Enfield and was taken to the boys' school. The teachers and students were then on summer holidays. I filled out the necessary forms and was given the particulars pertaining to the position. I would now be financially secure, I thought. One-half my burden had rolled from my shoulders. The rest was how to continue my academic studies.

Of all the Colleges of the University of London, Birkbeck was the only one which catered to the needs of people who work by day and wish to study at night. It admitted them not as part-time but as full-time students on the condition that they were engaged in full-time employment. This was tailor-made for me. I applied for admission, obtained it, and soon found myself rushing in the late afternoons on my motor-scooter from the school in Enfield to Birkbeck College in Central London, through rain or fog or sleet or snow, whatever the weather and whatever the season.

The Principal of the boys school in which I began to teach had been a Major in the Army and ran the school as though he was still in the Army. On my first day, he said to me:

"They tell me you can teach. We will soon prove that. Here is your time-table, Mr. Dale. My secretary will show you to the staff room and to your class room."

With that he dismissed me. I found his brusqueness downright impolite, if not uncommonly rude, altogether difficult to overlook.

But I soon found that he treated all members of his staff in a similar manner. Many were actually afraid of him. I told myself I was not going to be afraid of him; there would be no need for that if I executed my duties ably and professionally; and this was exactly what I tried to do. When I thought I should act contrary to the "orders" (and that was what they seemed to be) of the Principal, I did, and was proven right. Whereas other members of the staff would cringe at the Principal's demands, I would boldly tell him, whether in staff meetings or in his office, what I thought was wrong with them, if I thought they were wrong. The rest of the staff were aghast at my frankness. Two illustrations of my independent thinking may be mentioned.

The first had to do with an attempt by the school to raise sufficient funds to buy an expensive printing machine which the School Board could not provide. The Principal thought the school should raise the money by minor, small projects. He had called a small group of the staff, including me, to discuss the matter. I was candid in stating that the Principal's suggestion to attempt small projects would use up too much time and energy and brought in too little financial returns. We should aim instead to attempt larger projects. I mentioned that I had something in mind but needed a week more before I could bring it before them. Before going any further with their planning, would they give me a little more time and I would be back with something which, I thought, could bring in sufficient funds to buy the machine twice over. Everyone looked at me with amazement. Up to that time they did not really know me or much about me. The Principal fixed me a long, bewildered stare, then agreed to my request.

In less than a week, I returned to them with an ambitious scheme — a variety concert by the leading West Indian artists of the entertainment world, then performing in London. They would include Winnifred Athwell, the honky-tonk pianist; Lucille Mapp, a film star; Russ Henderson and his Steel Band; Boscoe Holder and his

Caribbean dancers; the Limbo Dancers; Olive Lewin and her group of folk singers; Al Timothy and his saxophone; Ivan Brown and his guitar; George Brown (Spirituals); Edmund Reid (violinist); Jay Thompson (Contralto). It would be a two-and-a-half-hour concert.

After I had finished reciting these names, I paused for the expected reaction from the Principal and the committee members appointed to raise the funds for the school.

"Mr. Dale," said Mr. Phillips, "you are dreaming. Almost all the people you mentioned top the London entertainment scene. How could we possibly get them, let alone pay them? Our campaign is a fund-raising one. I really thought you had something practical to suggest."

Before I could reply, the Principal chimed in:

"Mr. Phillips is right. Quite impossible! Whatever such a concert could bring in, assuming it was possible, and to me it is not, would be insufficient to pay such high-paid entertainers. That is quite out of the question."

"Well, gentlemen," I said, smiling, "generally West Indians are a kind-hearted people. If help is needed, they will give it (words which were to be repeated by the media). I have explained to each of the artists I mentioned what we are trying to do here, and each, every single one of them, has offered to do the show voluntarily, that is, without pay."

"What?" asked the Principal, "All of them?"

"Every one of them!" I said. "In fact, they were pleased that I asked them. I approached Winnifred Atwell first, and once the others heard that she and Lucille Mapp had agreed to help, they all wanted to do the same. Recall that I told you it would take me a week to sort matters out. Well, I visited each person in turn and obtained their promise which, believe me, they will honour."

"Amazing, Mr. Dale, simply amazing," said the Principal.

132

I ignored the compliment and emphasized the need for making arrangements for the concert if the committee approved my suggestion. They approved it gladly, and quickly set themselves to be concert promoters and agents. I undertook to convert the stage of the main hall into a tropical garden, using natural palm trees, tropical plants and flowering shrubs, to be borrowed from the City's greenhouse. The Principal's office was turned into a Box Office which handled the numerous calls for tickets after the local media carried the news. The seating arrangement presented the greatest difficulty, for the tickets were quickly taken up and more seats had to be installed to accommodate all who were phoning in for tickets. Yet, the fire regulations had to be strictly observed. Despite constant, careful checking, the seats were oversold. The demand for them was more than the 'Box Office' could cope with.

The night of the concert came at last. The hall was packed. All 800 tickets had been sold, and there were people standing at the sides and back of the hall. Seated in the front row were the Mayor and his wife, and other officials of the City of Enfield and the Enfield School Board. The Enfield Weekly Herald (Friday, 14th June, 1957) aptly described the scene and what followed:

> ...two boys turned the spotlights on to the stage as the curtains parted ... Dancers whirled, leapt and shook, their red, yellow and green costumes spinning against a tropical background of palm trees and sunsets. There were calypsos, rock'n roll, music from 'tuned' oil drums ... and everywhere the smiles were as wide as a slice of water melon. By the time the top-of-the-bill, Winnie Atwell, came on to the stage, the nearby park might just as well have been a sugar plantation.

In short, the concert was a huge success. As I had predicted, more than twice the amount required for the printing machine was raised. In publicly thanking the group at the end of the show, the Mayor pointed out that the tremendous contribution of the artists achieved not only the goal of raising money for the school but had greatly enhanced cultural relations in the area, and for that the City of Enfield was especially grateful.

Owing to limited space and limited pocket money, many of the boys could not attend, but a tape recording of the show brought it to them the following day before they left for the Whitsun holiday.

A second illustration of my independent thinking and contribution to the school was my organizing and conducting three educational tours of Switzerland for those students who could afford to go. These tours also proved to be very successful. The group flew from London to Brussels, Belgium, then took a through-train (night-sleeper) to Lucerne, Switzerland. On the return trip of the third tour, however, I planned to fly all the way. The Principal was opposed to the group flying and insisted that we should travel by train and boat. But I told him frankly that if I was going to be in charge of the group, I would insist on flying because many of the difficulties I had on the two previous tours could have been eliminated if the group had flown all the way. I held my ground and refused to give in to the Principal's wish. It was good that I had, for after what was an enjoyable tour, on our return trip, the French railway went on strike and hundreds of British students who were on holidays in France and had travelled by the railway were left stranded at various places in France. This caused their parents and schools frantic concern. My group, however, flew home without difficulty, to be met joyously by parents and the Principal. Shaking my hands and his head, the Principal merely smiled. Words were not necessary between us. He had already come to the realization that he had on his staff a teacher of independent thinking.

At all times I entered fully into the life of the school, but though the demands of teaching were heavy, I continued my evening studies at Birkbeck College, and was glad to be able to do so. I felt I had to be on top of my teaching all day, every day, also on top of my studies, and did not spare myself. The Principal, in one of his rare, friendly moments, had told me that my health would be impaired if I continued at the rate I was going. He had tried years ago to do what

I was doing, but he was forced to discontinue for fear of a nervous break-down. In his opinion, I would not be able to do what I was doing for long. I told him that one way, and only one way, was opened to me to obtain further qualifications, and I was obliged to take it.

In due course, I obtained the Bachelor of Science Honours degree, followed two years later by the Master of Science degree. On obtaining the latter degree, the Principal told the school of my academic successes at a morning assembly, and how he told me that I would not be able to do justice to my teaching and to my studies at the same time, and how I had proved him wrong on that and on other occasions. But what the Principal did not know was that the Commonwealth Missionary Society in London had been sending me to various parts of Britain over the week-ends to speak about its work in Jamaica and about Clarendon College. The spin-off from these visits were more invitations for me to speak at Boys' Public Schools, Girls' Public Schools, Women's Institutes, Men's Clubs, conferences and the like. It was fortunate that I was young, healthy and physically strong. A weakling would certainly have caved in as a result of the rigorous demands and the high standards I had set myself.

But why was I pushing myself so hard? True, I insisted on pursuing a university education. True, I had no financial support and had to make it on my own. And true, I had been fired by a fierce determination and a relentless drive to succeed. But more than that, I was acutely aware of the divisions, especially between ethnic groups, and wanted to help by example to remove at least some of them. At the first major student function I was asked to address, I made a passionate plea for racial harmony. The function was the closing ceremony of a Students' Conference on racial harmony, chaired by Miss Attlee, sister of Mr. Clement Attlee (then Prime Minister), and president of an organization whose mandate was to promote racial harmony. The Conference was held in Westminster Hall, a huge building opposite Westminster Abbey, later demolished to make room for a more modern structure. At this meeting, Miss Attlee insisted that representatives from the different countries attending the Conference should sit on the platform with her. I was invited to be one of them, to represent Jamaica. I accepted the invitation and took a seat at the back. The hall was packed with students, the stalls, the two balconies full to overflowing. It was a most impressive occasion. There was indeed an air of racial togetherness.

Miss Attlee introduced the platform guests, to the roaring applause of the audience. And then she said,

" I am sure you would like to hear from at least one of the guests."

The audience responded with thumping, whistles, cat-calls and applause — the way students usually behave at such functions.

"Well, let me see," she said. "Ah, Mr. Edmund Dale from Jamaica!"

The cheers were deafening. I heard my name but could not respond. I was terrified, dead but alive. I sat, glued to the chair; my heart pounding so loudly that I felt it would be heard a mile away. My mouth suddenly became dry. I could hardly breathe. It was too sudden; the shock was too much for me. But I had faced audiences before, so why was I so intimidated by this crowd? Perhaps it was the large number of them and the fact that I had not been prepared for what I was called upon to do. Miss Attlee walked over to me, took my hand and led me to the podium. At last the applause died down and I, facing what I later called the challenge of my life, opened my mouth but no sound would come from it. I held the lectern firmly and with tremendous effort said,

"Madam Chairman, platform guests, ladies and gentlemen, and you up there in the cheap seats (the upper balcony, called the 'gods') (laughter and uproarious applause), "if only you knew how my knees are shaking! (The applause and laughter increased in intensity). Believe me, I would readily change places with you. Would you like to exchange places with me?"

"No," shouted the whole house in chorus, and more laughter.

The convivial atmosphere, typical of a student gathering, helped me to get my breath. With lightening speed, words I once read in a book on the art of public speaking flashed across my mind: 'Breathe deeply and control the air that is being exhaled. Speak slowly at first'.

Striking an easy, comfortable, uninhibiting posture, I thanked and congratulated the organizers of the Conference for bringing together so many students, drawn from so many countries. In splendid accord, I said, free of the disease of racial intolerance, indeed, racial hatred, which took the lives of so many millions in the war just ended and which still holds so many millions in inexorable bondage, we were bound to profit from the rich experience offered by the Conference. If the Conference had done nothing else, I said, it had demonstrated with admirable conviction that race does not need to drive people apart (long, continued applause). Rather all who have attended the Conference should, like me, have caught even a glimmer of how people can live in racial harmony. Many of them, now in training, would be potential leaders on their return to their respective countries, and doubtless would be called upon to help to eradicate the fear and suspicion, the ignorance and prejudice that blind nations and bring them to arms. What I was saying was not mere hog-wash. The nations needed to be cleansed of racial hatred, and the job must be done by the young people of the world who should dedicate their lives to the cause. The Conference was making a singular contribution to their preparedness, and none of them should leave it without the resolve to do battle with racial prejudice whenever and wherever they saw it.

By this, I sensed I had the full attention of the audience, that they were with me, that I was their mouth-piece, voicing their feelings and emotions. The silence in the hall was almost audible, and I continued to make a vigorous, passionate plea for them to enlist their intelligence and talents in defeating injustice, grounded on racial ignorance and racial intolerance. I brought my few words to an end by asking them to stand and observe a minute's silence in memory of all the youths, students and others who, in the last war, were put to death in the most savage, barbaric manner simply because they were Jews. At the end of the minute's silence, I thanked them and walked back to my seat, and the audience thundered mightily their applause.

The impromptu speech to the hundreds of students gave me a degree of confidence essential for my continuing development. I felt I had all along been tested and had by then acquired the maturity with which to face head-on issues which I would later have to face and which would severely test my patience, humility, understanding, and what little wisdom I might have. I was thankful, very thankful for the experience and felt very humble.

It was not long after the Inter-racial Conference that my tolerance and understanding were to be tested. The incidence was humorous. One Saturday morning, I found myself along the Strand, in the heart of London, waiting for a bus to take me up to Tottenham Court Road, on my way to the Senate House Library of the University. First at the bus stop, I faced the direction from which the bus would come. Soon, two ladies came behind me and formed a queue, as was the orderly custom throughout the city and country. Obviously, they were Cockneys (from Southeast London) because they spoke Cockney. It was not long before the ladies began a running commentary on me. With considerable enthusiasm, the one said to the other,

"Ducks, do you see what I see?" ('ducks' being an endearing term of the London Cockney). Ducks must have looked in my direction, for she said,

"If it isn't a black man!"

Realizing that I was the topic of conversation, I listened without turning my head round.

"I wonder where he comes from," said one.

138

"You bet he is from some part of the **jungles**," said the other. (They laughed.)

"Doesn't he look strange?"

"But he looks intelligent," said the other.

It was good they could not see my face for here I was looking coy, if not pleased.

"Do you think he is married?"

"Yes, Luv (Cockney word for love), they are married from when they are very small. I suppose he has some **twenty** children by now."

They laughed uncontrollably and I had a hard time keeping a straight face. Although they thought they were not being understood, Ducks whispered something very 'juicy' to her friend, for they laughed so much that she had to hold on to the lamp post for support. I wondered what it was. I would have given anything to know.

"Suppose you had that hair, what would you do with it?" continued Ducks.

"I would comb it back and tie it up with a big ribbon bow."

Thus they continued until at last the bus came. Although first in the queue, I stood aside and allowed the two ladies to mount the bus before me. Pleased that they were shown such courtesy, one did not step high enough in mounting the bus and fell to the ground. Now it was my turn. Like a valiant knight, I rushed to the rescue, helped her to her feet, brushed her down, took up her handbag and gave it to her. Now, if someone thinks a person does not speak his/her language, he/she tends to speak loudly to him. And the damsel who fell did just that. She almost shouted, emphasizing every word:

"Thank you very, very much!"

Smiling, bowing with affected sophistication, and with a dramatic sweep of my right hand, I said,

139

"Not at all, madam, I assure you, the pleasure is all mine."

Then, in terrible consternation, she called to her friend:

"Ducks, he speaks English!"

And everybody laughed, I in particular. This incident became one of my fondest memories. I was never tired of relating it to friends. After all, I thought, the good Lord must have made his people black, brown, yellow and white for their own amusement.

But while some forms of racial ignorance can be humorous, others are less so, even unpleasant. Of the many I experienced, two may be noted, both occurred while I was boarding with two retired sisters in a large, beautiful home in Southgate, North London.

The first had to do with a little girl who, in the mornings, was usually out in the garden of her home which faced the street. My first encounter with her was while I was passing the house on my way to school one summer morning. I said, "Hello there" to her, and she fled into the house, crying. Exactly the same thing happened the next morning. On the third morning, the little girl stood her ground, and I said, "Aren't you going to run away this morning? What a beautiful dress you are wearing! And you are such a sweet little girl." She twisted her hands and shrugged. The fourth morning she had a flower in her hand. As I came along the side walk, she ran timidly up to the gate and timidly presented me with the flower.

"Oh, thank you very much. I see we have become friends at last. What is your name?" I asked.

"My name is Cynthia. You are not a bogey man," she said.

"Who is a bogey man?" I asked.

"A black man," came the reply.

"Well, I am a black man. Who said I am a bogey man?"

"My Mummy told me if I misbehaved, she would send for the bogey man, but you are not a bogey man."

"Then you must tell your Mummy that you met a black man and that you do not think he is a bogey man." I bent down and gave the child a rose which I had taken from the garden of the home where I was staying, especially for her.

As usual, I would return from the University after 11 p.m. On that evening, I was surprised to find a middle-aged woman and a man at the home waiting for me. The retired sisters with whom I was staying were looking extraordinarily pleased. They introduced me to their two guests who said they were the parents of the little girl I had spoken to that morning, and that they had come to thank me for being so kind to her and so understanding. But more importantly they had come to confess their stupidity in imparting, unknowingly, to their daughter the stereotype of the black person which they had held from youth. Although mentally and physically exhausted after a day of teaching and a night of attending lectures, I found strength to be patient and to be understanding. There was nothing to be gained by lecturing those parents, for they had come to realize the folly of their action. By being friendly with the little girl, I had convinced her that there was no need to be afraid of a black man, and the child herself had wrought the change in her parents.

Perhaps the most harrowing experience of bigotry that I could recall was that involving a family in North London. Always an admirer of English gardens, I had taken a Saturday morning walk through the nearby park. There I met Penelope Swithers, a member of one of my university classes. We sat on a bench in front of a bed of lovely roses and engaged ourselves in lively conversation respecting the courses we were taking and the problem of meeting assignment deadlines. A friend of Penelope's mother and member of her bridge club, Della Bathgate, had apparently seen us, and in prudishness and affected haughtiness imparted by telephone this information to Penelope's mother, Margaret Swithers. According to Penelope, the telephone conversation went like this:

"Was it Penelope I saw in the park this morning? But no, it

couldn't be. No, not really," said Mrs. Bathgate to Mrs. Swithers.

"What do you mean? Penelope took a walk in the park this morning, yes, what about it?" asked Mrs. Swithers.

"Then it **WAS** she I saw talking with a, with a — but no, it couldn't be her. I may not have seen properly. No, dear, I am sure I was wrong."

"Well, who was she talking to?" asked Mrs. Swithers, clearly becoming exasperated.

"No, Margaret dear, I am sure I am wrong. My eyes are getting bad. I do not see clearly these days."

"Della Bathgate, for heaven's sake, tell me what you saw," Margaret Swithers demanded.

"Well, Margaret dear, I thought I saw Penelope talking ever so friendly with, with, with a **black man!**"

Immediately she changed the topic, leaving Margaret to stew in annoyance. Mrs. Bathgate had scored. She 'had one over' Margaret Swithers.

Forthwith Mrs. Swithers confronted her daughter.

"Were you in the park with a black man this morning?" she asked Penelope.

"Yes, I was talking with a **black man** in the park this morning. What about it?" asked Penelope.

"In public? In the park of all places? I have tried to bring you up as a respectable young lady and the thanks I get from you is your consorting with a Negro in public."

"Wait a minute, mother, the person I was talking to was Edmund Dale, a Jamaican and a member of my class at the University. He hasn't leprosy or anything like that. Are you saying that I should not talk to him because he is black, or not to talk to him in a public place because the neighbours will see us? Really, mother, I didn't know your prejudice ran so deep."

Margaret Swithers, a pillar of rectitude in the area, had then become the epitome of mixed feelings by her daughter's comment. Social status to her was all important and she had nurtured hers carefully. Now, she felt, she was to be ridiculed by friends like Della Bathgate who, she told Penelope, had imparted the news, and **HOW** she imparted it.

Penelope was alarmed, indignant, disappointed and defiant. She came to realize that her mother, whom she loved and respected so much, was guilty of racism. She resolved to do something to purge her mother of this nonsense. She must, she thought, do something very effective and very dramatic, even if it was unpleasant to her mother, to make her and her friends see how foolish their bigotry was.

During the following week Penelope accosted and told me she wanted my help and co-operation. It was a very delicate matter and **no one else,** she stressed vigorously, no one else but me, could help her. She told me how her mother had heard of our Saturday morning talk in the park, her mother's and her mother's friends' objection, and how she, Penelope, intended to do something to make them realize the foolishness of their snobbery and bigotry. Every Wednesday afternoon, her mother's bridge club met at her home at 2 p.m., and her mother would serve tea after their game of bridge. Mrs. Bathgate, who reported our meeting in the park, would be present. Penelope would invite me to tea on the following Wednesday, a public holiday, and her father would be at home. I would be required to arrive promptly at 3 p.m., the time her mother would serve tea. I might be slighted at first by the ladies but her father would respect the rules of politeness and etiquette. I would be required to exercise understanding, not to feel slighted even if I was slighted, and to remain the "polite, charming, intelligent person" everybody knew me to be. She continued. She believed it was personal contact which would help to break down the barrier between races, as I had pointed out over and over again. She believed that her experiment would go a long way to enlighten her mother and her friends.

"I, to come to your house specifically to be insulted? Penelope, you are mad, mad, mad! Certainly not!" I said.

"But I thought I heard you tell students at conferences and elsewhere that one has to suffer insults and taunts sometimes to change the bigotry of people. Is it that you advocate, Mr. Dale, a policy of 'do as I say but not as I do'?" Penelope confessed to me that her motives were two-fold: to help in the struggle against bigotry and racial prejudice, and to help to make her mother in particular see how stupid the whole thing was. In the end, she succeeded in getting me to acquiesce to her plan and to accept the invitation.

On the Wednesday afternoon, neatly attired, as was my custom, I presented myself at Penelope's home, on time, and pressed the bell. Penelope was there to open the door.

"Oh, Edmund, it is good that you could make it. Please come in. I will take your overcoat."

It was like a bolt of lightning that struck Mrs. Swithers and her guests, as Penelope led me into the room. Mrs. Swithers actually looked like a ghost, outwardly white as death, and inwardly boiling like a volcano.

"Come, Edmund," said Penelope, "please meet everybody, my mother, Mrs. Bathgate who had seen us in the park from a distance, Mrs. Hargreaves and Mrs. Pinnock. And here is my father who, I am sure, is pleased to have another man with him, surrounded as he is by all women."

Mr. Swithers extended his hand to me, and Penelope placed me in a chair beside him. Everybody in the room looked and felt awkward except Penelope and me. Secretly both of us were enjoying the spectacle. Obviously Penelope had not told her mother that she had invited me to tea. The silence was broken by Penelope who asked her mother if she was pouring a cup of tea for me, and in the same breath said to the group,

"Edmund is from Kingston, Jamaica. He is teaching in Enfield and, like me, studying at Birkbeck in the evenings. We are both in the same discipline, Geography."

In a voice somewhat sarcastic but endeavouring not to be, Mrs. Pinnoch, who had been enjoying the intrusion with wicked delight, said,

"Mr. Dale, that is the name, isn't it? Mr. Dale, are you enjoying your stay in England and our English ways?"

Well," I said, "there is much here that I like and some things that I do not like. The weather, for example, presents a real difficulty for me — the fog, the cold, the air pollution, I find these most trying."

"And our English ways?" persisted Mrs. Pinnoch.

I smiled, knowing quite well that the lady was teasing, for she had been looking at Mrs. Swithers whose face revealed what was unmistakable annoyance.

"I take it that you mean general demeanour. I find this inordinately interesting, Mrs. Pinnoch. I have had to revise some of the views I held of the English, of course. But this is what happens when we get to meet and know people. Invariably our ignorance takes a battering. What we thought was, is not, and what we thought was not, is."

Mr. Swithers interrupted me to say, "I will say 'Amen' to that," and everybody laughed except Mrs. Swithers. She was still visibly upset and remained determinedly glum. As the lady of the house, and despite her rude shock, her behaviour was hardly above reproach.

Mrs. Pinnoch continued.

"You were not finished, Mr. Dale."

"I was going to add, Mrs. Pinnoch, that I have been privileged to see much of Britain and meet many people in their homes, as Penelope has kindly invited me to meet you here, as well as the different strata of English society. Usually I find that what you call 'English ways' are determined by education, upbringing, or generally, painful ignorance or lack of it. However, in most cases, the English do not seem to me to be much different from other peoples I have been fortunate enough to meet in similar circumstances. They usually change their ways— your word Mrs. Pinnoch — if and when circumstances permit."

Mrs. Pinnoch made a little cough and said, "Mr. Dale, I can see you are a diplomat, and an obviously skilful one at that."

Still smiling, I thanked her for the compliment but said that I was wholly deficient in the virtues and skill of the diplomat and that I could never aspire to becoming one.

It was I who directed attention away from myself to the game of bridge, as they sipped their tea and ate the buttered scone which Mrs. Swithers herself had made. I complimented her on the scones which I had eaten before in Scotland, while Mrs. Blake, who had been staring at me almost from the moment I entered the room, expressed warm appreciation of the strawberries, "so fresh and tasty," she said.

When Mrs. Swithers eventually spoke, she said:

"Ladies (with marked emphasis on **'ladies'**), let me show you the garden. My sweet peas have done remarkably well this year."

They rose to leave the room and Penelope, who had said very little after she had introduced me, looked at her father who took the cue and said,

"Well, Mr. Dale, I will show you my part of the garden, the vegetable section," and we all went out into the garden.

At 4.30 p.m. I thought it was time to take my leave, and with dignity — I was/am a stranger to affectation — I thanked Mr.

Swithers and Penelope — Mrs. Swithers had disappeared — and asked them to thank Mrs. Swithers for me for her tea and scone which I enjoyed, and I departed.

Two evenings after, Penelope caught up with me after lectures.

"Well," I said, "did your mother boil you alive?"

"I cannot tell you how grateful I am to you for coming," she said. "You brought off the whole thing with so much ease, naturalness and dignity. You left a marked impression on all of them."

"Impressed because I did not have a tail like a monkey, and my eyes were actually in the same place as theirs, my ears, mouth, nose and hands were all where they should be, and when I opened my mouth intelligible sounds came out?"

"Don't be silly," said Penelope, laughing. "It was actually your presence, your intelligence, your quiet dignity that impressed them. Mrs. Pinnoch was very taken with you, and Mrs. Blake confessed it was the first time she had sat in the presence of a black person."

"And he did not eat her alive?" I asked in jest.

Laughing, Penelope said that even her mother had off-handedly remarked that perhaps her views of the world and its peoples needed to be changed. "You see," Penelope said, "you made her realize that her views are now obsolete and must reflect those of the mid-20th century.

"Penelope, let me try to put your words in the right perspective, if I can. You are saying in an indirect way that there is one segment of your society which is of the pathetic view that any English girl who consorts with a black man is a slut; that he has one, and only one, thing on his mind, namely, to get her into bed with him. That is the stereotype, isn't? It was implicit in Mrs. Bathgate's telephone call to your mother, and your mother's belief that you had disgraced her by talking to me in a friendly manner in a public place for all to see. I rather think your main motive for inviting me to your home was to prove them wrong, above all to prove to your mother and your mother's friends that you are not really that kind of girl, isn't that right?"

Penelope suddenly felt embarrassed and flushed red in her face. She had not expected such plain talk. She did not know what to say. In the deep recesses of her mind, she knew I was right. The thought had crossed her mind, but her other motives took precedence. After a few moments of silence, she said,

"Well, anyway, thank you for coming. I do not know many black students but I hardly think another could have done what you did, and in the manner you did it. I am truly grateful to you."

"Pleased to be of service, Miss Swithers! Seriously, I congratulate you for your courage and ingenuity. You are quite a girl. You will one day be a great lady. Good luck!"

As Penelope went her way, she thought about my parting words, she later confessed. Was I being sincere or cynical or sarcastic or all three? If she was in my place, she thought, could she have been so magnanimous? Suddenly she sensed the trauma that must come from being black in a world so steeped in colour prejudice. This lamentable fact, cruel and repugnant to her sense of fair play and decency, gave her a new determination to fight the illusion that presupposes the white race is superior to all the other races and must therefore have ascendancy over them. In a very real sense, she admired the ceaseless struggle that I and others like me constantly face to win privileges and exercise rights that a white person would take for granted, or for no other reason than the fact that he is white. She admired my courage, my lack of bitterness, and other qualities of my character, she later tried to tell me, and later tried to explain to her parents. It was not romantic love she felt for me but rather respect and admiration. If her own mother in particular could not understand that, who else would, she wondered. And if her parents' world was loathe to accept the notion of racial harmony and strive to promote it, it followed, Penelope concluded, that the task falls, as I had said repeatedly, on the young people of the world, before they, themselves, become infected with the virus of colour prejudice. But it is such a huge task! It is all the more so because that virus is found even in supposedly enlightened camps, be it public places or comfortable drawing rooms, and it has been there for a very long time. What will it take to defeat it? The vast numbers of innocent lives it has consumed, and the very promising lives it has atrophied, the injustices that are so multitudinous for love to assuage, the fierce intransigence that constantly rebukes the incessant call for change!. The whole task seems to defy individual effort. The more I reflected on this matter, indeed, on the panoply of Western civilization from century to century, the more despondent I became. Yet, I told myself that there must be hope, for if there is no hope, humankind is sadly doomed.

CHAPTER 8

$\mathbf{M}$y thesis for the Master's degree in the University of London fell within the field of inquiry called 'political geography', a branch of the parent discipline of geography which is the study of the distributions and interrelationships of phenomena. Political geography focuses on the State, large and small, down to the mini- and micro-State, on the relationship between geographical and political phenomena, and on the fact that as politically organized communities, States inevitably have a territorial basis and a geographical location (East, 1960, p.122). Yet, this sub-discipline lacks a well-defined focus and specific boundaries, for which it is criticized. Nevertheless, as East declares, it allows two lines of approach: the effect of political action on present-day geography, and of the significance of geography behind political situations, problems and activities. Both lines of approach thus make for a distinct spatial analysis of the complex interaction between economic and political processes within an historic time-frame or sequence, and such analyses provide an enlightened background to understanding the many global issues of our contemporary world.

Consequently, the movement in the 1950s to establish a political federation of ten British island colonies in the Caribbean Basin readily captured my interest. It was a topic of debate at the very time I began my graduate studies at London, and as a native of the area, with a keen interest in its development, I thought I would examine some of the geographical bases of this primarily political union.

150

Besides, previous attempts to integrate the islands had repeatedly failed, owing in part to the narrow application of the union suggested — to parts of the region instead of to the whole region — in part to the lack of well-conceived policies.

In certain quarters, the proposed federation was seen as a prelude to the establishment of a new, small State. Expectations outside the area were high, but the difficulties of achieving that aim were numerous. Such difficulties were wrought by the physical fragmentation or dispersion of the area, and made manifest in its geography, history, economics, politics, population and culture. Yet, it was, and still is, federation, properly conceived, that is likely to overcome those difficulties. But even before I could complete the study and submit my thesis, titled "Some Geographical Aspects of The West Indies Federation", October 1958, the Federation was inaugurated, in January of the same year, followed in April 1958 by the formal opening of the Federal Parliament by Princess Margaret. The speed in which the final decision was brought about necessitated change in much of my study, if not in argument, certainly in tense.

The ten islands brought into the Federation were Antigua, Montserrat, and St. Kitts-Nevis-Anguilla of the Leeward group; Dominica, Grenada, St. Vincent and St. Lucia of the Windward group; and Barbados, Trinidad & Tobago (the second largest of the ten islands) and Jamaica (the largest, and some 1,000 miles from Trinidad & Tobago).

It seemed clear to many people at the time that the British Government wanted to relinquish responsibility for these colonies while retaining them in what was then the British Commonwealth, now the Commonwealth. Britain had attempted to use federation as a political device to solve problems in its dependencies in other areas, notably in Central Africa in 1953 — the Central African Federation, comprising Northern Rhodesia (now the independent State of Zambia), Nyasaland (now independent Malawi), and Southern Rhodesia (now independent Zimbabwe), but the attempt had failed.

151

The same policy was extended to the West Indies Federation, which inevitably would fail, too, and to the Malaysian Federation, initially comprising the eleven Malay federated states, Singapore, Sarawak, and Sabah. But by 1965 Singapore had pulled out and became politically independent. The others became the politically independent, federal State of Malaysia.

Aware of the many difficulties facing such a weak political union of ten poverty-stricken islands, I proceeded to examine some of the major ones — the facilities for communication by sea as well as by air, those factors that could promote inter-regional trade, agriculture (the mainstay of the region), fishing, forestry, mining, and the available raw materials for local industry. No less, I thought I would consider also the demographic problems, including an increasing birth-rate and a falling death-rate, population pressure on the resources of the land, and external migration. And I would attempt to examine the Constitution of the Federation to see if it had the beginnings of what is called a "state-idea" or raison d'être or justification for the existence of the State, which the people could understand and defend. Not least, since in modern political federations choosing the site of a capital is important, I would attempt an assessment of the capital site.

My study-outline was approved, and I plunged into the work with vigour and a sense of dispatch. Soon I discovered that much of the material I would need to analyze and from which I could make deductions and draw conclusions could not be gleaned alone from library records in London. Similarly, the views of many of the chief actors, decision-makers, influential private residents and, in general, the man in the street, essential for an investigation of this kind, necessitated local field survey in all ten islands. The financial cost, especially trans-Atlantic air fares and flights between the islands, since inter-island passenger shipping was virtually absent, was at first a major difficulty but was overcome in the end. I undertook the field survey in the summer of 1957 at a time when the discussions on the Federation were being finalized.

From the beginning of the survey, I discovered that although the idea of federating the British islands had been banded about for many years, few in the region knew what a federal system of government really was, namely, a division of powers between two levels of jurisdiction: a central government and several unit governments, each autonomous within the sphere allowed it by the Constitution. It is a division that provides more than a compromise between local and national demands, and has to be made so that neither the central nor the unit government is subordinate to the other. I found that the majority of the residents of the islands did not know this. The conclusion I drew from this was that the real preparatory work that should have been done to achieve an understanding of what a federation is had not been done, or if it had been done, it had not been done thoroughly. Unhappily, even many of the politicians themselves appeared not to have fully understood what they were soon to approve.

To illustrate, at a dinner party to which I was invited to meet key members of the Jamaican Government, some 15 or more, and to discuss with them questions for which I was seeking answers, I was unable to get those answers. The host, himself an influential Minister of the Government, had shown a keen interest in my investigation and had arranged the dinner to enable me to meet most of the government members in concert instead of individually, which otherwise would have been difficult to arrange and would have taken more time than I anticipated or had.

After the dinner, the host introduced me properly, told the group the purpose of my visit to the island and other islands. The first question I put to the group was whether the proposed West Indies Federation was a call from within (from the people themselves) or a call from without (imposed by the British Government). The question was met with an awkward silence which at first I found difficult to interpret. Was it that these key members of the government did not know or did not want to voice their opinions?

Then at last one said:

"I thought we were going to talk about the real issues of the Federation. What you are asking does not seem to me to be as important as where we are going to site the capital, for example."

Others joined in and voiced similar opinions, and I felt I was facing a class of students who were reluctant to think or to think deeply. The host Minister smiled at me when he saw surprise, if not consternation, covering my face.

"Gentlemen," he said, "Mr. Dale has floored you with his first question. That question goes to the very heart of the matter."

He proceeded to tell them that when the Federation was first mooted, he was a student at Oxford University, and that the question that I asked had exercised the minds of a group of his peers, for it was central to the whole matter, but their individual studies did not permit them to examine it to any great extent. He was thus pleased to see a Jamaican attempting an in-depth analysis of the issue and thought he would bring him and them together for an intellectual discussion, if nothing else, on the matter.

I decided then to change my tactics. Instead of asking questions, I would present a point of view for discussion and see if the Government members would support it or dismiss it. I pointed out that my first question needed to be answered by the politicians, for if the federal principle in general and the proposed Federation in particular were not understood by the people, they would not in the end support it or be prepared to lay down their lives for its cause. And if that was so, the Federation would not herald the new independent State it promised; most likely it would be short-lived, died the death of the Central African Federation which Britain had tried to establish in Central Africa. The host Minister fully supported my point of view; thereafter the discussion was free and easy, even though a few of the members tended to stray from the main point and had to be brought back to it. No one, however, opposed what I had said.

Next, I drew attention to the structure of the proposed federation — the Legislature, the Executive and the Judiciary — which claimed to be democratic, yet retaining elements of a colonial government. I pointed to the head of the Legislature, a Governor-General, **appointed** by and representing the Crown, who would **appoint** the members of the Senate, nineteen altogether. Although the House of Representatives, comprising forty-six members, would be elected, executive power would be invested in the Governor-General.

Then I turned to the division of powers, the chief characteristic of all political federations, and showed that whereas special powers would be given to the federal government and all other powers remain with the unit governments, the federal government, already dominated by an appointed, as opposed to elected, Governor-General, was free to legislate on subjects in two lists, an executive list and a concurrent list. Unit governments, however, could legislate only on subjects in the concurrent list. The main subjects of the exclusive list were defence, external affairs, the establishment of federal advisory agencies, the regulation of intra-regional shipping, the University College of the West Indies, and student services in the United Kingdom, the United States and Canada.

Clearly, I continued, the proposed structure of the Federation could never lead to independent status. The nominated Senate, a Council of State whose members were to include officials, and the Governor-General's wide reserve powers would ostensibly retard progress towards political independence.

"Think of it, gentlemen," I said, "the Governor-General could exercise his wide reserve powers without the advice of, or consultation with, his ministers in relation to defense and external relations, public order and the financial stability of the Federation. He could even veto a Bill. Clearly such powers would subordinate the federal government to a role similar to that of a colonial government. Given such a role, would it not challenge the sincerity of the British Government?"

On this issue there was spirited discussion. Again it was agreed that my assumption was valid. Their leader, Norman Manley, had been fighting desperately to have the reserve powers of the Governor-General and the appointed officials in the State Council removed from the Constitution and had, up to the time of the interview failed.

As for the economic difficulties, few of the government members present had any clear idea of how they might be resolved. Yet, these had to be faced squarely from the very beginning. Limited resources, limited circulation by sea, limited funding, and a sparsity of local technical expertise necessary for industrial development would pose immense problems. Each of the Ministers was acutely aware of the major problems but could see no easy way to solve them.

It was, indeed, an excellent opportunity for me to sound out members of the Jamaican Government as to their understanding of the proposed Federation. I left the meeting with the same feeling I had after interviewing other politicians and influential people in the nine other federal units I visited. The stark reality was that the cardinal issues of the Federation had not been fully understood. Nevertheless, the Federation was brought into being at the beginning of 1958, despite the strong reservations of a few, especially in Jamaica and Trinidad & Tobago.

Thus I showed in my thesis that many within the islands, ignorant of the working of the Federation and its claims but hopeful of its prospects, regarded it as the capital solution to West Indian problems. But after nearly a year of its working, optimism had begun to dim somewhat in the smaller islands, which had much to gain, and in the larger islands, which had much to lose. And this optimism, devoid of reality, could very well lead to disappointment as the real issues of the Federation were for the first time being understood.

My thesis highlighted the many difficulties of the Federation.

The decision by British Guiana (now the politically independent State of Guyana) and British Honduras (now the politically independent State of Belize) not to join the Federation was almost a fatal blow. Large in extent, endowed with potential resources of agriculture, mines and forests, and thinly peopled, with extensive undeveloped areas, these mainland territories could make an invaluable contribution to the Federation. And recall that the Federation was aimed essentially at the pooling of resources and energies in a united attempt to solve the many problems of the British Caribbean.

I showed further that as the Federation was little endowed with minerals, except bauxite in Jamaica and petroleum in Trinidad & Tobago, which were being developed by foreign capital, the federal units relied on agriculture as their mainstay. But this contributed to an agrarian economy, the common feature of which was the sameness of crops in more or less all the units. And as cash crops (largely sugar, bananas and citrus fruits), they were susceptible to climatic hazards (droughts and hurricanes) and the vicissitudes of fluctuating world prices. Moreover, they did not easily find guaranteed markets; they gave seasonal employment at low wages, invited the importation of costly foodstuffs, thus increasing the cost of living, and made for only a small though growing inter-regional trade. It was an economy that was weak and vulnerable.

Equally essential to the growth of a sound economy, I stressed in the thesis, but totally absent was an integrated trade policy. Consequently, the flow of goods within the region was severely restricted by differential tariffs. Each of the federal units imposed its own tariffs. Although the creation of a Customs Union within the British West Indies had been discussed, up to 1958 agreement had not been reached, and until such times when each of the component units dispensed with its tariff policy, the economic strength of the Federation would be weakened. This illustrated clearly why the Federation should have had stronger powers at the centre.

In like manner, the thesis emphasized that the economy was

affected by the lack of an inter-regional circulation, especially by sea. People and freight were not easily transported from island to island, owing to the insufficiency of ships, a problem that would need to be addressed quickly if the Federation was to be effectively developed, and by a strong central government which did not exist.

In respect of the tourist industry, I showed that it could very well strengthen the economies of the units, for the scenic beauty of the region, the historic shrines, the white sandy beaches, the blue sea and an abundance of sunshine and invigorating breezes were being exploited in almost all the units. But although the industry increased the US dollar earnings, it did not promote sound economic progress since the industry was sponsored by foreign capital. That meant that most of the profits were being spent outside the West Indies. Again the remedy required a strong central government to plan the profitable development of the industry for the region itself.

The rapid increase in the birth-rate was another major difficulty that I referred to in the thesis. It was estimated that the birth-rate would double itself in 30 years if it continued at the rate it was going. At the same time, the death-rate was decreasing, resulting from the increasing application of modern medical science. Recourse had been made by each of the islands to emigration, but former emigrants had not relieved congestion, owing to heavy repatriation after a decade or more. The problem invited government action in family planning, in the provision of a whole army of trained social workers to instruct the masses in an attempt to raise the living standards. Again this should be the purview of a strong central government, lacking in the Federation.

Disturbing, too, as the thesis pointed out, was the unrestricted freehold system of land tenure which arrested progress within the Caribbean world. Intensive utilization of the land for the purpose of increasing yield and food production was, in almost all the federal units, seriously affected by private ownership which kept large areas of land inefficiently used or lying idle. The custom of trading with land as though it were merchandize also checked the kind of utilization that was profitable for the local people. For example, during my field survey in the island of Antigua, I was barred entry to one of the most picturesque areas facing the sea in St. Johns, the capital city, called the Mill Reef Properties Ltd. Nevertheless, I evaded the guards and entered the premises. The area was indeed a natural paradise, with white beaches fronting the blue sea, with a number of structures built of white limestone blocks, quarried from the same area, with swimming pools and other facilities. The hesitancy of the employees to talk to me freely, and the prevailing air of secrecy sent me to consult the Title Deeds of the property in the Registry of Deeds in the city, with the help of two assistants provided by one of the government departments which was also interested in knowing how the land was acquired.

I discovered that the area, comprising 1,000 acres, was bought for the paltry sum of 3,700 English pounds or slightly over $11,000 US, that is, $11 US per acre. The transaction was done by three Americans, employed by a small group of wealthy Americans in the United States, who were sent specifically to purchase the land, piece by piece, clandestinely. The land was in small pieces, owned by poor, local residents who, in disposing of it were fooled into thinking that they were getting a good deal. To avoid suspicion, the agents exercised much care in not buying adjacent pieces at the same time. Rather, they bought them at random. As they bought each piece, they had it legally surveyed. After acquiring the whole area, they returned to the United States and transferred the whole to their employers who formed the Mill Reef Properties Ltd. Ostensibly, the Company declared itself to be a non-profit organization, but divided the land into small lots, varying in sizes from less than an acre to over six acres, and sold them to other wealthy Americans. By the end of January 1956, over 80 lots, totalling 320 acres (one-third the total area acquired), were sold at $500 US per lot. About five of the lots were slightly improved and sold for fantastic prices, ranging from $20,000 to $45,000 US. Clearly, a federation with a strong central government could prevent this kind of exploitation by formulating sound land policies beneficial to all the units of the Federation.

Not only in my Master's thesis but in papers, presented at national and international conferences and later published, I stated categorically that the problems of the region were too complex and varied to be successfully tackled by the kind of federation that the British Government relentlessly foisted on the region. Thus while some saw it as a hopeful panacea for the many problems of the region, others regarded it as an attempt by Britain to maintain control of the islands while shedding fiscal responsibilities — a federation in name only. Besides, the main financial problem was an insufficiency of federal revenue, particularly at the initial stage when a great deal of capital was required.

Yet, integration of the Caribbean realm has been the major focus of my writings on the Caribbean, and mine was only one of the many voices in a chorus calling for an economic union of some kind in the region, since unchanging conditions, historical and contemporary, have condemned it to poverty and underdevelopment.

Both in my thesis and a published paper titled, "The West Indies: A Federation in Search of a Capital" (Canadian Geographer, Vol. 2, Summer 1961) I discussed the two essentials of the capital site of modern political federations: centrality and political detachment. I explained that although in theory a central position in the geometric sense is best for a federal capital and makes for harmony between the federal capital and the component units, in practice, however, centrality of the geometric kind seldom exists, as the capitals of the largest and smallest federal States reveal. Moscow was thousands of miles from some of the Asiatic territories of the former Soviet Union. Washington was central for the thirteen American colonies, the commercial, industrial north and the agrarian south until the Louisiana Purchase in 1803 made it eccentric. Even so, that centrality was not of the geometric kind. It was no more than a junction between an agrarian zone on the one hand, and a commercial industrial zone on the other. Ottawa and Canberra are both located far to the southeast and east, respectively, of Canada and Australia. And even Brasilia, the new capital of Brazil, is situated to the southeast of that country, as is Rio de Janeiro, the former capital. Similarly, the capitals of smaller federal States attest the nullity of geometric centrality. Bern, the Swiss capital, is the only one of these that is more or less central, but this is a centrality that is based on culture rather than on geometry.

As for neutrality, the second essential of the federal capital, I showed that this requirement is sought by all modern federations because it satisfies the desire for the capital neither to be closely associated with the traditions and interests of anyone of the component units, nor to be influenced unduly by any one of them. Invariably then, a neutral capital implies a new town, illustrated by Canberra, instead of the well-established cities of Sydney and Melbourne, and by Brasilia.

Then I showed that neither centrality nor neutrality has any significance for the West Indies federal capital, owing to the curious physical sundering of the region and the distribution of the population. I illustrated by a map, showing all the islands of the Federation lying outside a crude triangle, with Jamaica at one end, Trinidad & Tobago at another, and Antigua at the other; and that none was geometrically central for the whole Federation. Thus the question of centrality could play no part in the siting of the federal capital. The same was true of neutrality. Since the federal units were all small islands, if the federal capital was placed in any one of them, it was very likely that the Federation would be influenced more by the interests of that island than by those of the others.

Having ruled out centrality and neutrality as factors that can exercise little or no influence on the siting of the West Indies federal capital, I then examined those factors, peculiarly West Indian, that might govern the choice of an island for the federal capital: adequate and available land suitable for building; ample water supply and

161

electricity; proximity to an existing airport, since funds were not available for the construction of a new one; proximity to an urban centre, especially during the construction and development of the site; general services, and those facilities associated with an urban area. And since the islands are by nature richly endowed with beautiful white beaches and scenic grandeur, of which West Indians are proud, the capital ought really to be sited in one of the most beautiful parts of one of the islands as a stimulus to self respect, dignity and pride, attributes essential to the making of a nation.

The inevitable conclusion of the analysis was that the smaller islands lacked the prerequisites of a federal capital and that the three largest islands of Jamaica, Trinidad & Tobago, and Barbados would seem to have stronger claims by virtue of their size and other cardinal geographical factors. An independent survey by the British Caribbean Federal Capital Commission also concurred with this conclusion, but listed the order of preference as Barbados, Jamaica, and Trinidad & Tobago. However, West Indian Governments agreed to site the capital in Trinidad, and a Standing Federation Committee was appointed to select the most suitable site in Trinidad. The Committee chose Chaguramas, the site of the American Air Base which, in 1941, was leased by the British Government to the United States Government (by the Churchill-Roosevelt Agreement) for 99 years. This was in exchange for some 40 battle ships. The choice initiated much heated discussion and raised serious international, legal and moral issues.

Legally, the US Government appeared to have had a dubious claim to Chaguramas, as well as to other bases in Trinidad for the full 99 years of the Churchill-Roosevelt Agreement. There was doubt as to the validity of the leases because the Trinidadian Government had not given authority for the disposal of Trinidadian Crown lands, such as the Chaguramas site.

Morally, the arrangement was made between two parties without reference to the people who were involved. It was an agreement which robbed them of their right to use their land in the way they desired for their capital.

My thesis showed that countries which had leased bases to the US Government in the post-war years had received considerable financial help from the US as compensation; for example, in return for the bases Spain leased to the US for two ten-year periods, beginning in 1953, Spain received US economic and military aid amounting to $700 million US. The agreement also secured Spanish sovereignty over the bases and the transfer of the installations intact if the US stopped using them. In contrast, Trinidad, and indeed the other British West Indian Islands of the Churchill-Roosevelt Agreement, received nothing. For 19 years Trinidad & Tobago suffered the loss of revenues, resources and amenities, and heavy damage to Trinidadian roads and its main airport, caused by US transport. Worse, it was the poor tax-payers of the island who had to finance the repairs.

The outcome was that in December 1960, two years after I submitted my thesis, representatives of the United States, the United Kingdom and the West Indies met in conference and discussed the revision of the 1941 Lease Agreement. A new agreement returned to Trinidad & Tobago 21,000 acres out of the 34,000 acres of land leased to the United States, provided Trinidad & Tobago with US economic and technical assistance, and reduced to 17 years the duration of the US tenure of the area retained.

From all the facts examined, I predicted the collapse of the Federation. Very clearly the thesis stated that it was not the kind of association required; admittedly, it was a federal union on a larger scale that might hold the germ of a successful solution of the major problems of the area. The thesis declared that unless the unsatisfactory division of powers drafted in the Constitution was amended so that wider scope was given to the central government, the West Indies Federation might not achieve what it was meant to achieve. Without that amendment, large-scale economic planning seemed impossible, and national will and national feeling or consciousness — essential props of the state-idea — would be frustrated, for surely the autonomous units in a federation do not always sacrifice local for national interests, as the history of modern federal States shows. Outrightly, I declared in the thesis that if the West Indies Federation was to be more than a 'union of victims of poverty, social backwardness and frustration', or merely colonial remnants yoked together by a common British Parliamentary procedure, then modifications in the division of powers between the federal government and the Governor-General were essential from the start. Failing that, the Federation was doomed to failure.

But despite the glaring weaknesses, the British Government remained intransigent and, as I accurately predicted, the Federation collapsed in 1962, when Jamaica opted for political independence, followed in turn by Trinidad & Tobago, also in 1962, and Barbados in 1966. Subsequently, each of the remaining units claimed independent statehood also.

The two external examiners of my Examination Committee — professors from the universities of Cambridge and Oxford — had tried to get me to modify the conclusion of my thesis, to make it less negatively predictive, but failed. I insisted that I had adequately substantiated my arguments and that it was only a matter of time before the Federation would become defunct. I was prepared to lose my M. Sc. on that point. The examiners questioned me on my prediction for nearly two hours of the three-hour oral defence, but I held my ground.

When at last I was told that my thesis would be accepted, and was complimented for producing "a well-documented thesis," I was advised to delay publication of any part of it, since the issue was at that time a controversial one and politically heated. I heeded the advice. It was not until after the Federation had fallen, which I had predicted, that I used the thesis as basis for three of the papers I published on the Federation. Thus what should have appeared as an accurate, predictive analysis tended to give the impression, from my point of view, at any rate, of being intelligent after the event. But that was in keeping with the pattern of my life. That which was important to me was always eluding me.

References:

Dale, Edmund H. (1961), "The West Indies: A Federation in Search of a Capital" (Canadian Geographer, Vol. 2, Summer).

East, W. G. and Wooldridge, S. W. (1960), The Spirit and Purpose of Geography (London: Hutchinson University Library), 6th impression.

CHAPTER 9

After obtaining my Master's degree, I faced the pertinent question whether I should proceed immediately to a doctorate or take a wife and settle down.   Angela Stubbs, a very attractive Jamaican girl, seemed interested in me, and those of my friends who were aware of her interest in me had done much to encourage the attraction.   However, I was not really in love with her and had responded to her display of affection coolly.   At no time and in no way my actions towards her could have been considered those of a lover.   I showed her friendship born of natural kindness, real and genuine, but more of the mind than of the heart.   This did not satisfy Angela who appeared to want from me romantic love.   And since it was not forthcoming, she decided to seek it elsewhere.

Was it that I had schooled or disciplined myself so rigidly that I could not think of anything else but academic work and my career? And how did I manage to escape the advances of so many attractive girls who came my way — lovely Monica of Kingston, Jamaica; Freda, a delightful Swedish damsel; Ruth of Denmark; Greta of Norway — girls I had met at international conferences in Copenhagen, Stockholm and Oslo?   In fact, Ruth's father, a banker, mistakenly believed that I was in love with his daughter (because he told me his daughter was in love with me and that he would approve the marriage only if I decided to live in Denmark).   The surprise that came over his face was painful when I told him I was not in love with Ruth and had given her no reason to think that I was.   At any rate, all these girls had seen in me, I suppose, what I could not see myself, namely, husband material.

At the back of my mind was the pledge I made to myself: I must reach the top of the academic ladder, the Ph.D., for which I had been preparing myself and making endless sacrifices. To take on the responsibilities of family life at this stage in my life was, in my firm belief, hardly the right thing to do. It was a matter which had required calm meditation and sober judgment, and I had come ultimately to the conclusion that I must aim for my Ph. D; and if I was to do that, I would need to devote all my energies to it. I had saved enough money to see me through a part of what would be a four-year programme. I thought I could support a wife and family if I discarded the idea of the Ph. D., but I would be always hankering after it and would certainly be a discontented husband and father. Nor would I want to take the divorce route if all did not go well. But did all this mean that I would not marry and become a family man? The years were passing. Yet, I had made my decision to go on, and that was what I set out to do.

There are moments in one's life when one gets a clear impression that there might really be a thing called destiny or fate. Sometimes in moments of uncertainty, a light shines to illumine the way, and one sees, if dimly, the path one should take. It is something that cannot be explained with exactness, but it is nevertheless discernible. It was during this period of reflection and self examination that I attended a public illustrated lecture on the Canadian North at the Senate House Lecture Theatre, London University. Both the lecturer and his beautiful coloured slides of the Canadian North captivated the large audience in attendance, particularly me. The lecture was thought-provoking, and the slides very revealing.

After the lecture, a few of my friends, who had also attended the lecture, and I went to the Refectory at Birbeck College to have a cup of tea and a chat. We had been so stimulated by the lecture that we discussed it and the lecturer all the way to the Refectory, even after we sat around the table to drink our cup of tea. Our discussion drew the attention of a young man, obviously not a European, or American or Australian, who asked if he could join us. I detected his subtle accent. Friendly, amiable, with an open-air expression on his face, he introduced himself as Shawn. Before he could say another word, I said,

"Canadian, isn't it?"

"Yes, but how did you know?" he asked.

"Your accent," said I

"But we (Canadians) do not think we have an accent."

"You certainly have," I said, and to make him feel comfortable, I added quickly, "most people have, you know."

Shawn asked what it was that we seemed to like so much about the lecture. He could not help hearing the discussion from the next table where he was previously sitting. The group explained that it was the northern Canadian landscape which was appealing — the melting snow in Spring, the rushing streams, the fish in the streams, the mosses and lichens, the spring flowers, the birds … . The Canadian obviously felt at home as the discussion proceeded. Then he reminded us that the lecture we had just heard was the first of a series on Canada that would be given every Wednesday afternoon at the same hour (5 p.m.), at the same place, for four weeks. He told us that the next lecture would be on the Rockies and he hoped we would attend it also. Attend we did, and were even more impressed than the week before. As geographers, we could readily identify excellent examples of glacial features, including cirques, arêtes, moraines, U-shaped valleys which were obviously deepened and widened by former glaciers. All these, we noted, were on a macro scale and most spectacular, compared with less significant examples of the same in Britain or in Scandinavia. But it was Lake Louise, the Columbia Icefield and the Athabasca Glacier, Peyto Lake, the Athabasca Falls, the Maligne Canyon that were the crowning beauties, also the blue skies and white clouds above. The scenes were breath-taking: stands of silent pine trees, black bears, grizzly bears and, generally, the wild life, mountain tops kissing the clouds! Martin Bernard, one of the group, summed up the feelings of all of us in saying, " Canada must be very beautiful!"

We had repaired to the Birkbeck Refectory again after the lecture and were in full discussion when Shawn, the Canadian, joined us. He sat listening to the group with delight. At the end, he said,

"Well, gentlemen, if you think Canada is beautiful, would you consider settling there?"

It was then he disclosed his true identity — a scout from Canada House in London, sent to find suitable teachers to teach in Canada, which at that time had an acute teacher shortage. When he left us the week before, he ran into the Registrar of Birkbeck, pointed us out to him and found out that we were teachers pursuing higher learning in the evenings. We were just the kind of people, he told us, that Canada was seeking as new immigrants at that time. Even by his brief meeting with us, he was confident that we would make good immigrants in Canada and get along well there. By then, he had moved into the role of the agent, ardently promoting his country. He had obtained from the Registrar valuable information about each of his new acquaintances. We listened to the attractions he listed but told him politely that we were not thinking of migrating. But before leaving us, he obtained our permission to send our names to Canada, and told us that Canada would write to let us know what it could offer us.

Within ten days after our second meeting with Shawn, I received six invitations from various parts of Canada to teach there — Montreal, Kingston, Ottawa, Winnipeg, Edmonton, Grande Prairie. A few days after, I was called by the Principal of the school where I was teaching and was shown a letter from the Winnipeg School Board, requesting him to give a reference on me.

"I did not know you wanted to leave us, although I should have expected it," said the Principal.

I tried to explain the events leading up to the letter, and that I, too, had received a communication from the Winnipeg School Board offering me a teaching position, but I had not applied for one, nor had I accepted it.

"Well," said the Principal, "I have to reply to this. I have to say that we do not want to lose you etc. etc. What I would like to know is whether or not you want to go to Canada."

"To tell you the truth, I had not thought of it before; it was only suggested to me a few days before the invitation came. Other friends of mine are invited to go, too, and they are all of two minds. I need time to think about this thing calmly before committing myself one way or the other," I told the Principal.

On the same evening at Birkbeck, I ran into Professor W. Gordon East, Head of the Geography Department, who took me to his office and explained that Winnipeg had requested of him information about me. Once more I had to explain what had previously transpired. Clearly Winnipeg was intent on obtaining my services and on finding out what they could about me. The speed at which Winnipeg was moving on this matter was laudable yet irritating, pleasing to a degree, yet bewildering. I had not given them the right to do so, nor had I so much as replied to Winnipeg's invitation. Clearly, it was Shawn, the Canadian agent, who supplied Winnipeg with detailed information about me. The overwhelming shock came ten to fourteen days later when I received a letter from the Education authorities in Winnipeg stating that I was appointed to teach in one of the City's high schools, beginning mid-August. An application form for 'landed immigrant status' — to be filled out and returned — was also enclosed. I was thoroughly bewildered and rang a few of the friends with whom I had attended the lectures on Canada at the Senate House Lecture Theatre. They, too, had received offers of teaching positions from Canada and were equally surprised. They were giving the matter serious thought. I was confused and could not make up my mind. However, Professor East, who had supervised my Master's thesis and had suggested that I should proceed immediately to the Ph. D. (he had shown a keen interest in me from my undergraduate days), now advised me to consider the Canadian offer seriously. He pointed out that as a geographer, I should try to see as much of the world as possible, that Canada was a Commonwealth country, a young country with enormous possibilities, that teaching there for a year or two would enable me to save a few pennies to begin full-time work on my Ph. D., and that I should ultimately aim at university teaching, for, he believed, I would do well at it.

For a whole week I pondered Professor East's advice. Such advice, born of intellect and experience, was too valuable to ignore. Repeatedly his words came back to me: "After a year or two, if you did not like it there, you could come back here to do your Ph. D., if you so desired."

Why was it so difficult for me to decide the matter? The thought of the perishing cold in Canada during the winter gave me the shivers. Could I, a man from the Tropics, stand up to it? The offers from Alberta were the most tempting. The letters were friendly; they made me feel I was really wanted and could certainly make a contribution. Grande Prairie's invitation was especially so. I did not know that it was an undeveloped area, northwest of Edmonton, which, with the town of Peace River, were far northerly outposts of the province. To my dismay later, I decided to accept Grande Prairie's invitation. My friends also decided to accept one of their invitations, too.

When it was known that I would go to Canada, the Commonwealth Missionary Society (CMS), which had also shown a keen interest in my career, wrote to the Education Authorities in Jamaica, verbally chastising them for not attempting to accommodate one of their trained young men who was to be absorbed by Canada.

Yet, so often they complained that their young people did not want to return to Jamaica. Before I completed my Master's degree, I had informed the Education Office in Jamaica that I would be free after November of that year and would consider returning to Jamaica if my services were required. The months had passed without my receiving so much as an acknowledgement of the receipt of my letter. Up to May of the following year, I had no word from them, and had written a second time, but still I received no reply. Then in June, the Canadian offers came. I thought if Jamaica really wanted my services, they would have replied to my letters. Since they had not, I accepted the invitation to go to Canada.

The letter from the CMS had roused the Jamaican Education Office to action, for the night before I was to leave London for Southampton to take the boat to Canada, I received a phone call from Wales, from a representative of the Jamaican Government, who said he had just arrived in the country. He stated that I should not to go to Canada, but to wait until he arrived in London when he would explain what Jamaica had to offer me. Too late! I had already signed a contract to teach with the Grande Prairie School Board, and had sent my luggage three days before to the boat in Southampton harbour.

The most difficult thing for me was to say good-bye to the school where I had been teaching for over seven years. Always I hated saying good-bye, and the Principal of the school was not making it any easier for me. He had assembled the whole school and recounted all that I had done there over the years, praised my courage and industry, my determination and drive, my intelligence and fortitude. He was deeply sorry to see me go, and he was sure he was speaking for the rest of the staff and school. He confessed that many were the times he had opposed my ideas and relented in the end because of the strength of my conviction, logic and argument.

When at last he asked me to step forward, a thunderous, deafening applause greeted me. To my utter amazement, the

Principal's voice broke when he expressed to me the thanks and good wishes of the school. This huge man, grey-haired, this seeming giant before whom staff and students were humbled, threw his arms around me in genuine affection while the hall resounded with the applause of students and staff. It was too much for me. I was choking with emotion. I had not expected this display of affection. When it was time for me to thank the Principal and the school for "tolerating me over the years," as I put it, and for all the nice things the Principal had said about me, I did so with the greatest difficulty, for I, too, was at the point where my voice could have betrayed my emotions. With remarkable brevity, I said I wished I did not have to say good-bye, but I had to. It was altogether a very painful exercise for me. I thanked them again and wished them well. Quickly, I took my seat again. I had survived the ordeal.

I was still somewhat dazed, in a dream, so to speak, when my train pulled out of Waterloo Train Station for Southampton, even more so when I climbed the gang-way of the Greek boat in Southampton harbour. Looking out from the deck, it occurred to me that significant phases of my life seemed always to be prefaced by departure by a boat. Twice before I had departed by boat from Jamaica in search of higher education; now I was to depart the shores of Britain for a new life in Canada. Was I being led, guided, directed? I thought of how in three short months I had come to decide what was to be a momentous step in my life. Was I doing the right thing? What did the future hold for me? Why had circumstances pointed me in the direction of Canada? Am I always to be moving on? Will I ever put down roots? These and other questions came to me in rapid succession. My English friends who had decided to go to Canada had changed their minds at the last minute, and I found myself standing there on deck alone, wondering if I had made the right decision. Yet, whether reason had supported my decision or not, my will to succeed was now to be my driving force. Moreover, I thought, life being the dynamic force that it is, every issue, somehow or other, gets settled in the end. My going to Canada might well be offering me opportunities denied me in the past. "Fate or destiny," I soliloquized, "if you are leading me on, I follow." With that I turned, looked to the other side of the deck and saw how I could be of help to others instead of dwelling on my future.

The scene that met my eyes at the other side of the deck was a group of passengers — new immigrants bound for Canada and the United States — wrestling with dictionaries in their attempt to put English sentences together. I walked over to them and offered my help. In no time, others joined the group, asking, "How do you say ... ?" I gave the answers, and repeated the words or sentences slowly. They repeated after me. Still others joined them. Most were from Germany and East European countries, while a few were from India. The purser, seeing me standing before a "class" of some thirty or more of the passengers, helping them with English, must have told the Captain, for a conference room with a blackboard was immediately made available for the purpose.

After lunch, a young German and his wife sought me out and requested me to give them an afternoon session because "we very, very want to learn eenglish." I went with them to the conference room where more than fifty of the passengers — the group had increased — were already seated, waiting for me. Obviously they had expected me to return there after lunch. Not seeing me, they sent the German couple to find me.

I took up where I left off, concentrating on vocabulary and pronunciation. I wrote on the blackboard twelve of the words that were giving them difficulty, explained their meaning, pronounced them and asked them to pronounce them after me. Next, I illustrated how they could be used in sentences. Tea was served at 3 p.m. on the boat, but when the bell rang, announcing that tea was being served, not one from the group wanted to leave or miss anything. But my throat was dry and was calling for moisture. I suggested that everybody should take a 30-minute break. Even before the half hour was up, the group had returned, as keen as little children. Their desire to learn the spoken language of the two countries they were about to enter and in which they would be making a living was overwhelming. Necessity, it seems, often drives or compels us to overcome major difficulties.

After supper and entertainment that evening, I returned to my cabin to find a bottle of excellent wine, a bouquet of carnations and a card from the Captain and the rest of his crew thanking me for "what you are doing to help the passengers on board ship." Naturally, I reciprocated my gratitude to the Captain by a card for the wine and flowers.

For the duration of the trip, I continued to help my new 'students'. This task earned me eventually an invitation to the Captain's dinner table, with other invited passengers, on the night before the ship docked in the harbour of Quebec City for a day before going down the mighty St. Lawrence River to Montreal. With four of the new friends I had made on the voyage, I spent the whole day on sight-seeing in Quebec City. Each member of the group wanted to see the Heights of Abraham where the French and the British had fought, and as much of Quebec City as we could see in one day. We returned to the boat that evening physically tired, but ready for the farewell dinner and entertainment that the purser had arranged. As we ate, an orchestra played dinner and sentimental music. Then followed games and dancing. During the intermission, the orchestra struck up, "For he's a jolly good fellow," and the Captain confronted me and led me to the spotlight in the centre of the room. Then he spoke appreciatively of my contribution to the boat's activities during the voyage and presented me with gifts — symbols of their gratitude. Again they sang "For he's a jolly good fellow," as students did at Elsinore, Denmark, years before. At such moments the recipient of the compliment invariably desires to wax eloquent in expressing his appreciation, but is invariably prevented from doing so by feelings of strong emotion. I succumbed instead to the prosaic expression of "thank you." Such was my experience. I merely bowed deeply and said, "Thank you very much." If I had said another word, I would have betrayed the emotions that welled up in me. These are feelings that money can never buy. The next morning we arrived in Montreal.

After the immigration and customs formalities, and all were standing firmly at last on Canadian soil, came the good-byes and good wishes. Some of the new immigrants were heading for Chicago, New York, and other cities of the United States, still others for various parts of Canada. Many boarded trains and many waited for trains. The first leg of our journey was over. We had arrived safely in a new country. Our hopes were high. A new life lay ahead of us.

In Montreal, I was told repeatedly to have my luggage checked for my journey to Grande Prairie. To my great surprise few of the train attendants knew where Grande Prairie was, and one who had a vague notion of the location asked, "Why are you going all the way up there to the North Pole, to that God-forsaken place?" My heart sank. "What have I done?" my heart was saying. The train was to take me to Calgary where I would take another train to Edmonton, and still another to Grande Prairie. I was advised in London to travel first class from Edmonton to Grande Prairie and, accordingly, had bought a first-class ticket in London for that portion of the journey. The trans-Canada train was scheduled to leave Montreal a few minutes before mid-night, and many of the new friends who would be leaving on later trains for their respective destinations came to my platform to see me off.

As soon as the train pulled out of the station, I inquired of one of the train attendants if I could have one of my suitcases. The attendant asked me if I had checked in my baggage. Pleased that I had done what I was advised to do, I told the attendant I had.

"In that case," replied the attendant, "I am sure it is not on this train. But even if it was, there are so many cases piled on top of one another in the baggage car that it would be quite impossible to get at it, even if it could be spotted." He led me to the baggage car to see for myself.

176

Frustration washed over me. All I had taken on the train with me were my type-writer and slide projector. My toilet articles and change of clothing were in one of the cases I checked in. What was I to do? It was a three-day journey. I wanted to change because I had spent the day touring Montreal, and my clothes had been soaked with perspiration. I had not so much as a tooth brush or a razor or comb with me. I was completely baffled. In soiled clothes, unwashed, unshaved, I could hardly sleep. I was wholly uncomfortable. My first night on that train would remain an unforgettable nightmare.

During the next day, the train passed through seemingly wild areas in Ontario. It would make brief stops at little stations along the line, and at such times, I would dash to the souvenir shops in the stations and buy a few needed articles. Unlike the British and European custom to blow a whistle to indicate the impending departure of the train, or for the station porters to shout "All aboard" or "Close the doors," or something of the sort, in Canada, it seemed, the departure of the train was unheralded by such warnings. The train simply pulled out of the station quietly. This was most disconcerting for me, for at every stop, I would rush to the souvenir shop to buy a few of the articles I needed. Afraid I would be left in these isolated places, I would run back to the train without obtaining all I wanted. At the first stop, I obtained a tooth brush, tooth paste, a razor and a hair brush and comb, at other stops underwear, pyjamas, shirts and a couple pairs of socks.

The next major problem was what to do with the soiled clothes. The answer came quickly — brown paper bags!. These were all I could acquire, for plastic bags, now ubiquitous, were not yet obtainable.

I spent most of my time high up in the observation compartment of the train, which gave a grand view of the landscape. Those sections of the route by Lakes Huron and Superior had special fascination for me, indeed for any geographer. Then, passing the

Lake of the Woods, the train hurled itself into Manitoba. What a spectacular, contrasting scene confronted the visitor! The wide sweep of the prairies, considerably flat, decidedly beautiful, ran away to the west on a macro scale, as far as the eye could see. The horizon was very much like that at sea. The sky was blue with cumulus clouds rising ever upwards, white, dazzling. Here and there were small clumps of trees, indicating the presence of a farmstead. The vastness of the wheat fields, the brilliant sun, and the lack of any sign of hurriedness presented a pastoral scene that warmed the heart and soothed the soul. I began to get my first real impression of the vastness and the grandeur of the Canadian landscape. From Manitoba to Saskatchewan to Calgary, I sat glued to the window, intermittently sighing and repeating, "What a country!"

In Calgary, I changed trains, as I was directed to do, and headed for Edmonton, a city in the first flush of modern development, resulting from the discovery and development of nearby petroleum and natural gas. As the train went over the High Level Bridge into the heart of the city, I was immediately impressed by what I saw — the beautiful valley of the North Saskatchewan River which winds its way through the city, and unmistakable signs of growing prosperity. Suddenly, I had a strange feeling that my future would have something to do with this city. It was no more than a mental flash, and it went as quickly as it came. I could not explain it.

As the train for Grande Prairie was not scheduled to leave until 6 p.m. and I had some eight hours to spare, I decided to see as much of Edmonton as I could by taxi. University Drive was at that time the residential pièce de résistance that the taxi driver was pleased to show. The houses along it were new and attractive; they clearly revealed affluence. That part of Jasper Avenue in the heart of the Central Business District, had begun to be transformed, indeed the whole downtown area was undergoing change from an agricultural-oriented market centre to a modern, vibrant metropolis, with a distinct character. The tempo of development was accelerating. The suburban residential and shopping areas were equally impressive. Everywhere land speculation was in striking evidence. Even the industrial areas showed signs of dynamism and far-sightedness, no less the university precinct. At the end of the tour I came to the conclusion that this was the city I would like to be in and whose invitation to teach in I should have accepted.

After climbing on to the train for Grande Prairie at 6 p.m., I asked the porter to direct me to the first class section.

"You are in it," came the reply.

I looked around shocked. I wanted to say "what!" but the word stuck in my throat. The porter asked for my ticket, and on receiving it, he said.

"OK! Your seat is right here," pointing to it.

In my estimation the compartment failed to qualify for even the dubious status of third class, and my misgivings about Grande Prairie returned. I sat down in complete bewilderment. Because I wanted to see as much of Edmonton as I could in the few hours I had, I had gone without lunch and was now very hungry. I asked the porter to direct me to the restaurant car. Greatly puzzled, apparently wondering where on earth this young man was coming from, the porter, in unmistaken desperation said,

"There is no restaurant car."

"What!" said I, "I have not eaten all day, and the train is not due to reach Grande Prairie until noon tomorrow. What must I do?"

"They should have told you when you bought your ticket. Where did you buy your ticket?" he asked.

"London, England," came the reply.

"No wonder," he said, and left the compartment.

Very tired, very dejected, very frustrated and very hungry, I sat back in my seat, and through the train window saw the rain descending heavily outside. I had been lost in the view outside and was in a state of semi-stupor when I felt a gentle touch on my hand. I looked from the window and saw the kindly face of a middle-aged lady before me.

"I could not help overhearing what you said to the porter. It is a long journey. You must have something to eat. Please take this (a sandwich, a slice of cake and an apple). I hope this will help."

"Madam, you are so very kind," I said, "but I would not dream of taking this, for you will need it yourself."

"No, dear sir, I have another sandwich and piece of cake. Please take it. I will feel much better if you did."

I took the offering and profusely thanked the lady. This was my introduction to Western hospitality. I had heard much about it. I ate the sandwich and slice of cake heartily and just as quickly ate the big, red apple. My hunger alleviated, I soon fell asleep.

I awoke in the morning to find myself alone in the compartment. The train, which had been standing at the station for some time, now pulled out. It was still raining, and from the window I could see only patches of wheat fields and patches of woods. This area was more wooded than the south. The roads on either side of the rail tracks were unpaved and fretted with deep mud furrows. Cars running on them were plastered with mud, and the few brave souls struggling to walk on them wore long rubber boots. The mud, I was later told, was called "gumbo" and stuck to everything. What would Grande Prairie be like, I wondered.

The train came to what might be called a siding and stopped for a few minutes in order to deposit and take on a few passengers. In my compartment came a young man of whom I took little notice, for I kept looking sadly through the window at the passing bush completely devoid of human habitation. I was now feeling I had definitely made a terrible mistake in deciding to come so far north. My face must have mirrored the look of regret because the young man, who had come into the compartment and had deposited himself in the seat opposite, inquired,

"The first time you have come this far?"

I had been miles away in thought and had hardly heard the young man. I looked at him, and he, thinking that I was having difficulty understanding what he had said, spoke again slowly, enunciating very clearly every word. I still looked at him bewilderingly, whereupon he said,

"Never mind; it will be all right. Just remember to say 'please' and 'thank you'. Say 'please'."

I tried to mouth the word, to the satisfaction of my new teacher.

"And, 'thank you'. Put your tongue like this, your tongue touching your upper front teeth."

I did as I was instructed. And the friendly young man began to lecture me on the Peace River District in slow English, I nodding to indicate that I understood. With another sudden jerk, the train pulled up at another siding and the young man jumped up, gathered his rain coat, wished me well, and was off the train in lightning speed.

Near to noon, the train pulled up alongside a wooden platform and a shed. This was the Grande Prairie stop. I dismounted with my type-writer, slide projector and some four brown paper bags with soiled clothes. I was to be met by the secretary of the School Board but there was no one in the shed, except a man stoking the wood fire at the other end. It was still raining, cold and very damp. I walked over to the wood fire, warmed my hands and struggled to fight down the disappointment that had by then infiltrated every nerve fibre in my body. I walked to the window to look at the gumbo outside. It was easily a foot deep. Just then a car drove up, ploughing through the mud. I wondered how the occupant would possibly get out. But the door was opened and out came a man. He sank his rubber boots into the mud as though he was stepping on hard concrete and heaved (that is the right word, for the gumbo does not readily give up what it captures) himself forward to the shed.

"Ah," he said, as he entered and saw me standing by the window. "Mr. Dale, I am sure. I recognize you from the photograph we have of you. I am John Hughes, the secretary of the School Board."

Stretching out his hand, he gave me a firm hand shake and continued.

"Welcome to Grande Prairie! The train was a little early and beat me to it. I am sorry I am late. Did you have a good journey? Coming from London, this must be quite a shock for you," he said, smiling.

If ever there was an understatement, I thought, but did not say it. I could hardly speak, anyway, for I was shivering and my teeth were chattering. Moreover, the paper bags caused me much embarrassment. I thought I was not making a good impression. I explained the dilemma of my suitcases and was told they would not arrive in Grande Prairie until three days later. That information served only to sink me deeper into despair.

Mr. Hughes looked me over, saw the pair of loafers and the light clothing I was wearing and said:

"You are not dressed for the North. I must get you fitted out immediately."

Unless I was going to be covered ankle deep in mud, I could not see how I could make it to Mr. Hughes's car.

"Here, put on these," came a voice from behind. It was Al, the station (shed) master, who had seen the practical difficulty and resolved it quickly by offering a pair of long rubber boots. Mr. Hughes promised to return them, and off he and I drove to a hotel in the centre of the town. Here I was to stay until I could find suitable accommodation elsewhere. I was glad to have a shower and a decent meal after four days of travelling. Later that afternoon, Mr.

Hughes returned to take me to a hardware store to obtain the indispensable pair of long rubber boots, and to a men's shop to get a parka and other articles of warm clothing. But if it was only the last week of August and it was already so cold, what would December and January be like, I wondered. Next, Mr. Hughes drove me about the town in order that I would get my bearings, so to speak. Only portions of the main roads — those through the town — were paved, and only for a short distance each way.

My plan was to find accommodation with a family until I could manage on my own, but since that seemed impossible, I scrapped the idea and opted to rent an apartment. Here, again, I met much difficulty. Without exception, all the places that were advertized for rent were, in my view, substandard. Often the outward appearances were enough to prevent me from leaving the car to inspect them. Finally, Mr. Hughes suggested that I should stay at the hotel, expensive though that would be, until I found a suitable place. I took his advice.

Until one experiences the difficulty of moving to a new place, that is, pulling up roots in one place and attempting to put them down in another place, one does not know the physical and mental anguish such an exercise involves. It was the day after I arrived in Grande Prairie that the full weight of the experience settled heavily on me. There I was in a hotel room, with four walls as my only companions, far in the northern reaches of Canada, alone, friendless, a stranger in a strange land. However hard I tried, I could not dismiss the thought that I was somewhat reckless in my decision to come to Grande Prairie when I could have gone to much less remote places. What had come over me to do this? I asked myself. Could it have been adventure? It is at times like these that the human spirit sinks into apathy and despair or rises to the challenge of making the most of what is, and summons strength from within to rise above the difficulties. Why expend energy in wishing we had done what we had not done? Why not channel that energy into seeking ways to improve the present? This was the pragmatic view I decided to take as I lay there on the hotel bed, looking up to the ceiling. I told myself I was not going to wonder anymore if I had done the right thing to come to northern Canada. The fact was that I was actually there, and I would throw my mind and strength into my work and all else, I hoped, would fall into place.

My difficulty at the hotel was the food. Lunch was a huge meal, and dinner a mighty feast. I just could not manage the huge steaks that were set before me — enough to feed a family of six in the London home from which I had come. I would eat a little piece of it and leave the rest. After two days of this, the person in charge of the meals, a warm, friendly if not motherly lady, joined me at the dining table and inquired what was wrong with the food why I did not eat it. She felt, she said, guilty for charging for food which was not eaten. I explained that it was the quantity, not the quality, that was the difficulty. Pleased to hear this, she said,

"Suppose we reduce the quantity by half. Would that help? Of course, we would charge only half the cost."

"That would certainly be most thoughtful and kind of you," I said.

"Is there anything else we could do to make you feel more at home with us?" she asked.

I mentioned that I was fond of dessert — fruit or a slice of cake, with tea, not coffee, as part of the meal. She thanked me for the suggestion and said she would bake me a cake that very day. She did, and I made a pig of myself eating the chocolate cake (much to her delight) even though I did not really like chocolate cakes. (I was to find out later that Canadians like chocolate cakes very much.) Thereafter, my food problem was resolved.

The high school in Grande Prairie was fairly new and large. I was assigned to teach Grade 12 English and Social Studies, and Grade 10 English. I was most displeased with the Social Studies course which was largely history and a smattering of civics. Geography was relegated to, what is, never "why", which is the bedrock of the discipline. Thus while I covered the content of the syllabus, I departed from the guidelines provided, and in so doing, gave a more rounded course which interested the students because it was meaningful.

The first day that I stood before my Grade 12 English Class A, a very bright, articulate group of fairly mature young men and women, I briefly introduced myself and was about to dive headlong into the English lesson when I looked towards the back of the class and saw the same young man who tried to teach me English on the train. Our eyes met, and the young man covered his face with his hands. The irony and the humour of the whole thing sent me into fits of laughter. Tried, as I had, I could not control myself. I laughed until tears rolled down my face. The class began to laugh, too, even though they did not know why I was laughing, and I would not tell them. The whole school was to hear about this later, and teacher after teacher wanted to know what the joke was, but I refused to tell.

From the first day, I would remain in my classroom after school to mark my students' exercises — seemingly the bane of teachers of English — and prepare for the next day's work. After school on the first day, I was alone in the room when I heard a gentle knock on the door. I opened it and found the young man of the train standing there. I began to laugh again, invited him in, and closed the door. He must still be nameless. He had come to thank me for not giving him away.

"I was really stupid," he said. "I don't know how I could have been so stupid."

"No, no, you were not," I said. "You were trying to be helpful, and I appreciated your intention which was really creditable."

"When I came into the room this morning and saw you, I wanted to hide. And when you actually recognized me, I wanted to evaporate. But you did not spill the beans and I am thankful. That is why I have come to thank you for not telling on me."

I assured him I would never do a thing like that, that he must rest assured that I would never do that. From that day he and I became good friends. It was a friendship that was to last even after I left Grand Prairie. I even became the god-father of his first born, a son.

What I soon learned was the remarkable friendliness of the people of Grande Prairie. Either through the School Board or the students, they learned that I was seeking a suitable apartment to rent, and the owner of a beautiful house, an elderly lady who was not using her lower floor offered to rent it to me. The house was on the south side of the town, beyond the paved part of the north-south axis. The unpaved road to the house was most trying when it was wet, but the lady's kindness, readiness and willingness to help me get settled more than compensated for any other difficulties, and typified the general attitude of the townsfolk. They made me feel I was one of them. They came in their cars every Friday evening to take me to Square Dancing, and would offer me rides to anywhere I wanted to go. For example, after leaving school in the early evenings, that is, after marking my students' exercises, a police car always caught up with me the moment I left the school grounds. The officer wanted to give me a ride home. The car always came along in the evenings at the exact time I left the school, though I varied my time of leaving the school. I asked the officer about this. He told me he could see me from his office window across the road, when I switched off the lights and left the room.

I might mention here that it was while walking home on one of these autumn evenings that I had a most extraordinary experience. Something, possibly a distinct popping sound above my head, caused me to look up into the night sky, and there I beheld a spectacle that caused my heart to skip a beat. It was the Northern Lights or Aurora Borealis playing (that is the right word) in the night sky. They were streamers, banners, shafts of light in arcuate formation, some, long lines, some, short lines, in colours blue, bluey green, greenish, yellowish and crimson. In the twinkle of an eye, they would change in form, direction and colour. They would run upwards, downwards, obliquely, horizontally, never at rest, ceaselessly creating patterns of indescribable beauty. I stood where I stood for more than an hour looking up, hypnotized, motionless, almost breathless. Never had I seen anything like that before. When at last my stiff neck screamed out in pain and my arms and leg felt like lumps of ice, I moved on, even so, looking up intermittently. Oh, the wonders of the universe, the terrible awesomeness of it, and the magnificent splendour of it! Surely, it must have been natural phenomena like this that compelled Joseph Haydn, the German composer, to declare in his oratorio, "The Creation", 'Die Himmel erzählen die Ehre Gottes'. (The heavens are telling the wonders of God.)

A few nights after my arrival in Grand Prairie and while still at the hotel, I was visited by a gentleman who introduced himself as a member of the local Rotary Club. He had come to ask me to address the Club at their noon meeting a month hence. I agreed, and addressed the Club. But unknown to me, the talk was taped to be broadcast by the local radio station. As usual, at supper that evening, I turned on the radio to listen to the news only to hear my own voice coming at me. Shocked, I felt that my approval had not been sought and should have been. Perhaps as a news item, approval was thought unnecessary. I was disappointed and felt I would need to know exactly how things were done up there in the North before agreeing to do anything of a similar nature in future.

The broadcast notified all in the Peace River District that new blood was in their midst or, to change the metaphor, a goat was there to be milked, and milked he was. Calls for me to speak to groups throughout the District came from Beaver Lodge, High Prairie, Peace River and elsewhere. By then, I had bought a car and was able to rush from one place to another. Church groups, women's groups, men's groups, youth groups — they succeeded in getting me to

187

address them on social issues, even conducting Sunday services at the United Church at the bidding of the minister.

Especially arduous for me was my school work. Outrightly I declared war on mediocrity, demanded a high standard of work and challenged my students to aim for excellence. I refused to accept sloppy or shoddy work, work that had been hurriedly done without much thought or care. I informed the students that it was a war I was declaring on them, that I was going to be the victor; and that whatever strategies they might devise to fight me, they would fail utterly, so they need not try. It seemed that they liked my style and manner of coaxing, cajoling, urging, prompting, encouraging, for they responded positively to my challenges.

I applied the same high standards even in the extra-curricular activities with which I was associated in the school. Representatives of the school's Drama Club had asked me to help them with their year-play, to choose, produce and direct the play, the main school event of the year, apart from football and baseball tournaments. Instead of giving a negative or positive reply, I requested to meet the Drama Club in person at an appointed time after school one day. Accordingly, the meeting was arranged.

In the meanwhile, I searched my papers for notes I had taken as I listened to lectures and watched demonstrations over a period of three or more years at the Royal Academy of Dramatic Art (RADA), located just across the street from Birkbeck College, London. Between lectures at Birkbeck, I would slip into RADA to listen to some of the special lectures that were given there. I had learned much from these lectures about acting and staging. But I had no idea then that the experience would be of some help in the years ahead.

When I met the Drama Club, I was well prepared. I explained to them that stage acting demands that every breath, every note, every tone and every syllable of every word must be given due value. It demands further that every word must be convincing and yet must be so controlled that the illusion of reality is not destroyed. The players must be heard by the audience, "the farthest ears being reached, without the nearest being shattered irreparably." I said I knew that these demands could not be met fully overnight. To increase the loudness of his/her tones and their beauty, the actor/actress must learn to breathe properly, and that requires instruction by the specialist in speech training. Yet, as a school drama group, with no formal training in voice production or in acting but are willing to try to entertain, they could try with whatever help I could give them. However, although they were amateurs, I would require of them acting bordering on that of the professional. I would not be interested in helping them to attempt the painfully amateurish production I had seen in the district, in which a change of scene took over twenty minutes, while the audience sat listening to hammering and banging behind the stage. I would expect the club to attempt a somewhat professional production, with proper stage properties (props) suitable stage furniture, according to the requirements of the play, and effective stage lighting — some of which may not be necessary for trained actors and actresses but certainly are for the untrained like themselves. Besides, the cast would have to live their parts, speaking naturally without the use of microphones which, I noticed, everybody seemed to want to use at public functions in the district. This was not necessary on the legitimate stage, I told them, for the players are expected to articulate and project their voices for all to hear in the hall. And to me, a change of scene should be accomplished in no more than the time it took the curtains to close and immediately open again etc. etc.

In laying out the parameters of what would be required if I was to help, I gave the Club a few days to think over the matter, for I would not commit myself unless they were unanimous in their desire to work hard to achieve the high standard I would demand of them. They wanted to decide the matter then and there but I would not agree to that. I insisted that the whole required calm reflection. I gave them a week to think it over.

189

Also, I needed a little time to search out a play that would capture the interest and imagination of high school students and a large enough cast that would allow many of the students to participate. Ultimately, I decided on "Stag Line", a comedy in three acts, by Anne Coulter Martens. The play involves a teen-age girl, Maudie, and her efforts to manage her sister's wedding, as well as capture the attention of the best man, a handsome older man. But all that Maudie's managing did was to get her into trouble, as her long-suffering beau from kindergarten days decided he was not going to put up with her fickle ways any longer. Yet, this comedy of love and marriage had a happy ending.

The week passed quickly and the Drama Club met me, as planned. Their consent to work with me, to strive for excellence was unanimous. I suggested that they might consider "Stag Line" and outlined the comedy to them. Their enthusiasm was immediate. I passed out copies of the play which I had prepared, attempted a preliminary casting with their help, and set a date for the next reading by which time, I hoped, they would be somewhat familiar with the play and their respective parts.

At the next meeting, I insisted that the cast should, from the beginning, imagine they were not reading but living the part.

"It is absolutely essential," I told them, "that you are convincing, that you make the listener feel you are the person you are playing, otherwise you will sound artificial; you will not evoke the emotion that the action seeks to arouse."

They listened attentively and tried to live their respective parts, to be the persons they were supposed to be. If their portrayal of a scene or a character was wrong or ineffective, I would make them do the scene or attempt the characterization over and over again until they got it right. Slowly, as the rehearsals continued, and with much encouragement and coaxing from me, they grew into the parts they were playing. It was gratifying to see this. They were even becoming their own critics, and very harsh on themselves.

I knew I had undertaken a major task; but I had learned over the years to tackle problems one by one. As I resolved one, I would turn to the next; and the next in the production of this play was designing the set — to provide something pleasing to the eye and suitable to the action and atmosphere of the play, yet allowing the cast to move freely, without difficulty. First, I marked out the acting area on the floor of the stage and the position of the doors and stairs. This enabled me to estimate how many pieces of furniture would be required. Then I set about constructing units of scenery or "flats", made of cloth stretched over wooden frames. These had not been used in the school before, and I hoped the School Board would provide the lumber and cloth, but they would not. Thus I advanced the cost of the materials myself, with the understanding that I would be refunded from the proceeds of the play. I insisted that the Drama Club appoint a treasurer (staff member) to keep an accurate account of the spending.

The play required a modern setting, hence modern furniture and fittings. I solicited the loan of these from retail outlets in the town, and was surprised to find the owners of these business places most co-operative and helpful. A furniture store lent all the furniture required (and I selected pieces with artistic merit and good taste); an electric store provided (lent) attractive lamps for the sitting room, the bedroom and the ceiling; a carpet store lent a huge rug to cover the whole of the acting area; a hair dressing salon volunteered its staff; the radio station gave publicity. Indeed, the whole town was wholly behind the project. I soon realized that this tendency to help one another or feeling of togetherness is characteristic of many remote communities, especially in northern Canada.

Encouraged, I threw every ounce (now gram) of my energy into the project, directing, supervising the making of the flats, helping with advertisements, and seeing to the thousand-and-one little things that had to be seen to. At last everything began to come together smoothly, especially the rehearsals.

Two weeks before the final dress rehearsal, the stage was put out of bounds to the rest of the school. This gave me a chance to get it ready. The flats were put in place, and the furniture and fixtures assembled and moved in one evening without the knowledge of any one save the Drama Club. Gradually, the stage was converted to an attractive living room where most of the action was to take place. The lighting was most effective, the furniture artistically arranged, the grand piano subtly occupying one corner of the room, near to which stood a small table with a magnificent arrangement of flowers (in pots, but the pots hidden from view). Little artistic touches (real and very large paintings, ornamental vases etc.) here and there, and the blending of colours gave the stage a very dignified, very pleasing appearance. Suddenly, everything had come alive, and the enthusiasm of the students quickened.

I had been waiting for a strategic moment to show off the stage to the rest of the school, and that moment came during the next week at the break in a basketball match in the hall, attended by most of the students of the school and the staff. Immediately after the break was called, I had the proscenium drapes opened very slowly, revealing this grand, well-lit, smartly-furnished, beautiful room. The effect was startling! "Ooh," the team, cheer leaders and students shouted. They rushed forward to get a closer look and cheered wildly. Then the curtains were drawn again, hiding the room. It was a deliberate publicity stunt, well timed, and very effective. It was to pay off handsomely. During the following days, there was a rush for tickets, and in a matter of two days all the seats for the two-night performances were sold. In fact, on each of the two nights, people were standing at the sides of the hall, two a breast.

The players were marvellous. They entered fully into their parts, shedding genuine tears when they should, laughed when they should, and showed feelings of anger or jealousy when they should. Imaginative, original, intelligent, they responded admirably to my guidance and direction. The School Board was ecstatic (though they

192

had refused to help), the parents proud and jubilant. I had demonstrated convincingly what could be done, given co-operation and encouragement. The local press declared that the students were a credit to themselves and to their school, and added,

"Mr. Dale, who understood the dramatic and the comedy, had coaxed his students into new depths of portrayal."

But this was extra curricula activity. What of academic work and academic excellence? Here, too, I was a hard task master. I insisted on excellence and challenged bright and weak students alike. This, too, paid off in terms of the final Grade 12 Departmental Examinations in which my classes scored some of the highest marks ever scored in the subjects I taught in the school. The average class mark was unquestionably impressive. But it was not the high scores of my students that pleased me as much as the realization that I had tried and had succeeded to inculcate in the students a desire to learn, to analyze objectively, to think rationally, and always to give of their best in whatever they do. I was demanding, firm, yet patient, kind and understanding. It was no surprise that the rapport between them and me was good. Many of them never severed links with me. Equally many of the parents and the School Board showed me much respect.

Yet, at the end of the school year, I resigned my position. This caused much alarm. Despite pleas from the School Board, parents, students, even the Mayor of the town, for me to withdraw my resignation and stay for even another year or two — reminiscent of my departure from Clarendon College and the London boys' school where I taught years before — I moved to Edmonton to fill a position that was offered to me there. It was sad as I took my leave of Grande Prairie, for the students and the whole city had accepted me warmly. It seemed I was always moving. But life is transient; there is no abiding. I said my good-byes and closed the Grande Prairie chapter of my life.

CHAPTER 10

It would be irrational to ascribe to my move to Edmonton confirmation of the prescience I had when I arrived there the year previous, but to that city I went and was to make a mark, howsoever insignificant. I was now to teach at the Jasper Place High School (JPHS). The Town of Jasper Place, later amalgamated with the City of Edmonton, bordered Edmonton on the west. Plans were already drawn up for the closing of JPHS and the building of a new school, the Jasper Place Composite High School (JPCHS) to cater to an expected increase in the population. It was planned to accommodate two thousand students, from Grade 10 to Grade 12. In fact, construction of the new school was already in progress. I would teach in JPHS for one year, then move to JPCHS the following year when construction was due to be completed and the school opened.

Once more, I was detailed to teach Grade 12 English and Grade 12 Social Studies, and once more I was to face an uphill struggle: the students were woefully unprepared for Grade 12 work. Whereas the Alberta educational system then required no Departmental final examinations (set and marked by the Department of Education) for Grades 10 and 11, it made them mandatory for Grade 12. Such a regulation carried the germ of dissatisfaction. It encouraged a laissez-faire attitude on the part of students of Grades 10 and 11 who, on reaching Grade 12, suddenly found they were not well prepared for the new work. And failure to pass the Grade 12 Departmental Examinations tended to reflect negatively not only on the students but on the Grade 12 teachers as well.

I was forced to go over much of the work that should have been mastered by the students in the two previous grades. Of necessity, then, I had to be teaching three years' work in one year. Worse, the initial unwillingness of the students to accept the fact that their work was below par hindered progress at first. It was not until I showed them copies of past final Departmental Examination papers that they came to realize that much more effort on their part was necessary if they were to be successful.

The whole year presented a major challenge for me. But I triumphed over the difficulty, eminently because I was persistent and used every strategy I could devise to get the best out of the students. The results of the Grade 12 Department Examinations (Finals) attested to this. There were no failures in the classes I taught, and many of my students had scored fairly high marks. Yet, I was not satisfied. The strain that the system posed on the Grade 12 teachers and the students was too severe, all because the tightening up that was necessary in Grades 10 and 11 had not been rigorously carried out.

When, therefore, the new Principal and staff of the new JPCHS met to discuss the curriculum of the school, aggressively I highlighted the difficulties I faced during the year that had just ended. I was fully supported by all the other Grade 12 teachers who had also experienced the same difficulties. I volunteered to teach Grade 10 English mainly to give the grounding the students should have. But the Principal would not hear of this, insisting that I was needed most at the Grade 12 level. But I was not to be put off easily. I offered to teach one class of Grade 10 English, even as an overload, to give and thus illustrate the background that these students should have before they entered Grade 12. I succeeded in the end in exacting a covenant from the Principal that allowed me to teach English to one Grade 10 class, and English to the same students in their Grades 11 and 12 years. I was intent on demonstrating how well students of average intelligence could do if they were challenged early to aim at excellence instead of mediocrity.

The main weakness of English at the high school level in Alberta at that time was its marked tendency to rely on multiple-choice questions and answers, which did not allow students to express themselves in full sentences or essays. It was customary for the students to fill out blanks with a word or phrase. Clearly what favoured this method was the enormity of the marking. For example, the Grade 10 English syllabus required the mere writing of a simple paragraph instead of a full-length essay; but even in Grade 12 many of the students could not write a well-constructed paragraph. I studied the English syllabuses of all three Grades, then threw them out. In their place I put my own, certainly incorporating the requirements of the 'official' syllabus but adding more challenging material. For instance, I included a thorough study of two novels (the classics) in each of Grades 10, 11 and 12 syllabuses. The study would encourage oral discussions and written work (essays) on the origin of the story, the plot, the structure, the purpose, the setting, the atmosphere, the characters, the style of writing. In general, by subtly combining English Literature and English Language, I hoped to add more meaning and depth to the language syllabus, and thus more interest, in the students' development of literary skills in thinking critically, speaking clearly, writing effectively, and gaining confidence — all at one and the same time.

Some ten months after I had introduced the revised English Language programme in the Grade 10 class that I was given to teach, the class was visited, quite unexpectedly, by a Superintendent of Schools. The students were so engrossed in what they were doing that they took no notice of him. They were discussing the characters in Dickens's Great Expectations. One student, Barrie Touchings, was in front of the class leading the discussion. Addressing the class, he was saying,

"In Great Expectations, Dickens portrays in a very unique way

196

two types of characters, the outcast and the eccentric, represented by Magwitch and Miss Havisham. Would you agree with that assessment?"

"Well," said Darlene Talbot, "Compeyson is a hidden villain, a third important character, who is definitely not one of your two types."

"You are right," said Barrie, "but I think he is no more than an agent who caused the two main characters to make their respective plans, also an instrument of fate, causing the arrest of Magwitch and indirectly the disappearance of Pip's fortune."

"Well," Frank Jasperse butted in, "if you are of the opinion that Compeyson is an 'agent', then surely Jaggers, the very impressive lawyer, and his very efficient clerk, Wemmick, must be 'agents' too …."

Just then, the Superintendent tip-toed over to where I was standing at the back of the class and whispered to me:

"Did you say these are Grade 10 students?"

"Yes, very much so," I replied.

"Impossible," said the Superintendent. "They sound like university students; and they appear to have so much confidence in themselves."

"I assure you," I said, "it has taken much effort to bring them this far. They were not like this at the beginning. This is the second novel they have read and are critically examining."

The discussion continued. Barrie Touchings, now a successful lawyer who throughout the years has kept in touch with me, had the unmistakable propensity of the lawyer to argue, and kept the discussion going. Refusing to allow any one member of the class to monopolize the discussion, he allowed as many of them as possible to present and substantiate their views, at the same time allowing for cross discussion. In this way, Peter Tchir, Eileen Wiebe, Beverley Etherington, Sue Hill, Bruce Bibby, Helene Chomiak, Erica Van

Soest — one and all expressed their opinions of the characters of the novel. I had insisted on their substantiating what they said with references to what others in the novel said about a character or characters, and what the characters said about themselves.

The Superintendent had taken a seat at the back of the class during the discussion and had been making copious notes. Not one student took any notice of him. They were too eager to participate in the discussion to pay him any attention, and his departure from the room was as unnoticed as his entry. But before he left the school that day, he returned to see me. He wanted to know, among other things, why I was not following the official syllabus, why discussing a novel at the Grade 10 level, why I was teaching literature when I should be teaching English Language.

This was the opportunity I wanted, and I exploited it readily. I showed the Superintendent the carefully-constructed English syllabuses for Grades 10, 11 and 12 that I had crafted and introduced, and indicated how they had incorporated all the requirements of the 'official' syllabuses. I reminded him that the 'official' syllabuses and guidelines were not orders or commandments to be obeyed, that I understood them to be what they said they were — guides — which implied that there was room for creativity, imagination, enterprise, even experiment.

Before me on my desk were written exercises by the students of my Grade 10 English Language class, whom the Superintendent had listened to earlier. Each student of that class had to write an essay on the character in Great Expectations that appealed most to him/her. The 'official' syllabus required paragraph writing. I had discussed what comprised a good paragraph, but instead of writing a simple paragraph, I went further to demand from the students an essay, which, clearly, is thinking and writing in paragraphs, and which, by far, is more interesting, stimulating and challenging.

I continued to explain to the Superintendent that the syllabuses I devised required the study of two novels, preferably the classics — in each of the three grades. Thus at the end of his/her Grade 12, the student would have read and studied six of the classics in the English language. I hoped that by then they would be more than merely functionally literate.

The Superintendent next asked how I was able to obtain copies of the novels for the whole class to read. I explained that was very easy. I had ordered the books (paperbacks) during the summer from a book shop in London, England, to arrive before the beginning of the term, and had informed the students at the beginning of the term that they had no more than three weeks to read the first novel. Two members of the class were assigned to distribute the books and collect the payment, as the Invoice showed, from the students.

"And they all bought them?" asked the Inspector.

"Certainly. The class was made to understand that if they did not obtain a copy right at the start and begin to read it, they would be at a serious disadvantage," I said.

Then I explained why I was doing what I was doing, the difficulties I had in the previous year with my Grade 12 English class, how I had obtained a firm promise from the Principal to allow me to teach English Language to my present Grade 10 students in their Grades 11 and 12. I wanted to demonstrate convincingly that if students were challenged, from the moment they entered the high school, to do serious and meaningful work, they would never be bored or do badly in the Grade 12 final examinations.

I also showed the Superintendent 'proofs' of the Literary Magazine which I had encouraged the same Grade 10 students to launch in the school, and which were right there on my desk. I had selected five members of the class to be the Editorial Board. Their task was to edit the contributions from other members of the class before I examined them. The contributions included essays, short stories, plays, poems. I would accept contributions from the rest of the school only after the first issue was published. What I wanted to do at the outset was to set a high standard. The general aim was to use the magazine as a vehicle for the creative, literary work of students who might be inclined (or encouraged) to attempt it. Printed in the Graphics Department of the school, the magazine also offered other students with an artistic bent an opportunity to develop their skills in illustrating by sketches, drawings and paintings many of the articles.

The Superintendent began to browse through some of the 'proofs' on my desk, and his browsing became reading of one of the short stories with well-constructed paragraphs. At the end he said,

"Most interesting! Very good work! Very good work indeed! Grade 10! Incredible! If I had not seen this myself, I would never believe it."

Then he made me promise to send him a copy "without fail" after the magazine was published.

The sequel to this was that the Jasper Place Composite High School Literary Magazine, which the student editors named The Quill, blazed a trail for many of the Edmonton high schools to follow.

To leap the years, the Principal kept his word and allowed me to teach English Language to the same students in their Grades 11 and 12 years; and my efforts and determination paid off handsomely if the results of the Grade 12 English Matriculation Examination (Department of Education, Alberta) of these students were any guide. The **average** mark of the class was 90 per cent (89.98 per cent, to be exact), and would have been higher if a new student had not joined the class a few months before the final examination. She had not the same background as the class she had joined, and her lower mark in the 70 per-cent range lowered the class average. Armed with these results, I walked into the Principal's office and engaged his attention. I began:

"…, you said to me some time ago that I was not co-operating with the other teachers of English in the school because I refused to adopt their teaching methods and marking scheme. Well, I am now in a position to tell you why."

I showed him the list of names of the students of my Grade 12 English class and their respective marks in the final Departmental Examination. I had copied these from the Examination Results which the Department of Education had published.

"My teaching methods and marking scheme produce these results, a class **average** of 90 per cent. As long as I can obtain successes like these, why should I change my methods to adopt others that have not given comparable results?" I demanded, and requested the Principal to compare the marks of my class with those of the other parallel classes which, during the year, were supposedly scoring very high marks but which in the Departmental Examination scored low marks. I continued:

"I do not come to crow or blow my trumpet. I have no need to do that because I know what I am doing. I am merely pointing out, convincingly, I hope, why I had refused to change my teaching methods for another that is obviously less effective. Marks aside, I have the great satisfaction in believing that I have taught the students, whose names are listed there, to think critically, to reason objectively, and to discriminate intelligently. I had asked you to allow me to teach this class from Grade 10 to Grade 12, and you agreed, though somewhat reluctantly. I now invite you to assess what I have done and to judge my action impartially."

The Principal found it difficult to respond to me. He shifted in his chair. At last he looked up from the list of names and the marks that I had given him and said:

"Well, Mr. Dale, your efforts have been most commendable. I congratulate you. And I must add, I admire your courage, the confidence you have shown in what you are doing, and your tenacious drive. That class of students were lucky to have you consistently throughout their three years here."

I responded by saying that I was not really seeking compliments. I felt, I repeated, it was my duty to explain to him why I refused to adopt the teaching methods and marking schemes of other teachers, which, the records showed, allowed high marks during the term but low marks in the final Departmental Examinations.

The same effort I gave to the English syllabus I also gave to the teaching of Geography. As included in the Social Studies course, geography was relegated to a listing of facts. As a trained geographer, I advocated the introduction of a sensible geography course that could capture the interest of students, and set about devising one. In conjunction with the Department of Geography at the University of Alberta (right there in Edmonton), I produced such a course, a blend of physical and human geography, showing the earth as the home of humankind, the manifold physical and human features it embodies, and the spatial relationships between the two. It involved, among other requirements, a local field trip, the establishment of a weather station in conjunction with the Federal Department of Transport, and an annual field trip to the Rocky Mountains.

The course was approved on a trial basis in the hope that if it was successful, it would be adopted in all the high schools of the city. Such a decision presupposed that there were many trained geographers in the school system who were qualified to teach it. But invariably what little geography was taught, if it could be called geography, was attempted by teachers who had no training in the discipline, not even an introductory geography course at the university level. It would then be the blind leading the blind. However, I thought I would not make a frontal attack of that notion until later. It was rational to introduce the course first and get it established. A special grant was approved by the School Board for the acquisition of wall maps, Canadian topographical map sheets at different scales, globes, and other equipment.

From the very start, the subject matter won the interest of the students. They were encouraged to be analytical and objective, to substantiate their views with reputable data from government agencies and government statistics, United Nations, and research material. To illustrate, one of the students, using data provided by the Federal Meteorological Office in the city, correlated temperature conditions on the prairies with the growing season. She showed that temperatures had increased markedly over the prairies between the 1880s and the 1960s, and this accounted for a longer growing season at the very time when experimentation with different strains of prairie wheat was being made to produce an early-maturing variety. She extended this study during her class field trip to the Rockies to show that the noticeable wasting away of the Athabasca Glacier corresponded with the increased temperatures over the same time period. Markings of the extensions of a series of recessional end moraines at the foot of the glacier by the National Parks people enabled her to measure crudely, very crudely, the rate of the wasting. As a nascent attempt at geographical analysis, it was a far cry from the former memorization or mere listing of facts. It was not surprising that this student proceeded to major in geography at the University of Alberta, and finally obtained both the B.Sc. and the M. Sc. degrees in the discipline.

The course was offered at the Grade 11 level, and the students' work was assessed by the Department of Geography, University of Alberta, and was found to be interesting, successful and commendable. It was adopted by other Edmonton high schools. I warned, notwithstanding, that the success of it mandated that it was taught by trained geography teachers.

Next, in attempting to help to widen the horizon of the students further, I organized and conducted, with the help of another member of the staff, Mrs. E. A. Laws, a three-month educational tour of Europe for the benefit of those students who could afford to go (and I saw to it that a native Indian was included), much the same as I did when I taught in England and repeatedly took British school boys on tours to Switzerland. The tour I planned for the JPCHS students (both sexes) included England (London), Belgium (Ostende, Brussels), the Netherlands (Amsterdam, Rotterdam), what was then Western Germany (including a boat trip down the Rhine from Cologne to Basle, Switzerland), Austria (Innsbruck, Salzburg), Switzerland (Lucerne, Geneva, Montreux), Italy (Milan, Piza, Rome, Sorrento, the Isle of Capri), and France (Paris). "Very educational and enjoyable, most successful and memorable" were the students' assessment of the tour. There were no accidents, no illnesses, except a slight fever of one of the boys in Rome, caused by the hot, Mediterranean sun. But this was soon remedied. I, myself, suffered, not surprisingly, a weight loss of some 15 to 20 pounds. The students returned in good health, with happy memories and a keen desire to learn French. During the tour, especially in Switzerland, they were repeatedly humbled by little nine- and ten-year olds who could shift from German to French to Italian to English with the greatest of ease. Totally disquieting for the Canadian students who, coming from a country with two official languages, looked on helplessly, feeling wholly inadequate and impotent with only one language! If the tour did nothing else, it removed the resistance which the students, like many other Canadians, had to learning French.

As if my energies were not being taxed severely, at the old high school, the Drama Club had sought my help in producing and directing their year-play. News of the success of the Grande Prairie year-play had obviously reached them. Perhaps for that reason they were keen to have my help. I accepted their invitation and did exactly what I did at Grande Prairie in producing and directing the play. Again the attempt was an overwhelming success, which only served as a prelude to a request from the Drama Club of the new Jasper Place Composite High School for me to produce and direct the first year-play in the school. I took time to consider the request.

The stage of the auditorium (with a seating capacity of two

thousand) of the new school was uncommonly large. It was almost frightening for amateur production because the play area itself was so huge. Unhappily the acoustics were poor; the voices of amateur players would fall flat or be completely lost in such a huge auditorium. As the building had not yet been officially taken over by the School Board, I pointed out the flaw, and the Board lost no time in having it remedied by the architect. They even went a step further to install the most impressive proscenium curtains that parted to the right and to the left. It might be too much to say that the Board's willingness to have the stage fitted out for dramatic purposes could have been interpreted partly as an act of contrition, for although they had refused to help with the production of the play in the old high school, they proudly accepted the accolades of parents and the general public that followed the successful production of it. They were now convinced that dramatics in the high school was good training for students. The sum of all this was that the first year-play in the school should meet expectations to which the previous play had given birth.

The major difficulty, in my view, would be to get the students to project their voices so that they could be heard in the huge auditorium, and at the same time to act convincingly. I did not doubt for a moment that I could bring this off successfully, but the hard work it would demand caused me to hesitate somewhat. It was not that I was afraid of hard work. I had been subjected to that all my life, but I knew what it takes to produce and direct successfully a play with untrained players.

At the meeting of the Drama Club, called to meet me and to hear whether I would help them, the interest and keenness of the students quickly removed what doubts I had. I told them what I told the previous Drama Clubs at Grande Prairie and at the Jasper Place High School: the severe demands of the stage, projection of the voice for all to hear, convincing the audience that the player is the person whom he/she is portraying, in other words, living the part; the high standard of acting I would demand of them etc. etc. Unless they were prepared to aim for high standards, I would not be interested in producing and directing their play; they could find some one else. No, no, it was I they wanted; they were prepared to work hard under my direction and make the venture a success.

Impressed by their obvious enthusiasm, I accepted their invitation. I selected a play which I thought they would like to act. It was "Stage Door", a three-act comedy by Ferber and George S. Kaufman, requiring a huge cast of 32 players. It would also give many of the members of the Club non-acting roles, such as stage hands, prompters, lighting technicians, stage manager, property designers and makers, indeed, a good many would be involved. I gave them a brief outline of the play. It revolves around a bevy of actors/actresses, all trying to become film stars. It is hilarious in parts, funny in others, and altogether good, clean fun — quite suitable and challenging for a high school drama group. Each Act has two scenes. The change of scene in the first Act, from the main room of an actors' club to a bedroom, if effected with lightning speed, should impress the audience greatly.

In my customary habit of being well prepared, I had obtained copies of the play which I then distributed and made a very tentative casting, with the help of the Club members. What followed next was what I had done before: play reading, then rehearsals with emphasis on voice projection from the first day, and doing a part over and over again until the players got it right. This took many months.

Next, I turned my attention to the designing and making of the stage properties. I was able to use some of the "flats" from the previous play; and again I thought of borrowing the necessary furniture and other fixtures. But of all the problems none was as monumental as finding a way to dress the players, to make them look like film stars, and having dressed them, to get them to walk with the poise and elegance, ease and grace, charm and confidence that the parts demanded. I considered the matter long and hard, then devised a strategy. I summoned courage, went to see the manager of The Bay Department Store, and dangled before him the publicity he would have if he could find a way to dress 32 students to look like film stars in their first year-play, in their brand new composite high school of two thousand students, and their new auditorium which seats an equal number of persons. The manager took the bait, and after two or three days agreed to help by offering everything that the cast needed (dresses, suits, hats, shoes, nighties, pyjamas and all accessories) at half price, and to lend the expertise of his cosmetics salon and hair salon to help with 'make-up' and hair styling on the night of the performance. The cosmetics would also be provided by the store. I felt I was walking on thin air when the manager told me this. His generous offer served to heighten my courage. I went across the street to the Scandinavian Furniture Store, and in like manner convinced the manager of the advertisement potential if he lent the furniture, lamps and other fittings for the stage. The manager readily seized the opportunity and promised to lend all the furniture required (Scandinavian). He even went a step further and volunteered to place the furniture on the stage himself, in strategic locations where they could be seen to good advantage, that is, advertize them, as well as to heighten the appearance of the room.

Still in high gear, I went to see the Director of a School of Charm and explained my difficulty in getting the girls (film stars in the play) to walk with the poise, elegance and confidence of film stars. Not until I told her that the girls were putting down their feet like elephants and almost waddle before lifting them up again, and all had a good laugh, that she offered to give the girls 13 complimentary lessons in deportment, each of an hour's duration.

In addition, the Imperial Lumber Co. Ltd. promised to lend ready-made doors and windows for the set; a flower shop, seeing the publicity that would be forthcoming for them, offered to provide (lend) real flowers for the sitting room. And three radio stations agreed to publicize the play free of cost. Indeed, the local community was incredibly supportive. They rallied to my appeal readily. Their generosity and community spirit were truly amazing.

When I told the Drama Club the successes I had with the local business outlets, they sat in stunned disbelief. How did I do it? they asked.

"Look them straight in the eye; explain simply and briefly what you are trying to do; show them how they could help and the publicity they would have; convince them of how much their help would be appreciated; and, above all, be honest in what you say. It is as simple as that, but you must also know how to make the approach, which is the real secret of success.

On both nights of the performance, the auditorium was full to capacity. Thanks to the radio stations which had sent scouts to the final dress rehearsal, all the seats were sold. It was an expectant audience, due in part to the "build up" by the radio stations, in part by the publicity of the students themselves. For me it was a happy reminder of the full houses at the performances in Grande Prairie and at the JPHS.

Exactly at the stated hour, the hall lights were dimmed, followed by the slow parting of the proscenium curtains, revealing a modern sitting room, expensively and elegantly furnished in the Hollywood and Scandinavian traditions, with subtle controlled lighting — a thing of sheer beauty that lifted one from the humdrum and the drab to the sphere of pure delight. The audience applauded so long and with such gusto that they delayed the action, and I would not allow the action to begin until the applause had died down. The performers were quite unprepared for this. The loud shouts of approval of the set unnerved them a little. But my encouragement behind the stage helped to restore their confidence and their timing of entry on to the stage. Each had to make an entry and had to be seen. They were well prepared for that. All was going well until disaster almost struck.

I had cast a native Indian girl for one of the parts. She was of striking appearance, tall, attractive in the real sense of the word. I thought she could bring off the part most effectively and had given her much help and encouragement to get rid of her shyness, to cross the cultural divide, and live the part she was to play. I had insisted that she should walk with grace and ease; the instructors at the School of Charm had spent extra hours with her; everybody had given her just that little extra help, perhaps because of her attractive looks. I had suggested she should wear a white dress with red trimmings and accessories which would enhance her appearance. The Bay people had gone to much trouble in selecting just the right dress for her. Also the cosmetics people had more or less perfected their art on her. She looked regal, queenly, magnificent! I had fully anticipated the audience's reaction when she made her entry on to the stage, and had directed her to walk somewhat slowly across the room to the piano before beginning her lines. As she entered, the audience registered their approval in the most remarkable way, first by loud gasps, then whistles, followed by a thunderous applause. There was no question about it, she **WAS** a film star. She walked across the room, as she was directed to do, while the applause continued, but on reaching the piano she broke down in tears. But I was right there behind her, out of sight of the audience, talking quickly to her and giving her the support she needed:

"Marvellous!" I said to her. "They love you. Do not let them down. Turn a few pages of the music sheets on the piano, then bend down as though you are picking up something and quickly dab your eyes with your handkerchief. Don't let them see you wiping your eyes. Be careful not to wipe away your make-up. You are doing splendidly. Now face the audience. Hold your head high like a proud Indian princess and begin. Show them what you can do!" She did. Her initial fright subsided. The crisis passed, and I could breathe easily again.

It was, however, the change of scene in the first Act, as I had predicted, that brought the audience to their feet. It was the speed at which it was executed, exactly one minute, that was the great surprise — from an elegantly furnished sitting room to a dainty, beautiful bedroom with a distinctly different colour scheme, with three beds, three dressers and mirrors, chairs, closets for clothes. How was it effected? At the end of the first scene, while the curtains were closing slowly, I had one team of stage hands with the bedroom furniture, moving slowly forward behind and with the moving curtains, but unseen by the audience. On the floor were markings where each piece should go. Thus by the time the curtains came together the stage hands rushed to put each piece in place, collected the sitting room furniture, and dashed back to the curtains to move out slowly with them as they opened again, again unseen by the audience. Their action coincided with the dropping of a curtain at the back to hide the rest of the sitting room. This had taken hours and hours of practice to get the timing right. In short, the moment the proscenium curtains came together at the end of the first scene, they were opened again immediately, revealing an entirely different scene. The efforts of the stage hands were amply rewarded by the resounding applause of the audience.

The second night of the performance drew an even larger audience. The school's caretakers, unknown to me, had defied the city's Fire Regulations and had placed another two rows of chairs down the main aisle way, at the back, and at the two sides of the auditorium. Even so, people were standing at both sides. Before the first night, the radio stations had been whipping up interest. One announcement ran thus:

"JPCHS year-play is going to be something. Mark my words! Jasper Place is about to be given a real treat."

And after the first night, the announcement said:

"You just must not miss it (JPCHS Year-Play). It is marvellous — marvellously produced, beautifully staged, beautifully acted."

The untiring efforts of everybody who helped with the play — players and non-players alike — were salutary and were greatly rewarded by the success of the play. It gave me yet another opportunity to point out to the students that when they attempt a project, whether it was their studies or anything else, if they worked hard at it, that is, put heart and soul into it, invariably success would crown their efforts. If, however, they expend little effort, or think they will fail, failure will result. In other words, to win success, one must strive very hard.

But although the demands of school work were heavy, I found time to continue my research work in Geography and published a few papers in Canadian and British refereed geographical journals. Equally, throughout my four years at JPCHS, I served in various capacities in the community. It was through my efforts that the Alberta Geographical Association was established, of which I was secretary, then president. I was also a member of the Robertson (later Robertson-Wesley) United Church choir in Edmonton. On many occasions I was invited to conduct the Sunday morning service there. With other members of JPCHS staff, I was also a member of the Board of the Indian Residential School near St. Albert, many of whose students attended JPCHS. Another JPCHS staff member and I did much to improve the physical and social conditions of the school.

I explained earlier that my intention was to go on to a Ph. D. degree in Geography. Without the financial means to do so, I was relegated to teaching in the hope of saving enough funds to keep me as a student again. Apart from that, the Department of Geography at the University of Alberta in Edmonton had not, up to the beginning of 1960, offered a Ph. D. programme. When it did in 1964, the Head of the Department encouraged me to seek admission to the programme. I did, and was admitted, with four other mature students. All five of us were more or less hand-picked to initiate the programme. We had hitherto published widely. I resigned my position at JPCHS, much to the surprise of the Principal who tried to dissuade me, pointing out the salary I would be giving up during the four years that the programme would require.

"You are one of the highest paid members of this staff," he said to me. "Are you going to give up four years of that kind of salary to obtain a Ph. D.?"

I looked at him in silence for an awkward moment, then said,

"Coming from you (he had his Ph. D.), such a question is painfully surprising."

"I am merely being rational, very practical," he said. "It would take ten years or more to recoup such an aggregate salary."

"As an educator," I countered, "surely you must know the satisfaction that comes from the quest for learning, from working not for material reasons alone but from pushing back, even by a little, the boundaries of the unknown."

It was now the Principal's turn to be silent for a moment, as he pondered the mild rebuke of the young man sitting before him.

"Well," he said, "I am not being rude; I am only trying to make you see the other side of the coin, and, in truth, I really do not want to lose you."

I thanked him, for his concern and told him I was quite willing to sacrifice four years of my salary and submit myself to the arduous work that learning demands in order to improve myself.

I doubted very much if the Principal could fully understand where I was coming from, my boyhood dreams, my bitter struggles, inextricably intermingled with disappointments? How could he understand the indestructible driving force of a young man to whom many doors, which he had tried to open, had been closed because of his ethnic background? I shut from my mind all that the Principal had said and resolutely proceeded with my plan to begin my doctorate. After I resigned my position, I was most surprised to read in the Christmas issue of The Quill, Volume 4, No.1, December 1965, the literary magazine which I had founded at JPCHS, complimentary remarks which the Principal had made about me:

> Mr. E. H. Dale, ... a truly creative teacher, has made a number of major contributions to the life of Jasper Place Composite High School: he directed the school's first year-play; he obtained the status of Department of Transport weather station for the school (JPCHS is the only high school in Canada which fulfils this role); he inaugurated the annual Geography field trip to Jasper National Park; with Mrs. E. A. Laws, he sponsored a student summer tour of Europe. Of all these projects, though he gave abundantly of his energy to each, I think The Quill was the achievement dearest to him. He spent many hours working with groups and individuals, coaxing, cajoling, and inspiring in a tireless fashion; he taught many students the value of serious literary effort. These students should be eternally grateful.

Thus ended my high school teaching days. I returned to university work with grim determination, which was to triumph over difficulties great and small.

CHAPTER 11

Although the allotted time span for the Ph. D. degree in Geography at the University of Alberta was stated to be four years, I thought that with much effort on my part, I could reduce the time to three years. Thus I set about ardently to achieve this goal.

The programme required certain prescribed courses germane to my research area (Urban Geography), a reading knowledge of two relevant languages (to be tested by examination), a candidacy or comprehensive examination, which reviewed the major areas of Geography, at the end of the first year or the beginning of the second, and research and thesis work for the rest of the time.

My background in French would be adequate, I thought, but would require about a month's brushing up before I would be ready for the examination. The second language, however, would impede my progress because I would need to begin it from scratch. From a boy I wanted to study Spanish, for Jamaica's neighbours are largely Spanish-speaking, but I did not get the opportunity to do so. At last, it seemed, the time had come for me to learn Spanish. I began in earnest, spent the whole summer preceding my return to university learning Spanish, and had made progress. Regrettably, when I enrolled in the Ph. D. programme, I was advised to substitute German for Spanish since more scientific papers in urban geography, which I would be required to read, were published in German than in Spanish. My hopes of learning Spanish went out the window and

I turned my undivided attention to German, night and day. After some six months or more, I was able to satisfy the reading requirement (translation of scientific papers in the language).

Next, I cleared the course work and Candidacy Examination at the beginning of my second year. All that lay ahead was now my thesis, the research for which I began in earnest from the beginning of my first year.

Of the cities of Canada, Edmonton had been growing with remarkable speed, although this phenomenal growth had been arrested by two world wars and two economic recessions. The speed of the growth had captured my interest. I wanted to unravel the forces behind this phenomenon, having regard to the difficulties that would be involved. I had examined the literature on urban geography and found that urban geographers up to the mid-1960s had done little work to reveal and assess the historical development and underlying political and social factors that shape, and thus explain, the development of towns and cities. In short, what was called political-urban geography was in its infancy. The few urban studies that had a political aspect failed to analyse intensively the political process at the urban level. The dearth of investigations into the many intricate processes of urban growth, especially those that arise from the decisions made by a town or city council, posed a challenge which I accepted. Thus I was to attempt an inquiry into this aspect of urban geography, focusing on the City of Edmonton. I submitted the parameters of my research work, which were approved.

Much of the research had to be done at the then City Hall, largely in the underground vault which housed the documents of the city. This was tedious, laborious work, time-consuming and dirty, for much of the material was covered by layers of dust accumulated since the Town of Edmonton was incorporated in 1892 and city status granted in 1905. Many of the documents were misplaced, a few missing, but the majority were intact. Soon, I acquired so much information about the city that on two occasions, I prevented the

City Council from making what would have been costly, legal blunders in land deals. On another occasion, armed with city maps, I showed the Mayor and his inner strategy committee land suitable for housing which had been by-passed by Realtors in the mistaken belief that it was underlain by gas and oil pipe lines. Quietly, without the knowledge of Realtors/land developers, the City acquired the land and used it to provide low-income housing for its residents, which was in great demand just then. More than that, the City's acquisition of this land brought down the soaring prices of land and housing in the city at that time, as well as putting into the city's coffers a few million dollars. The Minutes of the Council meetings of that period record the City's expression of gratitude to me. I was now given a spacious office, a departmental account number, and regarded as someone to whom members of the various departments of the Civic Administration could turn for verification of data respecting land deals — a grand, advisory position, flagrantly unremunerated, except for cups of morning coffee and afternoon tea quietly and justifiably pillaged from the Mayor's office.

Throughout, I focused specifically on the complex processes of public decision-making and on the effects of the decisions on the morphological evolution of Edmonton. I analyzed this by stages and at successive time periods, and found that these processes created in the beginning an industrial climate conducive to development by attracting railways which, in turn, attracted industries. Also, early public ownership of essential public utilities — the street railway, water and sewerage, the telephone system, electricity and electrical generating — greatly enhanced the industrial climate. Once the Council provided these urban utilities, it used them as inducements (free, or at cost, or at reasonable rates) to control the orderly development of the city, and refused to extend them outside the city limits. But the compact development which these policies ensured was adversely affected by land speculators who would buy land on the periphery of the city limits, divide them into residential subdivisions, and sold them quickly. Then they and the new owners would pressure the City to annex the lands, invariably after they were sold. One of the effects of this was to extend the city limits.

I showed in my thesis that the Council also ensured an ample, available supply of industrial sites at reasonable prices and, as well, devised a policy to attract immigrants by advertisement and other means. I found further that development was enhanced also by non-political factors, including an abundance and variety of natural resources, such as petroleum and natural gas, within the Edmonton district. But long before the exploitation of these resources, the Council's decisions to reserve lands along the railways for industrial sites, to extend spur lines to industrial sites as required, and to use lands along the river valley for parks greatly aided development. I showed, however, that the Council's decisions respecting tax-forfeited lands gave much of the impetus to Edmonton's growth; that, at the time of the land boom, between 1910 and 1912, the City attempted to raise the greater part of its revenue by a tax on land alone; that the ill-effects of the single tax were not felt during the period of intense economic expansion in Edmonton, when speculative land owners were said to be making fortunes over night and could pay their taxes; that these taxes were based on extravagantly inflated land assessment; and that when the real-estate boom came suddenly to an end in 1913 and the landowners were unable to pay their taxes, they were forced by provincial legislation to allow the City to sell the tax-forfeited lands to recoup the taxes that were owing. If the City could not sell them, it could acquire them without making a cash payment.

Painstakingly, and with a grant from the City Council to employ research assistants, I mapped the areas of tax-forfeited lands, lot by lot, and showed that between 1920 and the 1930s, over 50 per cent of the building (developable) land in the city passed into municipal ownership as tax-forfeited lands, much of which had previously been serviced, waiting to be developed. Thus when economic conditions improved after World War II and land prices rose simultaneously with the exploitation of natural gas and petroleum near Edmonton, the increasing demands for land in the city, fuelled by the development of these resources, caused the City to replot these lands quickly. They were then in small lots, and larger development sites and more space were needed to accommodate the drastic increase of population and industries that came to the city after 1947.

In very great detail, I showed further that (a) suddenly the city had become a magnet for industrial activity, based on petroleum and natural gas and their by-products; (b) the decisions of the City Councils were as numerous and rapid as the coming of the industries and people; (c) quick decisions were uncommonly a departure from the norm of the democratic process when the affairs of the community were urgent; and (d) decision-makers were then not allowed to employ delaying tactics to see how the wind blows in the community, or to play safe by taking no action in the hope of being re-elected.

I defended my thesis successfully and was awarded the Ph. D. Even the caretakers of the floor of the Marshal Tory Building in which my office was located were jubilant when they heard the news of my success. They had watched me as I worked by day and by night, even in the early hours of the morning, and were concerned that my health would be impaired. But at last, after years of bitter struggle, bitter disappointments, manifold difficulties, considerable frustration, and because of my unfailing determination, I had reached what some regard as the top of the academic ladder. But for the impediments, I could have reached there long before. Yet, they served to strengthen my resolve, my character, and conceivably made of me a more thoughtful, understanding person. In retrospect, I could look back with a degree of pride, much humility, and realize that I had beaten the odds. If only my parents were alive to share in the victory! They had died even before I could obtain my first degree. But who knows, as one of my friends remarked to me, if they were not looking on?

The Canadian Council on Urban and Regional Research had shown much interest in the research and, in fact, had provided financial assistance, after the first year, for me to do it. Completed, the Council regarded it as a thorough documentation of Edmonton's growth from 1892 to 1966, and a major contribution to Canadian geographical research. But it had to be to satisfy the requirements of the Ph. D. in geography, one of the first, at the University of Alberta.

A year before I was awarded the doctorate, I was appointed by the University to teach a course in the Geography Department, to alleviate a crisis which had developed there. At the end of the year, I was rushed to the University of Victoria to take a position there as a Visiting Associate Professor of Geography, to rectify another serious problem which had developed there. No sooner had I calmed the 'troubled waters' than I was invited by the University of Saskatchewan Regina Campus (later changed to the University of Regina) to head its Geography Department at the end of the academic year and settle a major problem that had occurred there also. (The mid-1960s was a troubling time for Canadian and US. universities.) After visiting the Department, I declined the offer for reasons which need not be mentioned here. But the insistence of the Dean of Arts, formerly a British Ambassador to South America, that I reconsider my decision, and the Dean's promise to help me make needed drastic changes within the Department, including the development of a sound undergraduate geography programme of studies leading to the B.A., B.Sc. General and Honours degrees, and the M.A. and M.Sc. degrees — the assurance of the Dean that I would be allowed to do this, made me change my mind and accept the position.

The next stage of my life thus began in Regina. Unafraid of facing challenges, I threw all my energies into the development of a viable geography department almost from scratch. In my first year, I concentrated on the appointment of faculty staff members suitable for the programme I wanted to develop. They were to come from different schools and cultural backgrounds — Canadian, British,

Swedish, South American — with a view to enrich the students' lives and extend their horizons. With the help of the new staff, I developed what was later regarded by other geographers as a sound geography programme. Yet, obtaining approval of it within the university was not an easy task. I came under intense, even fierce, criticism by the Division of Social Sciences (then a part of the bottom level of the decision-making hierarchy) of which the Department of Geography was a member. But I circumvented the difficulty by skilful diplomacy until the proposals came before the Faculty of Arts and Science, the next level of the hierarchy. Thanks to the full support of the Science section of the Faculty, the geography programme was approved. Not long after this, the first Rhodes Scholarship in the history of the University of Regina was awarded to one of the urban geography students, an act which gave the Geography Department some prominence.

Equally, in its formative years the Geography Department was to profit from my invitation first to my former professor, W. Gordon East, distinguished geographer at the University of London, as a Visiting Professor. Next, I invited the well-known American geographer, Dr. J. E. Spencer (now deceased), Emeritus Professor, University of California, Los Angeles, also as a Visiting Professor; next, Professor Kurt V. Abrahamsson of the University of Uppsala, Sweden. These visitors served to strengthen the international aspect of the Department, which I sought to achieve, and to widen the horizons of the students.

But the greatest difficulty for me was my attempts to introduce the Department's graduate programme. Every attempt was being made at that time to channel research work in the Social Sciences Divison into a questionable Social Studies Department. The Social Sciences Division comprised the departments of Anthropology, Economics, Geography, History, Political Science, Psychology, Sociology and Social Studies. There was clear evidence that the last named was attempting to control the Division. I quietly opposed this, and as quietly continued to work towards the development of my department. I had drafted the rationale for my department's graduate programme one early summer morning while visiting Tapiola, Finland's garden city, unable to sleep because of the early Finnish dawn. On my return to Regina, I discussed the proposal with the rest of my faculty members who had approved it with minor changes. Then I chose to try the top-down procedure of obtaining its approval, for I knew that if I had taken the other procedure of going from the bottom to the top, the proposal would be thrown out by the Social Sciences Division. I submitted it to the Dean of the Faculty of Graduate Studies and Research and explained why I had not followed the normal procedure. After discussing it with other members of his faculty, the Dean assured me that the proposed programme would be approved because it was well thought out, but only if the Faculty of Arts (Science had now become a separate faculty) approved it. Despite strong opposition by members of the Social Science Division, the Faculty of Arts approved the proposal on the condition that the Division of Social Sciences approved it. When at last the proposals came before the Division, I was almost roasted alive. I was indicted with the charge of attempting to Balkanize the Division. Throughout the ordeal, I remained stoically calm, smiling my peculiar smile, saying very little, because I knew that they could not reject the proposals without strong academic reasons, and they had none. I had them over a barrel, so to speak, and they knew it and were extremely angry. Geography was about to ruin their grand strategy to create an exaggerated, strong, leftist force in the University.

Such is the nature of pettiness or parochialism in sections of academia, the last place where one would expect to find it. It is not always that enlightenment is to be found in the halls of learning. And it is not surprising that the Division became moribund a year or two after. The actions of groups within it mercifully killed it, justifying the proverbial saying that if you give a dog a long enough rope, he will hang himself. But to return to the geography graduate proposal, the Social Sciences Division very reluctantly approved it. It could not do otherwise. Once the students could see where geography could take them, both the undergraduate and graduate programmes boomed, and soon the Department was turning out students with B.A. and B.Sc. (General and Honours) and M.A. and M.Sc. degrees in Geography. The faculty members of my department were now being rewarded for their hard work, courage and dedication.

It was altogether a busy, challenging time for me. Yet, despite my administrative and heavy teaching duties, I succeeded in continuing my research, writing and publishing papers. I also presented invited papers at geographical conferences held in Buffalo, Los Angeles, Vancouver, Kingston (Jamaica), among other places, supervised numerous Honours and Master's theses, and was External Examiner on a few occasions for Master theses in History. In addition, I was frequently asked to assess research proposals presented in Canada, the United States, Nigeria and China, as well as evaluate the works of others with a view to their promotion to the status of Full Professors. The many-sided aspects of my daily life taxed my energies to the full. Surprisingly, in all my years at the University of Regina, I suffered no serious illnesses nor miss a class, except once — one day only — when an eye operation prevented me from seeing my students and using the blackboard.

Meeting challenges was the pattern of my life from youth. Two of the most outstanding of these challenges, coming soon after I had taken over the Headship of the Department, were in connection with the 22nd International Geographical Congress, held in Canada in 1972 for the first time since 1871, when the first Congress of this world-wide association of geographers was held in Antwerp, Belgium. The main meetings were held at McGill University, Montreal, in August of that year. At the end of the formal sessions, the delegates were taken on field trips throughout the country. Two of these were associated with the prairies.

The first, the Trans-Canada Field Trip, was to pass through

Southern Saskatchewan, and my Department was asked by the planning committee of the Congress to be responsible for the delegates from the time they arrived at the Manitoba-Saskatchewan border until they departed at the Saskatchewan-Alberta border. Altogether, they were to spend two days in Saskatchewan.

The second was a Southern Prairies Field Excursion. This was to be a ten-day field trip, beginning in Winnipeg, Manitoba, moving in a circuitous route across the southern part of Manitoba, Saskatchewan and Alberta, and ending in Calgary, Alberta, after reaching Banff and Lake Louise in the eastern Rockies. My Department was asked to plan and conduct the Saskatchewan portions of both field trips, and to co-ordinate the activities of the Southern Prairies Field Excursion with the other participating Geography Departments at the universities of Winnipeg, Brandon and Calgary. This was a considerable undertaking.

Initial preparations for both field trips, financed by the University of Regina, saw me and one of my senior students dashing about the province, planning the routes; documenting features of geographical significance; arranging for visits to small, medium-sized and large farms; checking restroom facilities, stops for morning coffee, lunch and afternoon tea, and a host of other mundane but important matters which, in hosting large groups in rural Saskatchewan, tend to present major difficulties. This work took the whole summer of 1970, and was completed only the day before the Fall Semester began and the rest of the staff returned from their summer vacation. I sacrificed the whole of my summer vacation for this work.

In the next stage of the preparation, I allocated to each of my faculty members sections of the routes for which they would be responsible, so that they could study them, prepare material for two proposed publications, a Tour Guide and Background Papers, in conjunction with the other participating Geography Departments.

Next, I solicited and obtained the support not only of the University of Regina, but of the Saskatchewan Government and its various departments and agencies, including two experimental farms, also the City of Regina and various municipalities through which the tours would pass, as well as other groups. All were pleased to offer hospitality. The preparations were thorough. Nothing was left to chance. Even at a coffee break, west of Moose Jaw, on top of an area of the Missouri Coteau which runs from the United States through the southern part of the province, I arranged for a mobile canteen to be there at 10.00 a.m. to serve coffee, cinnamon buns and fruit pies!

The careful preparations explained in part the success, especially of the Saskatchewan parts of the two field trips. The warm hospitality, for which Saskatchewan people are noted, left an indelible impression on the visitors, judged by their repeated expressions of gratitude during and after the tours.

Yet another challenge for me and my Department was hosting the annual meeting of the Canadian Association of Geographers in 1975. With the same thoroughness and industry, we succeeded in hosting the conference to every one's satisfaction, as the deluge of letters to the Department after the Conference attested.

Challenging, too, was the twin difficulty of informing the general public that there was a Department of Geography at the University of Regina, and explaining to the public and private sectors what trained geographers do in their specialist areas of competence, for example, geomorphology, meteorology and climatology, hydrology, glaciology, biogeography, human geography, cultural geography, historical geography, urban and rural planning, urban geography, economic geography, resource management, outdoor recreation, population studies, air photo interpretation, remote sensing, cartography, water management, among other geographical specializations. Ignorance about the discipline on the part of both the public and private sectors at first made for their reluctance to employ graduates of the Department. I attacked the problem and sold my discipline to the local public. My strategy was to get one or two of the Department's graduates placed in the City's Planning

Department, the City's and the Province's Parks Departments, the Saskatchewan Housing Corporation, the Canada Mortgage and Housing Corporation, the Map Division of the Federal Government in Regina, and other government departments in the city and the province. My success in this was entirely the result of the 'grape vine' connections I had established with these departments. I was informed when vacancies occurred, or about to occur, and my strong intervention and endorsement of suitable candidates from my Department for the jobs, often in person, prevailed. By their competence, the successful candidates soon dispelled the ignorance or erroneous views that the employers had of geography and geographers. Thereafter, it was easier for the Department's graduates to find employment in civic, provincial and federal departments, and to some extent in the private sector in southern Saskatchewan.

I remained Head of the Geography Department at the University of Regina for nearly ten years and could look back with a degree of pride and satisfaction on all I did to establish the viability and international connections of the Department — a seemingly thankless but rewarding job. And for another ten years I remained the senior member of the staff. Nevertheless, I did not and would not allow my heavy administrative and teaching duties to inhibit my research work and publications. Soon after I assumed my duties in the university, I was promoted to the rank of Full Professor.

What is surprising is that I found time to help with community work. For three years I served in a voluntary capacity on the Regina Planning Commission, an advisory body to the City Council on planning matters, as one of its members. I resigned my position on the Commission only because I was invited to teach for a year in China — an irresistible challenge, as I said at the time, which I accepted. Also I helped to establish the Transitional Area Community Society (TACS), one of the many community societies of the city which help to devise and shape policies for the development and improvement of parts of the city. First, as a member of the Executive Board, then as Vice-President, and finally as President of TACS, I wrestled, in conjunction with the Board, with those private developers whose avowed intent was to change by bulldozing this former high-quality residential area of the city into a commercial area, with highly undesirable commercial structures. It was to prevent this change in land use that TACS came into being. It arrested the change that had been previously initiated. We fought a valiant fight and won the day, but only by maintaining constant surveillance of the area. TACS vetted plans for new construction and for the alteration of buildings in the area, and recommended to developers, the City's Planning Department and Planning Commission alike changes that would satisfy the local residents or designed to improve the plans or designs they submitted for approval. TACS also made briefs to the City Council and held endless discussions with private developers. In retrospect and with consummate pride, I can look back and see the positive results of TACS's endeavours in which I played an important part — attractive reconverted residential dwellings (with heritage status conferred on many) which were slated for demolition; preservation of trees along avenues, which were to be removed to allow the building of new structures; a reduction of boarded-up houses as a prelude to their sale as commercial properties; and other successes.

However, the success that has brought me intense satisfaction is the development of Central Park in the Transitional Area. This open space occupies a whole city block. It had been left undeveloped for many decades. It was used largely, but not entirely, as the playground of the Central Collegiate, directly facing it on the south side. The School was later closed because most of the families who lived in the area had moved out to the new and more spacious suburbs. The closing of the school led to a move by land developers to pressure the City to rezone the open space to 'commercial use'. On behalf of TACS, I quickly made a detailed study of the area and presented it to the City. I followed this up with a brief in person to the City Council in which I showed that more than two thousand senior citizens were spending the evening of their lives in proximity to the open space; that they required developed park space for passive recreation — walking, quiet contemplation of nature (especially flowers and flowering shrubs), rest benches — in short, a little world of beauty and inspiration. Surely, I argued, these senior citizens had made contributions in various ways to the development of their city. It would be shamefully remiss of the present Council not to allow them to enjoy a modicum of the fruits of their labour in their senior years.

I went further to show that the City could not but accede to the request of a well-developed park in the area; that according to Saskatchewan planning legislation, all new subdivisions in the province are required to devote ten per cent of the total area to open-space development, that is, recreational use; that because of this ruling all the surrounding new subdivisions of the city, less densely settled than the Transitional Area, were provided with well-planned, well-developed open spaces; and that in bewildering contrast, the Transitional Area, where most seniors live because of easy access to facilities and services in the downtown area, had no open-space facilities. I acknowledged the fact that the development of the area antedated the planning legislation, but that there was no reason why the anomaly should not be corrected.

The brief was punctuated by applause from a large number of senior citizens (voters!!) who, at TACS's insistence, had attended the meeting, leaving the Council members in no doubt that they supported the views that the President of their Area Association was espousing. The upshot was that the Council passed a motion at that very meeting to retain the open space, and another motion to develop it quickly. The applause which followed the passing of the motions assured the Council members that they had satisfied the local residents. Now developed, Central Park may not fall into the category of a Chinese or Japanese park/garden, but, especially in the summer months, its flowering shrubs, flower beds, pavilion, benches facing the flower beds now give the whole area a quality, indeed an

227

appeal, which hitherto was missing. A part of the park is given to active recreation. Central Park is, most assuredly, a resounding success of the democratic process.

In addition, during the mid-1980s I found myself taking part in a local debate concerning the twinning of Regina with a Chinese city. I had sounded out the Municipal Government of Jinan, capital city of Shandong Province, on this matter while I was lecturing there in the summer of 1984, and had found members of the government eager to twin their city with the city of Regina. Dr. Hsieh, a Professor of History at the University of Regina, had previously taken this matter up with the Regina City Council. But members of the Council were more inclined to twin Regina with Changchung, capital city of Jilin Province, since Jilin was already twinned with the Province of Saskatchewan. I was opposed to twinning with Changchung. Knowing this, Larry Schneider, the incumbent Mayor, invited me to address a few members of the Council who were appointed to go to China to investigate the matter.

I explained to the delegation that it would make more economic sense if Regina was to twin with Jinan. This was not only because the University of Regina was already twinned with the Shandong University in Jinan, but because Shandong, then with a population of some 88 million people (increased to over 92 million by 1993), and Jinan, with a metropolitan population exceeding 4 million (increased to over five million by 1993), provided a huge consumer market for Saskatchewan's wheat, potash, telephone and computer software technology, agricultural technology, agricultural-manufactured products and, generally, technological expertise. In contrast, Jilin's population was only 18 million and Changchung's a mere one million. Besides, Shandong was by far a more progressive province than Jilin Province.

The members of the delegation seemed impressed with my argument but appeared not to be dissuaded from their tentative inclination to twin with Changchung. But on visiting China, they were soon convinced that it was more economically advantageous for Regina to twin with Jinan. On their return to Regina, they apparently had difficulty in convincing the rest of the Regina City Council that a sister relationship with Jinan was more advantageous for Regina than with Changchung, and again the Mayor invited me to present a brief to the Council on the matter — the same argument I presented to the delegation before they left for China. I obliged. With Dr. Hsieh, who spoke on the educational and cultural advantages of twinning with Jinan, I proceeded to point out the economic advantages, and urged the Council to accept the challenge. With the exception of one member, the Council voted for twinning with Jinan. By the end of 1993 Regina was beginning to see the positive effects of twinning with Jinan in terms of contracts in water treatment, air pollution, cattle breeding, housing and other economic activities. My assessment of the matter has been justified, suffice it to say that economic arrangements with China or any of its provinces or cities are usually slow, if not altogether frustrating.

There is no doubt that I tried to give my community my "time, effort and service," as cited by a Volunteer Recognition Award given to me by the Central Zone Board, one of the Zone Boards of the city. As well, I was always addressing groups in the city who repeatedly invited me to share with them my experiences on my travels throughout Europe, the Caribbean and South America and Southeast Asia, especially China, countries that I had visited repeatedly.

My first visit to China was with a delegation from the University of Regina in 1983. It was arranged that the visit would be a cultural exchange, sponsored by the Chinese People's Association for Friendship with Foreign Countries. The aim of the Association, as its long name implies, is to promote and enhance friendship and mutual understanding between the Chinese and other peoples of the world, and to maintain peace. The professors in the group were asked to give guest lectures at the universities in the various cities we visited.

In this 1983 tour, no one knew what to expect, for as a result of a 'closed-door' policy which China introduced centuries before, the country was effectively isolated from the rest of the world. When in 1978 the leader of the country, Deng Xiaoping, replaced the 'closed-door' policy with an 'open-door' policy, the mystique that shrouded this ancient land was to be removed. Even so, it was not until about two years later that small groups of Westerners began to enter the country. By 1983, the penetration was being accelerated, although there were still areas which were declared 'restricted' by the Chinese government, that is, barred to foreign visitors.

It should not have been a surprise, but it was, that the University of Regina group would find that they were the objects of intense curiosity in China, particularly me, the only Negro in the group, and Mrs. Golding, a white-haired lady and staunch supporter of the University. The reason was simply that it was the first time many Chinese were seeing people from a Western country. Understandably, the rural people seemed to regard foreigners as people from another planet. Wherever the group went, whether walking on the street or sitting in a bus or car, or shopping in a store, we were quickly surrounded by curious onlookers. It was a friendly curiosity that involved the Chinese touching our hand or hair, sometimes with a smile, and even peeping into our wallets when we opened them. This was somewhat disconcerting to some members of the group, but they were encouraged to replace their embarrassment with understanding.

I found much in China to impress, fascinate and enjoy. There are, of course, other things that do not evoke the same emotions, but for me, standing on the Great Wall for the first time was a marvellous thrill. I was fully aware of the long, unbroken, recorded history of the country, spanning some five millennia, and of four of the greatest inventions of the Chinese — the compass, gun powder, paper making and the printing machine — which greatly influenced and profited the Western world. But seeing the impressive legacies of a rich cultural past — monuments, buildings, instruments, relics — I was profoundly impressed. Visiting the Observatory atop Purple Mountain, overlooking the City of Nanjing, political capital and economic and cultural centre of Jiangsu Province, and observing the many ancient instruments of measurement exhibited there, I felt compelled to ask: "What caused China to lose its early ascendancy among the nations of the world and eventually succumb to a Third World status?" Various answers have been given, including the debilitating effects of the age of the 'Warring States', feudalism, foreign imperialist invasions, and a corrupt national government. While these may or may not have been contributing factors, they seem to me not to tell the whole story. The psyche of the Chinese people, difficult to analyze intelligently, seems to tell another story. From later visits, I surmised, and this is no more than a surmise, that complacency was perhaps the most telling contributing factor that halted major development in China up to the birth of the new nation in 1949. I assume also that geography had something to do with it.

The country is huge, territorially the third largest in the world after Russia and Canada, and demographically the most populous, with 1.2 billion people. It has a diversity of regions and a variety of industrial materials, sufficient to meet its internal and commercial needs. And its people have learned and handed down skills to one another from century to century. In concert, these factors had made China independent of the outside world in earlier days, revealed by the often quoted Chinese Emperor's rebuff of the British proposal in 1793 for closer trade relations:

> Our Celestial Empire possesses all things in prolific abundance, and lacks no products within its own borders; there is therefore no need to import the manufactures of outside barbarians.

(Tawney, R.H., 1964, Land and Labour in China, London: George Allen and Alwin Ltd.)

This first visit to this amazing country was to leave so intense an impression and evoke so profound a curiosity in me that I wanted to see and experience more of China. Speaking about this first visit, I was asked:

"What was it that impressed you most?"

"That is a very difficult question to answer," I replied. "The history, the culture, the cultural relics, the people, their amazing skill, their remarkable engineering and other spectacular technical feats, the physical landscape, and the human fashioning of the landscape ... all these impress me greatly. There is so much that is awe-inspiring and immensely interesting. I seem always to want to see more and more of it."

My next visit came soon after the first, the following year, 1984, again with a delegation from the University of Regina. On this occasion the group toured the northeast and southeast, and again gave lectures at universities to those students who could speak English fluently, usually the senior students. The Regina professors' inability to speak Chinese was a constant source of embarrassment to us. Although English is a universal language, ability to speak it and no other language is not always satisfactory. True, the Chinese language is not easily learned; the many characters, tones and nuances are not easily mastered, to say nothing of pronunciation. Yet, this is not a sufficient excuse for not learning the language that nearly a quarter of all humanity speaks. Many Canadians, it would seem, particularly those who resent learning the one or the other of Canada's two official languages, English and French, are yet to appreciate this fact.

At the end of my second tour of China and according to previous arrangements, I remained in China for another month, lecturing at the Shandong Teachers' University in Jinan, Shandong Province. I was astounded by the enthusiasm and keenness that the students brought to their work. There seemed to have been an insatiable hunger for knowledge; specifically they wanted to hear about the outside world, doubtless because of their long isolation from the peoples of the West. One of the lectures in particular drew a large number of people from the municipal and the provincial governments. It was on "Housing in the West", a topic that had been suggested by the local people. Very broad in scope, it called for much generalization. But I illustrated the lecture generously with coloured slides of housing in Saskatchewan, in other parts of Canada, and in selected countries which I had visited — Finland, Norway, Sweden, Denmark, what was Western Germany, England and Scotland, the United States, the Caribbean and Brazil. It was unlikely that those who attended the lecture would have had the opportunity to see pictures of these homes and their interiors. Thus the interest of those who attended was overwhelming. The lecture began at 1.30 p.m. and continued until 5.30 p.m., with only a ten-minute break. After the lecture, I was still bombarded with questions and though hoarse by this time and utterly exhausted, I was exhilarated. I could hardly satisfy the curiosity of those who attended this lecture. It was yet another memorable experience for me.

My third visit to China was in 1987, yet again with a delegation (which, this time, I helped to organize) from the University of Regina. After Beijing and Xi'an, the tour kept to southern China — Chongqing, a two-and-a-half day cruise down the Yangtze River (Changjiang), Wuhan, Kunming, Guilin and Guangzhou (Canton). To a geographer, the spectacular karst (limestone) features of the Guilin area are of considerable interest. I considered Guilin one of the most impressive areas of China, as is Huangshan Mountain.

The fourth tour, in 1989, incorporated centres that I had visited before, as well as others new to me: Beijing, Jinan, Yantai, Qingdao, Qufu (Confucius's birth place), Shanghai, Suzhou, Hangzhou, Guilin and Guangzhou. In Beijing, our group was discreetly kept from Tiananmen Square where students were protesting, and from other student demonstrations in most of the cities we visited. However, we had not anticipated the debacle of June 4. On that day our group was in Guilin, the last Chinese city of our tour. We were to fly from there to Hong Kong at 4.30 p.m., but news had come that morning that Air China was likely to use all its planes to rush troops to Beijing where civil war threatened. Foreign Embassies there were advising their nationals to leave Beijing, indeed China, for fear of being caught in a possible protracted civil war. Three or four groups of frantic US citizens had descended on the small Guilin Airport (a new, very modern airport has since been built). All were in a panic to leave China. Two members of one of their groups had fainted even before they reached the immigration control barrier. It was not necessary to advise my group to remain calm, as sensible persons should in such circumstances, for Canadians are not easily flappable.

The Airport's cooling system had broken down, hardly an uncommon phenomenon in a developing country, and the heat in the waiting rooms was oppressive. Our group waited patiently, and waited, and waited. At last, just before midnight, an aircraft arrived; it was the aircraft to take us to Hong Kong. An hour or so later, we were airborne and soon found ourselves in Hong Kong. Much of the city was in pandemonium — demonstrations; taxi companies on strike; radios blaring out news about a Tiananmen massacre and students being shot, douched with gasoline and cremated on the spot; while large public television screens showed pictures of some of what was going on in Beijing ... . Indeed, much of Hong Kong was in mourning, with black banners, edged with white, hanging from many of the buildings. It was a troubling time for the residents of Hong Kong who had relatives in China. Our group was equally alarmed and did not feel relieved until we returned to the relative calm and stability which characterize Canada.

But earlier in the year, I had received and accepted an invitation to teach for a year in Jinan, Shandong Province, beginning September 1, 1989, and had signed a contract to that effect. The arrangements were that after I returned from the tour, I would go back to China during the last week of August, that is, two months after the Tiananmen trouble; but the latter called for serious reflection. I was undecided as to what I should do. My friends advised caution, stating that I would be insane to return to China just then. I sought the advice of the Foreign Affairs Office in Ottawa and was told by telephone that Canada had then temporarily severed all but cultural ties with China. The government representative who spoke to me said he could not advise me to go or not to go to China to teach for the year, but that if I went, I should report to the Canadian Embassy in Beijing the moment I arrived there, and give them my address and telephone number.

Despite the advice and concerns of friends, I returned to China during the last week of August and was promptly met at the Beijing Airport by a representative of Shandong Teachers' University, who whisked me off by taxi to the city. Nearing the city proper, the taxi was brought to a stop by four military men with guns at the ready. Two advanced to the taxi while the other two covered them with their guns. The guards asked to see the taxi driver's papers and those of the university representative. Then they searched the front and rear (trunk) of the taxi, completely ignoring me who sat at the back silent, with pontifical dignity in manner and bearing, not wanting to reveal my inner feeling of mounting dread. Finding no arms, obviously what they were checking for, the soldiers allowed the taxi to proceed.

The arrangement was for me to rest off in Beijing for a day before taking the eight-hour train ride to Jinan. (A super highway, recently opened, now reduces the distance to four hours.) As I toured Beijing that day, I noticed the conspicuous presence of the military everywhere. The people were going about their business quite calmly, as if nothing had happened, yet they were under the strictest surveillance. At every 'fly over' or bridge were four armed soldiers, facing each other from the four cardinal points. Tiananmen Square was closed to traffic and pedestrians. Not a single foreigner could be seen on the streets. Thus I drew much silent, curious stare. I reported to the Canadian Embassy, as I was advised to do, gave the address and telephone number of the university where I would be, and departed Beijing the next day.

In Jinan, too, all was calm compared with the chaos when I was there two months earlier. At that time the streets were clogged with students of the Democracy Movement, and movement of traffic was chaotic. As I was to be informed later, few people in Jinan knew exactly what took place in Beijing. Most people went about their daily tasks seemingly unconcerned. In public gatherings, however, the few visiting professors and teachers were heavily guarded. It was clear that China wanted to avoid an international scene. Never had I felt as safe as I was in Jinan!

My year's teaching in a Chinese university was most rewarding. I found the students friendly, co-operative, attentive, eager to please and eager to learn. They gave their studies maximum effort, perhaps because they realized that among the millions of students seeking university admission, they were lucky to gain entry. Their positive attitude to study drew from me a keen desire to give of my best to my teaching. What I did not expect was the many students who came to me for counselling. I wondered if the University had a counselling service or if the students' coming could be interpreted as their acceptance of and trust in me. They asked for my advice and counsel even on the most private matters. I was also sought out by teachers of the university and other institutions in the city who wanted my help with various matters. Even before I could sit at the breakfast table in the mornings, there was often a knock at my door — someone wanted my help. I gave to the best of my ability, and confessed readily that my teaching in China gave me a great deal of satisfaction. I was particularly pleased when the University, in characteristic Chinese politeness, elected me "Honourable Model Teacher of the Year" (1990).

Before the end of the year, I was able to satisfy a long-held desire to visit Tibet, one of the five Autonomous Regions of China, to stand on "the roof of the world," as I once told my boyhood friends. After the uprising there in 1988, the Chinese Government had banned foreigners from visiting Tibet but removed the restriction about a year later, perhaps because the Tibetan tourist trade, which formerly brought in much needed foreign exchange, was too adversely affected by the ban. Thus in July-August 1990, in company with two American professors, then teaching at Shandong University, also in Jinan, we headed for Chengdu, Sichuan Province, gateway to Tibet, and flew from there to Gonggar Airport which serves Lhasa, the capital and largest city of Tibet, and the highest in the world.

The drive from the airport to Lhasa took more than two hours and passed over the most spectacular landscape. It warranted many photo stops, but the slightest exertion on the part of any one of the three of us made for dizziness, a gasping for breath and general discomfort. It was the height, some 4,000 metres (13,200 feet), that accounted for the rarefied air and depletion of oxygen. Yet, the mountain peaks gave the deception that they were not very high, if their base elevation was not considered.

Arriving in Lhasa, all three of us were advised to lie in bed for the afternoon, or until we were adjusted to the height. This process of adjustment took more than a day, and even then, I was constantly losing my balance and falling to the ground.

For me, the most impressive sight in Lhasa is Potala Palace (Monastery). It rises majestically, and spreads itself dramatically and horizontally along the Potala Mountain range for about 400 metres (1,320 feet). It looks down peacefully on the town below as if bestowing a blessing upon it. The whole structure is built of wood and stone which are said to characterize Tibetan architecture. The centre is referred to as the Red Palace and the two sides the White Palaces. The whole is topped by six golden turrets which glisten in the sun. The Monastery can be seen for a considerable distance. The deep blue sky and contrasting, white cumulus clouds above render the scene an unforgettable one, a sight which more than compensated for whatever effort that was made to reach this

237

Buddhist domain high above the world.

I was greatly impressed by the Red Palace's halls containing stupas or Buddhist shrines, and by the various Buddhist chambers. The stupas, eight in all, contain the embalmed bodies of eight Dalai Lamas: the Fifth and the Seventh to the Thirteenth, inclusive. One of these stupas, with either the Fifth or the Thirteenth Dalai Lama, I cannot remember which, held my undivided attention for some time. Before it sat about twelve monks in red robes, playing Tibetan instruments and chanting sonorously. The embalmed body of the Dalai Lama, sealed in a glass chamber, sat on a cushioned chair. He was splendidly robed, and his face glazed, flesh-coloured and smiling, looked down on the chanters. For long I contemplated the scene before me, lost in thought. I felt I had entered into a world I did not understand but which, nevertheless, held me in strange fascination.

The White Palace also had an equally strong fascination. This structure contained the residential quarters of the Dalai Lama, as well as the administrative offices. The rich, gold trimmings against the white stone of which the Palace is partly constructed, made for a truly pleasing sight.

Also impressive were the Zuglakang Monastery in the centre of the city, and the Drepung and Sera Monasteries. Again, in traditional Tibetan wood and stone, they are decidedly an attraction. They are adorned in strong colours (chiefly dark reds and strong yellows), and with decorations showing intricate designs. They have an overwhelming, indeed delightful appeal.

From Lhasa, the three of us travelled by road in a vehicle similar to a landrover, with huge wheels, to Xigaze, the second largest urban centre in Tibet, some 340 km (over 200 miles) to the southwest. To reach it, the road ascended heights exceeding 5,200 metres (over 17,000 feet) where breathing was most difficult for all three of us. Relief came only when the vehicle descended to lower levels. Xigaze itself is about 3,800 metres (12,500 feet) above sea level. As a political and religious centre, it boasts the splendid Zhaxilhunbu

Monastery, a large complex, built, it is said, by the first Dalai Lama and subsequently expanded by Panchen Lamas (second in administrative authority after the Dalai Lama).

We were greatly impressed by most of what we saw in Tibet. The exquisite workmanship of Tibetan handicrafts (produced at the cottage level), the Tibetan attractive blending of colours, women in Tibetan clothes walking with prayer-wheels twirling around in their hands, the extensive pastures over which herdsmen and their herds of yak, sheep and goats roam — all have left strong impressions. The single irritant of the whole visit was the powerful smell of yak butter (made from the milk of the animal). Hardened somewhat, it is used to light many of the monasteries and for domestic purposes. It has a nauseous smell, yet the butter is added to Tibetan tea, a brown, strong brew which is greatly favoured by the people.

I left Tibet thankful that I had seen this mysterious land which I had dreamt about for so long, but with questions, born of ignorance, about the Buddhist faith and Buddhist way of life.

It was after the 1987 tour that the Chinese People's Association for Friendship with foreign Countries asked me to organize future China tours from the University of Regina. Clearly the Association wanted to maintain cordial relations with the University. I agreed to the request, and organized the 1989, 1992, 1994, 1996, 1998 tours and, at the time of writing, planning the tour for the year 2000. In short, I have been privileged to visit many places in China, some more than two or three times, summarized in the list below:
NORTH CHINA:
  Beijing, Chengde, the Great Wall, Hohhot (Inner Mongolia)
NORTHEAST CHINA:
  Harbin;
EAST CHINA:
  Shanghai, Suzhou, Wuxi, Nanjing, Hangzhou, Zhenjiang, Jinan, Mt.Taishan, Qingdao, Weihai, Yantai, Qufu, Dalian; Quanzhou, Xiamen (Amoy) Huangshan Mt.;
CENTRAL-SOUTH CHINA:
  Wuhan, Luoyang, Zhengzhou, Kaifeng, Guangzhou, Haikou

(Hainan Island);

SOUTHWEST CHINA: Guilin, the three Gorges on the Yangtze, Kunming, the Stone Forest, Xishuang Banna;

NORTHWEST CHINA:The Ancient Silk Road — Xi'an, Lanzhou, Dunhuang, Turpan, Urumqi, Kashi (Kashgar).

Each of these tours served only to quicken my interest to see more and more of this amazing country and to learn more about Chinese culture, traditions, customs and great achievements. And now, having seen much of the country, and the spectacular changes that have taken place there since 1983, the year of my first visit, I am wholly convinced that China has a great future and that it is ultimately and inexorably bound up with leadership and control, especially population control — a leadership that is intelligent and courageous, far-sighted and understanding; and a control that is humane and flexible. Given these conditions, China could assume a world-power status that is globally admired and globally respected.*

* I have expressed some of the views stated immediately above in a book which I organized with Canadian and Chinese authors, and edited: <u>Trade Opportunities, Saskatchewan/Canada—Shandong/China,</u> Western Geographical Series, University of Victoria, Vol. 28, 1993.

CHAPTER *12*

$\mathcal{C}$onsidered from either an academic or professional point of view, my experiences, as recounted in the preceding chapters, have been uncommonly varied. Whether the setting was Jamaican, British, European, Asian or North American, these experiences have been testing, some vexing, always challenging though sometimes pleasing. More often than not, the way was strewn with difficulties of one kind or another. Always they required of me strength of will, determination, courage. Faced with similar hardships, others might have given up but I refused to. Every drop of my blood rejected acceptance of the status quo in my early years, which relegated the young, the ambitious and the would-be progressive in colonial Jamaica largely to stagnation and despondency. Nor could the calls of my young body for fun and pleasure deviate me from the course I had charted to reach my goal. In fact, from I was a boy my parents had inculcated in me a disciplined approach to life and the need for disciplined perseverance. These were to sharpen my vision and develop in me an assiduity that rescued me from the temptations that sought to distract.

Without financial support, and, having to earn money, young as I was, to pay for my post-primary education, scholarships being few or non-existent in my early years, I was constantly struggling to forge ahead. Added to financial difficulties and a dearth of opportunities, which in themselves were restricting, were other hardships imposed by society at large because the Almighty determined that I should be a Negro, or to put it bluntly, the colour of my skin is black, more accurately brown. Thus from childhood, the confused and tangled issues of race, used here very loosely, and colour have weighed heavily on my mind. I saw these issues as a phenomenon in which prejudice has more often than not outweighed reason. Throughout my adult life I have tried to unravel the causes of this phenomenon, having particular concern for its inhibiting consequences.

I admit readily that the mental capacities of individual persons are not all the same. It is an irrefutable fact that some people are more mentally endowed than others. But it is quite a different thing to assume falsely that because a member or some members of a race or ethnic group are deficient in innate intelligence, the whole race or ethnic group is also lacking in intelligence, exceptions ignored or their existence denied. There is no evidence for this, neither biological, nor anthropological, nor genetic. Thus to discriminate on the basis of ethnic groups or the pigmentation of the skin is nothing short of gross stupidity. Yet, that stupidity is rampant in many countries even though the cost of it in terms of money, property and lives is alarming, notably in the United States, South Africa, the Middle East, the Balkans and elsewhere. Admittedly, racial intolerance in the Middle East and the Balkans is also tied to religious intolerance and politics. In plain words, to say that a person is inferior because he is black, or is of the Jewish or Moslem or other faiths, a view that is widely and stubbornly held and exploited precociously, is clearly the pitiful manifestation of the prejudiced. That a certain section of humanity attaches marked importance to the colour of one's skin; that a dark pigmentation condemns a large percentage of the world's peoples to contempt, ostracism, oppression and humiliation; that the lives of so many of these people have been wrecked by this odious concept is infamous injustice which reason and fair play will, I strongly believe, eventually overturn. But for the present, those who suffer the injustice and the personal insults must, survival insists, aggressively resist them.

In calm deliberation over a period of many years, I have examined race and colour prejudice from both the Christian and the secular points of view. In the teachings of the New Testament, I see no dubiousness about this matter. The words and actions of Christ and the teachings of Paul clearly show that differences which divide people are insignificant compared with the larger similarities among them, to say nothing of their considerable unity in Christ. Witness, and this is often emphasized, the kindliness with which Christ dealt with the Samaritans, his healing of a Syro-Phoenician woman's daughter and, in general, his dealings with peoples of other races. Hear his command to his disciples: "Go into all the world and preach the gospel to every creature," including their own. Then listen to Paul's ringing, anti-racist declaration: "There is neither Greek nor Jew, circumcision nor uncircumcision, barbarian, Scythian, bond nor free, but Christ is all and in all." Jew and gentile, freemen and slave were the social distinctions of the day, not black and white, otherwise Paul would most certainly have included them. And hear again another of Paul's firm declarations: "He hath made of one blood all nations of men for to dwell on the face of the earth."

Not altogether a stranger to theology, for Divinity was one of my ancillary subjects in College, I have accepted what eminent theologians and others have repeatedly emphasized, namely, that while the New Testament teaching does not contradict, it surpasses, indeed enhances that of the Old Testament. The New Testament, they insist, reveals that Israel, a nation, is chosen by God for his purpose, and when this nation proved unable or unwilling to rise to their calling, they yielded to a more fitting instrument, the Christian Church. And the Old Testament is shown to lead Israel from particular to universal sympathies. In particular, theologians say books like Ruth and Jonah, as well as other biblical passages, were to rebuke those who attempted to confine God's favour exclusively to the chosen race. Thus those who try to give the white race dominion over the black race for ever do injustice to the Scriptures by extracting words from their context to savour their prejudice, such as Noah's

243

angry outburst to his sons, "Cursed be Canaan; a servant of servants shall he be unto his brethren." The implication, theologians continue to argue, is that because of its blindness or disobedience, the nation may forfeit its election, that is, will not fulfill the purpose of God. No race has a permanent privilege over other races. To subscribe to the opposite view is blatant prejudice. The New Testament and most religions ignore physical differences and declare the universal brotherhood and sisterhood of humankind. The Mormon Church and the Dutch Reformed Church may be regrettable exceptions, and even they are beginning to change their views.

As for the scientific point of view, I have accepted the authoritative statement prepared for UNESCO by a group of scientists as far back as 1941 at the height of World War II — "Aspects of the Race Problem," 1941, London: Longmans Green and Co. In part the statement reads:

> ... for all practical social purposes, race is not so much a biological phenomenon as a social myth ... There is no proof that the groups of mankind differ in their innate mental characteristics, whether in respect of intelligence or temperament. The scientific evidence indicates that the range of mental capacities in all ethnic groups is much the same. The likenesses among men are far greater than their differences.

We may add that colour is the least of these differences.

I have found no other **reputable** scientific evidence since 1941 (apart from pseudo-scientific statements which the informed have dismissed) that has repudiated this finding. It runs counter to those who regard racial prejudice or colour prejudice — they are hardly separable, for they are much the same and much involved — as "an antagonism planted by God in people to preserve the distinction of the race he has created." Such people project their fear of the dark on the Negro, equating 'black' with evil, illustrated by such terms as black magic, blackmail, black sheep, black market, black hole, black list, blackguard, and an infinite number of other terms prefixed or prefaced by the epithet "black", all meaning something evil, or bad, or sinister, or wicked, or discreditable. Simply put, the racially prejudiced develops colour feeling for social, economic and political ends.

I agree with the notion that colour prejudice is not natural, that it is a preconceived opinion, and that if it were not, it would be seen everywhere. Certainly historical records, anthropological and other studies show that it was not practised by the Greeks, nor by the Romans, that the motives of even the Crusades and the Inquisition were allegedly religious and not racial, and that its advent came with European expansion and the slave trade. Michel Leiris, in charge of Research at the National Scientific Research Centre, UNESCO, Paris, 1951, tells us that the picture began to change with the opening of colonial expansion by Europeans. It became necessary then, he states, to excuse violence and oppression by decreeing the inferiority of those enslaved or robbed of their own land and denied the title of men, the task being made easy by differences in custom and the physical stigma of colour.

Leiris shows further that the white nations secured power over the blacks, inculcated in colonial populations the feeling that they were inferior to the colonizers, prevented part of the population from rising in social scale, eliminated competition in employment, and neutralized popular discontent by supplying the people with a scapegoat.

As one who has taught, guided and helped black and white youngsters for decades from their teens to adulthood, I am totally convinced that racial prejudice or colour feeling is not instinctive. From my teaching experiences in Jamaica, Britain and Canada, I have noted that white children consider themselves racially superior to black children only when they are taught to do so or conditioned at home. Even so, after they have been with children of other colours for some time, they soon get rid of it. This latter trend, I contend,

245

is seen both in young and in older children, no less in teenagers who may even rebel against it when they come to see for themselves how iniquitous it really is.

I also support the scientific view that racial prejudice is not hereditary, that is, no more than a 'prejudice' in the strictest sense of the word, a cultural value-judgment with no objective basis; that it is simply propaganda by special interests.

I acknowledge the fact that racial intolerance in the contemporary world still promotes acute tensions, yet I realize that since World War II, the world has become or is becoming more enlightened about racial issues. It was on December 10, 1948 that the then 56 members of the United Nations committed themselves to a Universal Declaration of Human Rights, one of the Articles of which reads:

> Everyone is entitled to all the rights and freedoms set forth in this Declaration, without distinction of any kind, such as race, colour, language, religion, political or other opinion, national or social in origin, property, birth or other status.

By 1993, the membership of the United Nations Organization had increased to 171, all of whom had accepted the Declaration. In fact, the equal rights of citizens were enshrined in the Declaration of the United States at the birth of that nation. The Fifteenth Amendment of the Constitution explicitly stated "that it shall be illegal to deny or restrict (those rights) in any state of the Union on the grounds of race, colour or former condition of slavery." But words are words, and action is quite another thing, as the shocking history of race relations in the United States subsequently revealed. Nevertheless, many States have now passed their own human rights legislation and have been trying to dismantle the physical, social and cultural barriers that aim to separate one ethnic group from the other.

Notwithstanding, I acknowledge that there is still a stubborn tendency in members of the white race to discredit or discriminate, even hate, on the ground of the colour of one's skin. Racism (that is, inter-group antagonism) still manifests itself overtly and covertly, and continues to exert a negative influence by many who still believe that the white group of the many ethnic groups in which humankind is divided is at the top of the species, endowed with the best capabilities and virtues. They hold obstinately the alleged superiority of their 'white' colour as if it were something they had achieved by their own effort, like education or a skill, or something of the sort.

The folly is heightened all the more when the white, colour-prejudiced person burns himself in the sun to obtain the dark skin he despises or against which he is prejudiced, and ends up with cancer of the skin, caused by excessive exposure to the sun. The irony is not laughable; it is singularly pathetic.

No one but those subjected to racial discrimination knows how excruciatingly painful, how truly maddening, how utterly humiliating that discrimination is. And no one but the black person knows the rebellion he experiences when, because of his black skin, he is denied rights and privileges which whites, because of their white skin, reserve solely for themselves. The assumed 'right' of the whites to have ascendancy over the black person because they are white is an insufferable arrogance that makes for rebellion of the fiercest kind in the black person; for the latter to remain calm when faced with this painful affront requires of him iron self-control and discreet sagacity — the very qualities that appear alien in the prejudiced. But I maintain that unless such qualities are summoned or exercised, acute indignation is likely to get the better of those who are humiliated. So while the prejudiced wallows in his assumed superiority, indeed bigotry, he who suffers the indignity which racial prejudice imposes must repulse it with every lawful means at his disposal and use every weapon (short of guns and bombs) he possesses to convict the conscience of those given to racial prejudice. This is my dogma. I have wrestled with and repulsed racism all my life.

I firmly believe that the most effective way for the black person, especially of the Americas, to deal with racial prejudice is first to know and understand his past. He must know that racial prejudice was and is motivated by raw avarice, blatant self-interest, if not deep-seated fear of retribution. He must know that racism was at first the overwhelming catalyst of slavery which plucked his ancestors against their will from West Africa, clamped them in chains as though they were wild beasts, transported them under the most reprehensible conditions to the New World to be sold as slaves, to work on sugar and cotton plantations. He must be aware that the sweat, blood and tears of his forebears brought untold wealth and privilege to those who kept them in bondage, while such wealth and privilege served all the more to sharpen their greed, warped their personalities, and made them determined to preserve the heinous practice of racial injustice. He may rightly ask, "Why has God allowed this?" The answer has to be that God has given us a will free to do what we want to do, and God will not undo what He has done, not even to prevent the heinous crucifixion of His Son.

Because the history of the West cannot be rewritten, the shame of it is often shunned by descendants of slave-owners who are often ready to advise the black person not to think of the past. (Examined closely, advice of this kind is hardly different from the slave-owners' ruthless suppression of the previous history and culture of the slaves.) But tell that to the Jews, for example, whose history of suffering at the hands of others nearly parallels that of black people and witness their volcanic indignation. Advising black people of the New World to forget the treatment meted out to their forebears at the hands of white slave owners is understandably an attempt to calm troubled waters, doubtless the result of a sense of guilt or remorse. Nor is anything to be gained by the black person in harbouring resentment, difficult though it is for him to exercise charity towards those who want to subject him to a life of inferiority. Happily, the black person of the New World is not readily given to the revenge and the deep-seated hatred, held for centuries, that has been witnessed so poignantly in the Middle East, the Balkans and elsewhere in Europe, resulting in two world wars and the most savage massacres from the close of World War II to the present time. The illumination cast by history is simply ignored and we continue resolutely to uphold the policy of ethnic intolerance.

But knowing his past, that is, the little that is recorded of it, the black man in the New World must resist the temptation to hate or to resort to violence or revenge. Arguably, there should be little fear that the black man's awareness of his sad past would so inflame tempers to engender revenge. It is not the nature of the majority of black people in the Americas to respond to the cruel past of their ancestors by hating, for they know that hatred is counter-productive. It is definitely not the tool with which to fight racism. It would merely breed more racism. By far, what a knowledge of the slave trade and its manifold injustice should reveal to the black person today is that the institution stripped the slaves of their dignity, destroyed their morals and inculcated in them a complex conducive to making them believe they were inferior. What is more, this complex has been passed down to many of their children, grand children and great grand children — the three generations of slave offspring since the official abolition of slavery in the mid-19th century. Knowing this, I would continue to argue, these descendants should strive to rid themselves of the complex if they have it. It is perhaps the worse legacy of the slave period.

I see the disease of inferiority complex as a negative factor that must first be recognized, then attacked. The tendency for some black domestic workers, among others, to hold their heads down when talking to their white employers is agonizingly reminiscent of the subservience demanded of their forebears by the slave owners during the slavery period. I have often been incensed about this, and rightly claim that there is no reason for the black person to do this. If anything, the shoe should be on the other foot. It was not the black man's ancestors who cheated and exploited. There is therefore no reason for any black person, especially of the Americas, to hang down his head, shameful of himself and/or of his history. Nor, can it be over- emphasized, that he should not allow anger for what was done to his forebears to goad him to harbour feelings of resentment and hatred. Rather, he must find enlightened ways to defeat colour prejudice. I would advocate that perhaps the most effective approach might be for the black person to focus his gaze first on himself, to see if his behaviour offends — that is, his speech, manners, dress and actions — because if it does, it will serve only to heighten the prejudice he seeks to remove. If he is rude, crude, loud, vulgar, coarse and offensive (usual traits of the uneducated or little educated), he will rightly be repelled in most quarters. He cannot command respect or be accepted if he is uncouth, unpolished, indisciplined. Black or white or brown or yellow, such a person is wholly objectionable, and his undesirable habits or behaviour will most assuredly add to the prejudice shown to him.

Above all, I would emphasize strenuously that the black person should strive to educate himself, if not at full-time, certainly at part-time institutions by day or by night, at every opportunity he gets, despite the manifold difficulties which may negate his doing so. It is education that gives him the dignity and poise that bring admiration. It is education that inspires in a person self esteem and confidence, and equips the black man in particular to combat more effectively race prejudice. It is education that qualifies him for a suitable position in the job market. And it is lack of a good education that renders him idle, redundant, or forces him to do the menial tasks which the racially prejudiced expects him to do. I admit that in the past many black persons were denied quality education — in some places they are still denied it — and this lack of education was then looked upon as a mark of their inferiority. This was a wicked practice. However, opportunities now exist for them to improve themselves. Instead of degrading themselves in objectionable pursuits, they should be flocking to educational institutes in an attempt to improve their education or learn a new skill or improve what skills they may have in order to become more employable or more useful citizens.

Without a doubt, education is an effective weapon that the black person may use against colour prejudice, not scurrilous behaviour. I am convinced that what education imparts, especially disciplined control, together with the avoidance of hatred and vindictiveness, usually triumphs over racial prejudice.

But while I, the academic, the educator, stress the importance of education in the black man's fight against racial animosity, I admit quite readily that the educated black person is also the target of racial discrimination. One has only to read the newspapers to learn of manifestations of this here and there. I give two instances from my own experiences. The first was in Switzerland. I had taken to the Lucerne area a group of British school boys, aged 13 to 18, on a geographical field excursion. On a tourist boat in Lake Lucerne, I was pointing out to them certain glacial features along the surrounding landscape, and how they occurred, when other passengers on the boat drew near and listened to my exposition. At the end, unheard by me but reported to me by a British tourist, was a brief dialogue between one of the boys of my group and a boy from the United States, himself a tourist with his parents.

"Hi there," said the American boy, "you have a Nigger for a teacher."

"Wrong," said the English boy. "I do not have a Nigger for a teacher. I have Mr. Dale."

Saying that, the English boy walked away with a superior look on his face, leaving the American boy to ponder the meaning of his words.

The second instance was in the Italian city of Milan. On this occasion I was with a mixed group of 33 Canadian students, aged 17 to 22. I had organized a European tour for them and, as leader of the group, I would discuss the day's itinerary with them after breakfast each day. I was doing just that one morning in the hotel where we were staying when a man and his wife came slowly up and joined the group, even though it was quite obvious to them that it was a private group. The students were completely surprised and greatly amused. As the couple came nearer, I lowered my voice. At last, they were standing with the students, listening to me. I quickly brought my talk to an end and dismissed the students. Just then, the couple walked up to me, and in an unmistakable southern US accent, in manner rude, in annoyance obvious, the woman said:

"You, a teacher?"

I replied that I was, and in flaming disgust, she looked at her man and said,

"Lard, what the world is a coming to?"

The students looked incensed but I laughed heartily and said:

"Well, madam, I am delighted to see that your education has begun at last. Congratulations! Travelling is a good way to improve one's education, don't you think?"

The students laughed and cheered, and the couple walked away puzzled.

There is no doubt about it, racial stereotypes, racial slurs, racial prejudice are levelled at both the educated and uneducated black person. However, my point is that the educated black person is often better equipped than the uneducated black person to counter the arrogance that he may encounter, hence my contention that the education of the black person is paramount. I can reel off instance after instance when my education and training helped to insulate me from, or to combat effectively, racial prejudice.

I am equally convinced that the black person in his battle against racial discrimination should refuse to take a position or play a role in any endeavour that is demeaning to his race, for instance, on the legitimate stage or in the cinema. His pride should be enough to make him reject the part, attractive though the remuneration might be, if his playing the role is likely to reinforce the prejudice that created the part or role in the first place. If his economic situation is bad, rejecting the part may mean a great sacrifice on his part, but it is only by sacrifice that the battle against racism may be won. Always, I would insist, the black person has to appear in a good light in his battle against racial prejudice.

It is true that some of the dross of colour prejudice has been blown away in recent decades, but much of it remains and poses one of the most challenging problems of the modern world. By skilled efforts, as also by sharp vigilance and monitoring, I would plead the ultimate overthrow of race and colour prejudice. Legislation or enforcing compliance with the law or laws may help somewhat, but it will not ultimately defeat racial bias or colour prejudice. Rather, it is the removal of those false racial concepts that will bring about meaningful change. Among them are derogatory statements about people, the exaggerated importance given to skin pigmentation, easy condemnations of and sweeping generalizations about people, the exceedingly foolish notion of superiority based on being a member of the white group, among other false beliefs and stereotypes. So, too, should law enforcement officials be compelled to cleanse their minds of bias and racial antagonism.

Equally, black people should not accept the status quo that suppresses in subtle ways their economic, political and cultural evolution, for more often than not, the status quo maligns their worth and hinders their growth and progress. I believe that black people have no other recourse but to fight prejudice, advisedly, to **repeat**, not with sticks and stones, or guns and bombs, or overt loathing or hatred of white people, but with intelligence, consummate skill, persistence, and an indestructible spirit, grounded on hope and a desire to usher in the dawn of a more racially-accepted world.

I have arrived at this conclusion through my dealings with the racially biased and the racially unbiased. The generosity of spirit shown by members of the latter group, their genuine concern, kindness and often fearless actions to counter racial discrimination shown by their friends and others, their understanding, often sacrifice, have been outstanding. Notable among these people was the Head of the Geography Department at Birkbeck College, University of London, England, where I studied. A gentleman in the real sense of the word, and a distinguished scholar, Professor W. Gordon East (recently deceased) treated me with marked respect, understanding, kindness and patience. The influence on me of this remarkable man, known for his lucid and elegant writing, as indeed searing analysis of what he investigates, was enormous. He advised, guided, counselled, inspired me; he made me appreciate the finer points of rational thinking and coherent writing. He even allowed me, while I was his student, to use his personal library when he was out of his office. The confidence and trust which Professor East placed in me, and the genuine interest he showed in me could hardly be matched. He was to me almost like the father he was to his own two sons and two daughters. Altogether, his support gave me courage to withstand periods of stress, despondency and loneliness. Properly considered, Professor East's treatment of me was either a conscious or unconscious attempt to help right past wrongs. The Professor's humility and warm regard for his former student even allowed him to accept a temporary Distinguished Visiting Professor's position in the Department of Geography, University of Regina, when I was the Head of that Department. I revere greatly this venerable scholar whose quiet dignity and marked sincerity high-lighted his total lack of racial bias. Most assuredly, Professor East was balm for whatever racial discrimination I had experienced in Britain. Unquestionably, he was the catalyst for change in me during my student years. Years after, I could say with conviction that not all members of the white race are infected with the malady of racial superiority, and that there are angels among them.

In like manner, other goodly English folk showed me genuine friendship and warm regard while I was a student and later a teacher in London. Charlie Roberts and his mother, both now deceased, shared the warmth and comfort of their home with me, as their paying guest, and treated me as an important member of it, as also Mr. and Mrs. Hamilton. The Spalding sisters, Anne and Ruth, the former a retired civil servant, the latter a retired teacher, courageously faced the negative criticisms of their neighbours for inviting me, a black man, to live with them over a period of two years. Their home, spacious and comfortable, was located in a very conservative neighbourhood of North London, which seldom admitted black residents. Silently the sisters battered the wall of local obstinacy and prejudice, took me in as a paying guest, treated me with respect and kindness which I can never forget, and, with my help, successfully demonstrated how sterile and irrational were the existing stereotypes, how culturally poor were those who discriminated on the basis of race, and how, when injustice is meted out, it affects not only the unjustly-treated person but also the person who acts unjustly.

I am able to draw parallels from Canada, too. The supervisor of my Ph. D. thesis, Dr. Peter Smith, formerly Head of the Department of Geography, University of Alberta, Edmonton, and a distinguished geographer, well known in Canada and elsewhere, has also impressed me greatly by his complete lack of racial bias. The many white, black, coloured and Chinese students whom he taught and whose work he supervised readily admit this. Dr. Smith treated all alike, irrespective of our race or nationality, and guided and helped all equally. His positive influence on all of us has been considerable.

And if I was to single out one or two of my former students who abhorred discrimination on the basis of race, they would be Barrie Touchings, now a successful Barrister and Solicitor in Edmonton, Alberta, and Allan Schmidt, now a school teacher in Regina. There are many others, of course, but these two especially have never ceased to show me genuine regard. Uncompromising, untouched by the malaise of race, Barrie and his wife, Cherry, have a healthy attitude towards race relations, and for over thirty years have consistently held the view that all persons must have the right to determine for themselves what their liberties are, and that all are of the same value and should be treated alike. Wisely, they have passed this on to their daughter and son. I strongly believe that it was Barrie Touchings' strong beliefs in racial equality in his student years that led him to his vocation in jurisprudence.

Allan Schmidt and his wife, Sharon, have been my close friends for over twenty years. We have held each other in marked esteem and treated each other as we would a relative. I have tried to reciprocate friendship and have helped, I would like to think, to widen their horizon and that of their daughter and two sons to the extent of their offering hospitality to Chinese and other international students in their home, and providing tangible help to many of them.

Cameron and Jean Kennedy, Stuart and Yvonne Mann, and Anne Rigney, among others, have shown me similar friendship. Modestly, I might add, with a little push on my part, Anne Rigney has demonstrated a certain measure of realism about race relations, namely, that the stronger should help and respect the weaker, that wealth must be a servant and not a master. So convinced is she of this notion that, at my suggestion, she has established two permanent scholarships in her name at the University of Regina, the one solely for Chinese students, the other for Canadian students. In the same generous spirit, she, the Schmidts, the Kennedys, the Manns, and many others of my friends have helped me to sponsor Chinese students to do advanced studies at the University of Regina. Further, they assisted me in finding and furnishing suitable accommodation for these students before they arrive in Regina, and on their arrival, join me in welcoming them at the Airport, subsequently entertaining them in their own homes. In general, they have taken an interest in these students while they are in Regina — very much in conformity with Western Canadian hospitality in particular, and Canadian tradition in general. It is in the realm of such actions, I contend, that racial discrimination will be defeated.

So I know from experience that there are many members of the white race, not just in Britain and Canada but in many parts of the world who are accepting opportunities open to them in their social and economic lives to live in racial harmony with their neighbours, to love them as themselves, to regard what is right and necessary and good for themselves as right and necessary and good for their black or coloured or yellow neighbours.

I conclude my discourse on racism by declaring my belief that howsoever rampant racial prejudice may be at present, it will be defeated in the end. It is my belief that God is a God of justice and fair play, opposed to man-made inequalities of opportunity and power which, while securing the benefits of life for themselves, deny those benefits to others. I believe that which is evil ultimately has no ascendancy over that which is good. I confess, however, that I do not yet fully understand why evil, indeed, racial hatred, is allowed to cause so much harm, and so much suffering and loss of life before it is ultimately defeated.

Finally, I must add that now in retirement, I am given to reflecting on the life I have been given. I admit readily that despite hindrances, I have succeeded in surmounting some of the hurdles that had confronted me, and I am thankful that I was able to do that. But there is a recurring thought that I seem unable to suppress or expunge completely from my mind. It is that the hurdles I could not surmount have prevented me from developing my full potential, from achieving more, from reaching heights to which I had aspired, from being a better servant of humanity. And the realization that this was not due to a lack of ability, or industry, or determination, or persistence on my part intensifies the mental anguish that I feel so often. Nevertheless, by battling adversities we become more human, more understanding, more tolerant, more compassionate. It is my hope that I have acquired a modicum of these traits while painfully and persistently battling a life of relentless struggle.

ISBN 155212308-1

9 781552 123089